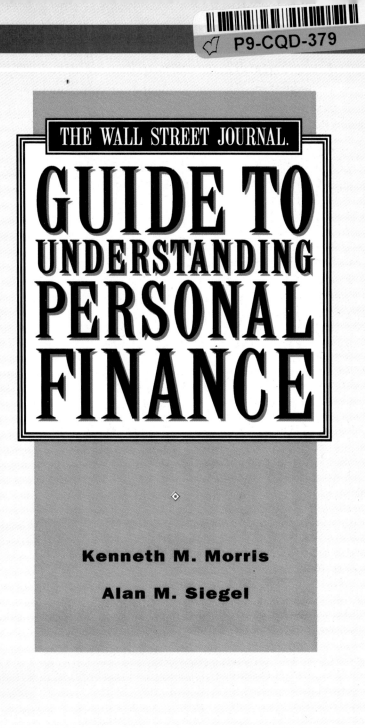

THE WALL STREET JOURNAL.

GUIDE TO UNDERSTANDING PERSONAL FINANCE

Kenneth M. Morris

Alan M. Siegel

LIGHTBULB

PRESS

CONTENTS

BANKING

Traditionally at the center of personal finance, banks now offer a wide range of checking, savings, and investment accounts. They're also one of the first places to look when you need a loan. Through your local branch, you also have access to national and even global financial networks.

BANKER'S HOURS
Originally, banking hours were Monday – Friday, 10 a.m. – 2 p.m., probably to allow bankers time to handle the paperwork manually.

The first public bank in the world was opened in Barcelona in 1401. The first savings bank in the U.S. did not open until 415 years later — in 1816. It was the Provident Institute for Savings in Boston.

A Chronology of American Banking History

1791 Bank of the United States established; lapses in 1811

1816 Second Bank of the United States chartered; out of business in 1841

Choosing an Account

Most banks offer four basic types of accounts: checking, savings, money market accounts, and certificates of deposit, plus some hybrids like checking with interest.

What Do Banks Offer?

You can usually do most of your banking in one place, choosing the accounts and services you need. Often the more money you keep in a bank, the less it costs you to do business there and the more options you have, such as:

• *Direct deposit* of your pay check or Social Security check into your accounts

• A *bank card* to let you use Automated Teller Machines (ATMs)

• A *credit card* linked to your bank account that includes a line of credit to use in an emergency

• *Overdraft privileges* to insure that all the checks you write will be paid

Today many banks have Saturday and evening hours. And, of course, ATM machines have made 24-hour banking the norm.

Though most banks offer similar products, there may be important differences — so be sure to read the fine print. For example, some banks do not pay interest on small savings accounts of less than $500. Others impose large service charges, or monthly fees, or limit your withdrawals from certain accounts.

What You Need to Apply

Banks make it easy to open basic accounts like checking and savings.

You need:

• *Money to deposit*—either in cash, check, or money order

• *Some form of identification*—official documents like a driver's license or passport are the best, but you can often use official letters or financial statements sent to you at your current address

• *Social Security number*—you can't open an account without one (Today, many children born in the U.S. get a number at birth, but you can apply for one through any Social Security office)

• *Your signature*—on a signature card— to identify you when you cash a check or require other services

1836–63 Banking regulated by states only

1863 National Banking Act establishes national standards for currency and banking

1913 Federal Reserve Act establishes a central banking system

Where to Bank

Banks offer full services; their competitors offer fewer options, but often cost less. You can choose the mix of convenience, cost, safety and service you want.

For most people, the differences between banking at a traditional commercial bank, savings bank, or S&L (Savings and Loan) have disappeared with deregulation. But competition from other financial institutions continues to intensify.

Banks	Pros	Cons
Commercial Banks	They serve individuals and businesses, usually have multiple, well-located branches and offer the full range of banking services. Deposits are FDIC insured up to $100,000 per depositor.	Fees are generally highest, and service is often impersonal.
Savings Banks and Savings and Loans (S&Ls)	Their fees may be lower than at commercial banks. Personal service may be better, especially at the smaller banks. They may be open evenings and Saturdays. Most are FDIC insured.	They can require you to notify them before withdrawing from checking. Most have only a few branches. The most bank failures have occurred among S&Ls.
Credit Unions	Their fees and loan rates are usually lowest because they are non-profit. Earnings are paid out to members at year's end.	About 10% aren't federally insured. Checks aren't returned to you; instead you keep a carbon copy for your records.
Mutual Funds, Brokerage Firms, and Insurance Subsidiaries	They offer limited banking services: low-cost or free savings and checking coordinated with investing. Checking usually earns high interest, even tax-free, if requested.	They tend to require larger minimum balances. Not FDIC insured but may have private insurance.
Private Banks and Private Banking Departments	They provide full-range, individualized financial services, as well as banking, to affluent clients. A personal representative handles all your banking needs, including loan authorization.	Services can vary. You need substantial assets to qualify for the full range. You're usually expected to generate a certain amount of business or pay a minimum annual fee.

1933 Glass-Steagall Banking Act limits banks' rights to deal in securities

1933 FDIC established to resolve the banking disaster of the Depression

1970 Bank Secrecy Act requires reporting all cash transactions over $10,000

THE BOTTOM LINE

Shopping around can save you money on what it costs to bank—sometimes lots of money. For example, if you wrote 25 checks one month and used your ATM 15 times with an account that charged a $7 monthly fee and 30 cents a transaction, it would cost you $19 a month or $228 a year. If you could get free checking by keeping a savings account balance of $1000, you'd save the charges plus earn almost as much in interest. In the end, you'd be ahead about $500.

1978 Electronic Funds Transfer Act passed

1980 Depository Institutions Deregulation and Monetary Control Act removes many restrictions on S&Ls and savings banks

1990 Banks permitted to deal in securities, which had been prohibited since 1933

Checking

Checks are the hub of the banking system. Most of us are paid by check. We buy our groceries and pay our bills with checks. On average, we write about 20 checks a month. Our checkbook is often the most complete financial record we have.

What Is A Check?

Originally, checks were hand-written notes telling your banker how much money to pay out of your account, and to whom. Today's standardized, computerized, magnetically imprinted forms are so common, we can't imagine a penciled note having the same effect—though technically it could.

In 1990, Americans wrote checks for more than $30 trillion against their accounts, also called *demand deposit* or *transaction accounts*. Demand means that your money is available when you want it. Transaction means that you can tell the bank to give your money to someone else.

Reading a Check–There are three kinds of information on the front of a check— some preprinted, some written-in, and some added when the check is processed.

Pay to the order of makes a check negotiable, or transferable, which means that the person who receives it can demand the amount the check is for. No other wording requires your bank to pay out the money.

Your name and address are included for convenience, since many stores that take checks require that information. They have no bearing on the legal standing of the check.

The name of the person or company who can demand the amount of money from your bank. To get money yourself, you can make the check out to yourself. Making a check out to "Cash" is risky because the bank may honor it—even if the check is stolen.

KENNETH M. MORRIS
VIRGINIA B. MORRIS
187 RIVER

PAY TO THE ORDER OF

MARINE MIDLAND BANK, N.A.
TAPPAN OFFICE
16 ROUTE 303
TAPPAN, NY 10983

FOR

The amount to be paid both in numbers and in words. If the two don't agree, the words usually take precedence—though the bank may return the check. If you correct an error on the check, initial the correction; that may satisfy the bank's questions. If the check is altered by somebody else— like making a $10 check a $110 by inserting a "1"— and the check is cashed, the bank must refund your money—provided you were not negligent (like signing a blank check) and notify the bank within a year.

The check routing number is used when the check is processed. It identifies your bank, the collection arrangement for its checks, and the Federal Reserve Bank for your area.

Your bank account number and the check routing number are printed in magnetic characters that bank scanners use when processing your check.

MICR Codes The strange computer digits you see on checks are called MICR codes (Magnetic Image Character Recognition). The digits actually have iron in their ink so that a scanner can read them magnetically. The numbers have this unusual shape because each image must be a certain height and width to hold enough iron in the ink to be readable.

American banks have routinely returned your cancelled checks to you. Some are experimenting with **TRUNCATION** (also called check safekeeping) which means your checks stop either at the bank where they are deposited or at your bank. Some banks send reduced-size facsimile copies with your statement. The checks themselves are photocopied and then destroyed. Banks like the process because it saves money.

The date your bank debited your account, or your check clears. The number of days between when you write a check and when it clears is called a *float*.

The date and bank where the check was deposited are important proof against claims a check was late—or that it never arrived.

Endorsement, or signature, is required—and by federal law must appear within the top inch and a half, on the left end. To be sure that checks you deposit are credited to your account, write "For deposit only," and the account number above your signature—if you can fit all that in the space you're allowed. You also have the option of using a stamp with the relevant information.

The Back of the Check— Processing information on the back of the check provides a record of its travels. When the check is paid, it is *cancelled*. Cancelled checks are proofs of payment.

The check number makes your record-keeping and the bank's processing easier.

14 May 19 92 3744

$ 402,39

DOLLARS

Virginia Morris

The date—get it right, because a time limit—usually six months—can be imposed on how long a check is *fresh*, or valid. The bank can refuse to pay *stale*, or old, checks. If you *postdate* a check by writing in some future date, it may be paid sooner than you intended because the electronic scanning equipment can't read the date.

Your check number and the amount of the transaction are MICR-printed when your check is processed so that bank computers can read them. Now the bottom of the check contains all of the information necessary to debit your account and record the transaction.

Your signature authorizes the transaction. It can be legible or illegible—as long as it corresponds with the signature card you signed when you opened the account. If someone else signs your name, it is forgery. If the bank honors a forgery, you are usually not responsible and can demand that the bank credit your account.

The first recorded use of a check dates back to 1374, but checks were rare until 1700. They became really common only after World War II. Today, about 55 billion checks are processed in the U.S. every year, and the number keeps growing.

How Checking Works

Knowing how checks are paid and when deposits are credited can help you manage your money better.

When you deposit a check in your account, it's sent to the bank of the person who wrote it. The bank *debits* (or takes money out of) that person's account and transfers it electronically to your bank.

If you both use the same bank, the amount is credited to your account the next day. If another local bank is involved, the process takes a day or two. And if the two banks are far apart, the transfer usually goes through the Federal Reserve System.

How Checks Are Paid

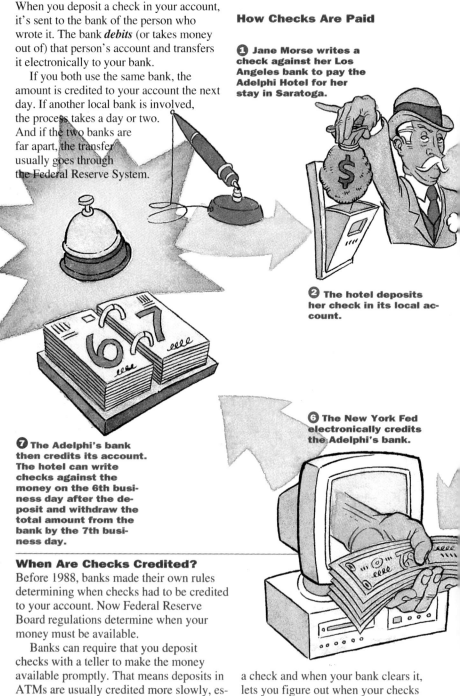

❶ Jane Morse writes a check against her Los Angeles bank to pay the Adelphi Hotel for her stay in Saratoga.

❷ The hotel deposits her check in its local account.

❻ The New York Fed electronically credits the Adelphi's bank.

❼ The Adelphi's bank then credits its account. The hotel can write checks against the money on the 6th business day after the deposit and withdraw the total amount from the bank by the 7th business day.

When Are Checks Credited?

Before 1988, banks made their own rules determining when checks had to be credited to your account. Now Federal Reserve Board regulations determine when your money must be available.

Banks can require that you deposit checks with a teller to make the money available promptly. That means deposits in ATMs are usually credited more slowly, especially when you use a machine that isn't owned by your bank.

Your bank can charge you a fee for paying checks that you write against uncollected funds—deposits that haven't been credited yet. Correctly estimating your *float*, the time lag between when you write a check and when your bank clears it, lets you figure out when your checks will clear.

For example, if your paycheck is deposited directly into your checking account on the 15th, checks you mailed to an out-of-town address on the 13th probably won't clear before there is money to cover them.

Why Does a Check Bounce?

If there's not enough money in your account to cover a check you write, your bank can refuse to *honor* (or pay) it. The person who cashed it gets the bad check back, and usually has to pay a fee. You're also charged a fee—sometimes as much as $30. If several checks bounce on one day—as they might if you've made an error—the charges can be staggering. It can hurt your credit rating as well.

The best way to avoid "rubber checks" is to apply for *overdraft protection*, a special line of credit that covers checks you write when there isn't enough money in your account. The bank automatically transfers money to your account to cover the check—though it charges you interest on the full amount transferred. In the long run, overdraft protection can save you money and aggravation.

❸ **Morse's check is routed to the New York Federal Reserve Bank, which forwards it to the San Francisco Federal Reserve Bank, which forwards it to her bank in L.A.**

❹ **Morse's bank verifies her check and takes the money out of her account, but keeps her check to return to her. Then it tells the San Francisco Fed to credit the amount to the New York Fed.**

❺ **The San Francisco Fed electronically transfers money to the New York Fed.**

How Can You Stop Payment?

If you write a check you don't want the bank to pay, or write a check and lose it, you can—for an extra fee—put a *stop payment order* on it. An oral order—either in person or on the telephone—is good for 14 days. A written order lasts for 6 months. The bank must honor your order if it's "timely," which generally means before the check is paid. If the bank pays the check anyway, you can demand your money back, but you'll probably have to show proof that you ordered the stop payment.

If a $1,000 check you deposit is:	You can withdraw the following amounts:			
	1 day later	2 days later	3 days later	5 days later
A federal, state, or local government check	$1,000			
A bank, certified, or travelers check	$1,000			
A check from your own bank	$1,000			
A local check	$100	$400	$500	
A non-local check	$100			$900
An electronic transfer	$1,000			

Deposits in ATMs often take longer.

Choosing Your Checking Accounts

With so many checking options available, you can target the kind that's best for you. The key is to balance the costs and limitations with the services you get. You may even find that having more than one account makes sense.

Checking Accounts	How They Work	Fees and Balances
Regular Checking	You can write as many checks as you want, but you earn no interest on your account.	*Banks impose a fee for each check, or monthly charges, or both. Typical charges are $7.00 a month and 30¢ a check. If you keep a certain minimum balance in your checking or savings account, you may get free checking.*
Negotiable Orders of Withdrawal (NOWs)	You can write as many checks as you want. You earn about the same interest on your balance as you would on a regular savings account. NOWs are often package deals, with small discounts on loans, free traveler's checks, and no annual fees for credit cards.	*If you don't have the required minimum balance, the fees are usually higher than those on regular checking accounts.*
Money Market Deposit Accounts	You earn a changing rate of interest to reflect market conditions. When rates go up, they pay well. Banks may offer high initial rates to attract business.	*You need a large minimum balance, and fees are high if you keep less than the minimum required. Some accounts limit you to 3 checks per month and restrict money transfers.*
Money Market Funds	Available through mutual fund companies, these pay market rate interest and rarely charge fees for checks. There is no limit on the number of checks you can write.	*The funds may require a minimum opening balance. Checks must be for $250 or $500 minimum, and you may have to wait 14 days to write checks against deposits.*
Asset Management Accounts	Checking accounts are offered by brokerage houses or banks that handle your investments. You can write an unlimited number of checks and you get a comprehensive year end statement, plus the advantage of using one account for all your banking and investing.	*You need a relatively high balance, often $5,000 – $25,000, to open an account and you usually pay an annual fee, plus fees for investment services.*

Some banks offer extended-warranty and loss protection for goods purchased with their checks, just as credit card companies do. Goods don't have to be registered, but a loss will be paid only if it's not covered by insurance.

What is a Minimum Balance?

A minimum balance is the least amount of money a bank requires you to keep on deposit to qualify for certain benefits like reduced fees or free checking.

Some banks figure your average minimum balance. That means the money on deposit each day must average above the minimum. Other banks charge a fee if your balance drops below the minimum at any time during the month.

Some banks define the minimum as the combined amount in all your accounts (checking, savings, money market, even CDs). Others don't.

Taking advantage of minimum balance options can save you money. But you'll want to compare what you save with what you could earn by investing your money elsewhere.

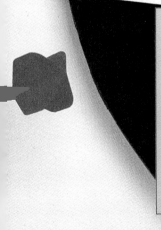

THE ART OF CHECKING

Choosing personalized checks today no longer means deciding between pale blue, pale yellow and pale green—although those old standards are still available. Banks offer checks in multiple patterns, type faces, and sizes, and charge extra for special orders. You can also get checks directly—and often more cheaply—from other sources, like printing companies and nonprofit organizations. As long as the checks have the correct information, format, and MICR coding, they work.

Guaranteed and Special Checks

There are times when your personal checks are just not good enough—especially when large amounts of money are involved. That's when guaranteed checks are convenient—and necessary.

Cashier's Checks—sometimes called *bank checks*—guarantee that the check is good because it is drawn against the bank's account.

How They Work: *You give the bank money for the amount of the check you want them to write, along with your name and the name of the recipient. The bank officer makes out the check—which is usually machine-printed so it can't be altered—signs it, and hands it to you. You also receive a carbon copy as a record, since the cashed check is not returned to you.*

The charge for a bank check is usually half the charge for a certified check. You can't stop payment once the check reaches its destination.

What's the Charge?
A retailer can't charge your purchase to a credit card if he's used the card number simply as identification—even if your check bounces. That's one reason you might have to use a check that your bank guarantees.

Money Orders—are useful if you don't have a checking account. They cost about $2.50 at banks and 75¢ at post offices, making them the least expensive guaranteed checks.

How They Work: *You pay the teller or clerk the amount you want the money order made out for, plus a fee. The amount is printed on the money order. You fill out the requested information, sign it, and send it. (A bank will sell you a money order even if you don't have an account there.)*

Money orders are a reasonable alternative to checks if you need them occasionally, but they have limitations. The money order is not returned to you, so you don't know if or when it's been cashed. Also, you can't stop payment once you've sent the money order, and there are restrictions on the amounts—up to $250 on a bank money order and $700 on one from the post office.

American Express Traveler's Checks first appeared in 1891. A century later, traveler's checks have become a $40-billion-a-year market.

Certified Checks—are personal checks that your bank guarantees it will honor. People who don't know you may want assurance that your check is good—especially if it's for a large amount, or they think you might change your mind and stop payment. These people want your check guaranteed so they can be confident of being paid.

How They Work: *After you write the check, your bank puts a hold on (or freezes) your account for the amount of the check and stamps the face of the check "certified."*

There is a fee for each certified check, but there is no limit on the amount of the check, provided you can cover it. Also, you can't stop payment on certified checks after they reach their destination.

Traveler's Checks—are popular when you're away from home, since local merchants may be reluctant to accept your personal checks. Traveler's checks are less risky because they are guaranteed by the issuer. You can get them from banks, credit card companies, or travel companies. A great advantage: you can replace them if they're lost or stolen simply by calling the issuer.

How They Work: *You can buy the checks in various denominations or amounts and in local or foreign currencies. You sign your name when you receive them, and again when you cash them. Once you use a check, it is returned to the issuer, and you have no official record of using it.*

There is usually a 1% charge for buying the checks, unless they are free for keeping a lot of money in your account or as a perk of membership in certain groups.

Some merchants and some banks may refuse to take traveler's checks or charge an additional fee for cashing them.

ATMs: Tellers Go Automatic

Automated Teller Machines have changed banking radically —in most cases for the better. Instead of waiting during banking hours for a teller to make a deposit, you can do basic transactions—and even some complicated ones—24 hours a day. All you need is an ATM card, a Personal Identification Number, and a machine that accepts your card.

ATMs have flourished in recent years. Most regional banks belong to a system that gives their customers access to every bank in the region and beyond.

The New York Cash Exchange (NYCE) is one example, with member banks in New England and the MidAtlantic. Regional systems are linked, in turn, to national and international networks like Cirrus and Plus.

You can get cash anywhere the system exists: dollars in Utah, francs in Paris, or pounds in London, whether you bank in Atlanta or Timbuktu. You can use the ATMs to complete as many separate transactions as you want. Usually the only limit is the amount of cash you can withdraw on any one day. Different banks have different limits, ranging from $200 to $500.

If the role of the ATM keeps expanding, traveler's checks and money changers may become obsolete.

The first ATM appeared in 1978. Today there are more than 70,000 nationwide, and the number is still growing. To be competitive, almost every bank that offers checking accounts offers an ATM card.

What If Something Goes Wrong?

The most common problem comes from customers—and clerks—who write down the wrong amounts. But if you spot a problem, contact your bank quickly. The bank must respond within 10 days and resolve the problem within 45 days. If you still have a complaint, they must give you a copy of their report to review.

If you discover your ATM card is lost or stolen, report it immediately. You have two business days to report an unauthorized withdrawal listed on your monthly statement to limit your potential liability to the first $50 withdrawn. Waiting 3 to 60 days to report the problem extends your liability to $500.

Waiting over 60 days can cost you everything in your account.

These rules are different than those for credit cards. That's because ATM cards are *debit cards*—the money is deducted from your account immediately.

Fees for Each Use

Many banks charge for using an ATM, especially for using your card at another bank's machine. Fees can range from 75¢ to $2.00, and are increasing despite customer resentment.

If you use ATMs frequently, fees should be part of your analysis when shopping for a place to bank.

How ATMs Work

1 The ATM card has your name and a 16-digit account number embossed on the front and a magnetic tape, or strip, on the back that identifies your bank and account number.

2 When you insert your card, the screen asks for your personal identification code. If you enter the correct one, you can access whichever accounts are tied to your card.

If a PIN is entered incorrectly three times, most machines swallow, or won't return the card, because they assume an unauthorized person is using it. To get it back, you should notify your own bank. They'll return it or replace it for you.

3 The machine displays a series of screens that walk you through a number of transactions. For example, you can:
- withdraw cash
- deposit checks
- transfer money
- pay your credit card bill
- check your account or credit card balance

4 The machine returns your card and a record of what you've done.

The record shows vital information. Check each one against your monthly bank statement and follow up immediately with your bank if you uncover any errors.

ATM Cards as Debit Cards
Many retailers now have ATMs in their stores. The amount you purchase is automatically transferred from your account to the retailer's. Stores like it, because they get their money immediately.

You may be more reluctant: some banks charge a fee for using the card this way—plus you lose the float—the time between your purchase and the time your check clears or your bill is due.

What Next?
ATMs issue rail passes in Portland, gift certificates in Tacoma, postage stamps in Pittsburgh, and grocery coupons in the Midwest.

Who Owns the Networks?
Cirrus is owned by MasterCard. Visa owns about a third of Plus Systems. Most banks connect through one of these two. Citibank has linked all its ATMs worldwide and is also part of the Cirrus network. And the Hong Kong & Shanghai Banking Corporation has linked all its Midland Bank (U.K.) and Marine Midland Bank (U.S.) branches worldwide.

The Monthly Statement

Balancing your checkbook each month—which can be surprisingly tricky—helps you keep tabs on your cash flow. It also shows you the fees you are paying for the bank's services, and warns you about problems such as over-drawing your account.

Instead of returning your cancelled checks, many banks now send "images"—electronic reproductions of the originals. While some people feel more secure with the originals, the imaged versions will be equally acceptable as electronic documents become the norm—the IRS, for example, already accepts them.

PlainView Bank
Statement of Accounts

Test Customer
14329 Beechwood Blvd.
Milwaukee, WI 53214

December 24, 1990

Direct inquiries to:
Lakeside Plaza Branch
4900 West Brown Deer Ave
Milwaukee, WI 53202
(414) 123-4567

Closing balance
$598.

3,647

6,97

Summary of Account Balances

Account	Number	
Regular checking	123-456-789-0	
NOW checking	234-567-890-1	
Money market	345-678-901-2	22
Savings	456-789-012-3	
Certificates of deposit	567-890-123-4	
Line of credit	678-901-234-5	

Get more for your money. Consider a deposit to an interest-bearing account and earn current money m

Get more for your money. Consider a deposit to an interest-bearing account and earn current money market today.
Contact our customer service department today.

Additions

Subtractions

Regular Checking
...count number: 123-456-789-0
...number: 123-45-6789

100.00
150.00

Keeping Track of Checking

All checkbooks come with ledgers to record the checks you write as well as your deposits and withdrawals. They let you keep a fairly accurate record of your financial transactions. And they help you locate errors by comparing the records against your monthly statement. You can choose from three types of checkbook ledger systems.

Separate Ledger uses a separate booklet which fits into your checkbook. It lets you easily see a running balance along-side the details of each check.

As banking services expand, monthly statements have become important records for managing your daily finances. Besides being a record of the checks you wrote, the statement shows your deposits and withdrawals—both cash and ATM transactions—and may also provide helpful information, such as when your CD will mature.

Some banks have developed *relationship statements* which show you all the accounts you have with the bank—checking, savings, CDs and even loans. The advantage is convenience: you have a monthly "snapshot" of your dealings with the bank all on one document.

What if There's an Error?

In most cases, bank statements are right. But you should compare your records—such as ATM receipts and deposit slips—since errors do occur. Generally, you have 60 days to report errors involving electronic transfers, but only 14 days for other kinds of mistakes. The sooner you notify the bank, the better.

How Long Should You Keep Cancelled Checks?

The simple answer is, as long as you need the check as proof that your payment was made. Credit card statements, as well as phone and utility bills, show when the payment was credited to your account. But insurance and mortgage companies usually do not send confirmations—your cancelled check is your receipt. You should always keep checks you write for taxes or for items that are part of your tax records, such as home improvements.

Balancing the Plusses & Minuses On the back of your monthly statement you'll find a worksheet for balancing your account.

▼

If the balance doesn't tally with your checkbook—and it often doesn't—here's what to look for:
• fees the bank charged for checks or other services
• checks or withdrawals you forgot to enter or entered incorrectly
• writing the check number twice
• transposing numbers (writing $97.50 instead of $79.50)

To balance your checkbook

Update your checkbook.
• Make sure all deposits shown on this statement, such as interest credited or direct payroll deposits, are added to your checkbook.
• Make sure all withdrawals shown on this statement, such as maintenance or ATM fees and automatic payments, are subtracted from your checkbook.
• Determine the current balance of your checkbook.

$ 598.77
$ 15.21
  50.00
  29.81
  35.00
  25.00

1 Enter the ending balance shown on the front of this statement.

2 List all checks or other withdrawals recorded in your checkbook but not shown on this statement (or previous statements).

$ 443.75
$ 50.00

3 Subtract withdrawals listed in step 2 from line 1 and enter the total.

4 List all deposits added to your checkbook but not shown on this statement.

$ 493.75

5 Add line 3 and all the deposits listed in step 4. Enter the total here. This total should match your current checkbook balance.

9
.29
9.74
04.14

r rate

Balance
$29.45
45.55
54.55
204.45
858.45
770.57

Check Stubs are attached to checks that are usually packaged in a ring binder. The stub is left in the binder after the check is detached.

Carbon-copy System provides a copy of each check you write, but you have to figure your balance separately. It's the standard in credit union checking accounts.

CD: Certificate of Deposit

If you want to earn the most interest with the least risk, consider a CD. You always get back the amount you invest, plus interest. The drawback is that you must leave your money on deposit for a specific period of time and pay a penalty for early withdrawal.

To own a CD, you simply deposit as little as $500 and agree to leave it for a specified period of time (ranging from a month to 5 years). In return, you get back all your money in the end (at *maturity*) and earn interest that may be higher than many other savings products.

What Happens at Maturity?

You decide what you want to do with the money when the CD matures, but generally you must tell the bank in writing. If you wait too long, the bank can *roll over* (reinvest) your CD into another one of the same length at the going rate. The bank can also *sweep* (move) it into another of your accounts, wire transfer it to another bank, or mail you a check.

Who Sells CDs?

You can buy them through almost any bank or broker and can often do the entire transaction by mail.

Brokers buy CDs in bulk and then parcel them out to individual investors. Because you buy only part of one of these huge CDs, you aren't locked into holding it until maturity and can sell at anytime. The tradeoff for this flexibility may mean paying a commission (banks don't charge commission). But you may also earn more on your investment.

Finding the Best CD

Generally, the longer the term, the higher interest a CD pays, but that's not always the case. The table below, which appears monthly in The Wall Street Journal, lists the best rates offered nationally on the most common CDs. Notice how some banks are offering higher interest on CDs with shorter terms.

Lenders may be flexible, though, if you ask for special terms. For instance, if you owe a tuition payment in 7 months, you may be able to get a custom 7-month CD, at a better rate than the regular 6-month CD.

HIGH

Small min

Money Market Investments*	Rate
JC Penney NB, Harrington De	4.41%
Columbia First, Arlington Va	4.25%
Metropolitan Bank, Arlington Va	4.30%
New South FSB, Birmingham Al	4.15%
First Charter, Beverly Hills Ca	4.10%

One Month CDs	Rate
Valley View State, Overld Pk Ks	4.00%
Topa Savings, Los Angeles Ca	3.80%
Chase Manhtn USA, Wilmtn De	3.70%
Colonial Bank, Santa Ana Ca	3.75%
New South FSB, Birmingham Al	3.75%

Two Mo		Rate
Valley Vi		.00%
Colonial		.00%
Topa Sav		.80%
Chase Ma		.70%
New Sout		.75%

Three

Compounding Methods. These codes tell which compounding method is used. For example, interest can be compounded daily, monthly, quarterly, or semi-annually. Whichever method is used, you'll earn more with compounding than with simple interest.

Plusses of CDs

▶ Your investment is insured up to a total of $100,000
▶ The yield is higher than on other bank accounts
▶ Knowing what you have and when you can take it out lets you plan for known future cash needs
▶ You can get very good yields when banks want cash to make loans
▶ You pay no charges for your investment
▶ Changing economic conditions do not affect what you earn

Yield—Compounding Is Key

What you actually earn on your CD, in dollars and cents, is the *yield* or the *annual effective yield*. To calculate it, you have to know whether the interest is *simple* or *compound*, and how it's compounded.

Simple interest pays you a straight percentage—for example, a $10,000, one-year CD paying 9% would earn $900. But you make more money when interest is compounded—your interest is added to the initial investment so that it earns interest as well.

For example, the CD that pays $900 in simple interest would pay you $995.12 with interest compounded quarterly.

How Compound Interest is Calculated	1st quarter	2nd quarter	3rd quarter	Maturity
Base	$10,000.00	$10,240.00	$10,485.76	$10,737.42
Interest	+ 240.00	+ 245.76	+ 251.66	+ 257.70
Value	$10,240.00	$10,485.76	$10,737.42	**$10,995.12**

Yield. The total amount you earn, as a percentage of what you invested, is the yield. The best yield is not always from the highest advertised rate.

Interest Rate. This is the percentage of your money added to your account each time you are paid interest.

What if the Rate Is Flexible? It means your interest could change in either direction. Some flexible rate CDs have a *floor* (a limit on how low the rate can drop). Without a floor, a big drop can reduce the earnings you expect. Sometimes banks offer CDs that let you choose a different (presumably higher) rate once during the term. That carries less risk, since the rate can't go down, but the reward may be less if the initial rate is low.

Floating Rates. The interest rate on a floating rate CD is "pegged" to another interest rate, like the prime or Treasury Bill rate: when that rate goes up or down, the CD follows suit.

IELD SAVINGS

num balance, generally $500 to $25,000

	Yield	Six Months CDs	Rate		Yie
A	4.51%	JC Penney NB, Harrington De	4.41%	dA	4
C	4.40%	Topa Savings, Los Angeles Ca	4.45%	siA	4
A	4.39%	Colonial National, Wilmington De	4.31%	dA	4
A	4.22%	Olympus Bank, Salt Lake City Ut	4.25%	qA	
A	4.18%	Fidelity Federal, Richmond Va	4.25%	qA	

	Yield	One Year CDs	Rate		Y
		Topa Savings, Los Angeles Ca	4.80%	siA	
iA	4.00%	JC Penney NB, Harrington De	4.65%	dA	
siA	3.80%	Fidelity Federal, Richmond Va	4.65%	qA	
dA	3.77%	Olympus Bank, Salt Lake City Ut	4.60%	qA	
siA	3.75%	Colonial National, Wilmington De	4.55%	dA	
siA	3.75%				

	Yield	Two Years CDs	Rate		
		Washington Savings, Waldorf Md	5.50%	qA	
siA	4.00%	JC Penney NB, Harrington De	5.41%	dA	
siA	4.00%	Equity Bank, Oklahoma City Ok	5.30%	qA	
siA	3.80%	Fidelity Federal, Richmond Va	5.25%	qA	
dA	3.77%	Olympus Bank, Salt Lake City Ut	5.20%	qA	
siA	3.75%				

	Yield	Five Years CDs	Rate		
		Astoria Federal, Lake Success NY	6.55%	dC	
			4.65%	qA	

CDs Are Seasonal

October and April are the two big months for CD investments for several reasons. Regulation of interest rates on CDs ended in October 1983, and 1-year and 6-month CDs—the most popular—are rolled over (reinvested) regularly. Tax deadlines make April a natural time for investment decisions—and 6-month April CDs mature in October.

Minuses of CDs

▶ Your money is locked in at a specific rate, even if interest rates go up
▶ You pay large withdrawal penalties if you take your money out early
▶ You may earn more with other, non-bank options
▶ CD interest is taxable

▶ The new interest rate when you reinvest (or roll over) your CD may be lower
▶ If your bank is taken over by another bank, your CD term or rate may change

Savings

Putting money away for a rainy day is the basic idea behind savings accounts. With something in the bank, we breathe a little easier about unexpected costs. But the appeal of traditional savings accounts has eroded because there are so many other options.

When your money is in a regular savings account, you can withdraw it or move it into another account at the same bank, but you can't write a check against it.

Banks pay interest to encourage you to leave your money on deposit since deposits are the main source of their loan money. Regular savings accounts—also called *deposit accounts*—are the most common. Most banks offer several versions of the basic account, each with different fees and different interest.

Statement accounts are increasingly common. You deposit, withdraw, and earn interest, and the transactions are reported either monthly or quarterly on a statement. If you have more than one account with the bank, they may all be shown on one statement.

Passbook accounts are the traditional savings accounts. You get a booklet when you open your account showing the amount of your deposit. Each time you deposit or withdraw, the teller records the amount, adds the interest you've earned, and figures the new balance. Your booklet is your record. If you lose it, you'll probably be charged a fee.

Money Market Accounts are savings accounts that allow you to write a limited number of checks—usually 3—each month. You can also transfer money to a regular checking account to pay your bills, either automatically or as you need to.

Money market accounts pay more interest than regular savings or NOW accounts, as long as you maintain the required minimum balance in your account.

Holiday savings clubs require a weekly deposit of a fixed amount of money so you'll accumulate a desired amount in time for holiday spending. You can make the deposit yourself or have the amount transferred from another account. Some holiday clubs pay the same rate as a regular savings account, *but others pay no interest.*

Plusses of Savings Accounts
- You can get your money any time
- Money in a savings account can reduce—or eliminate—charges on your checking account. You save more on fees than you lose because of low interest
- Bank savings are FDIC insured for up to $100,000 per depositor

Minuses of Savings Accounts
- Other kinds of accounts, such as CDs and Money Market funds, pay more—sometimes much more—interest
- Most banks discourage small savings accounts by not paying interest below a minimum balance and/or by charging service fees that can erode the interest you earn
- Interest on savings accounts is fully taxable

How Much Interest Will Your Money Market Account Earn?

Specialty accounts, like NOWs and money markets, often pay different rates of interest on different balances or different parts of your total balance. If the rate is *tiered*, you earn the highest rate on your entire balance once you meet the minimum. If it is *blended*, you earn different rates.

Take, for example, an account with a $1,000 minimum and a $12,000 balance.

Tiered—you earn the highest rate the bank offers on the entire $12,000.

Blended—you earn one rate on the first $1,000, a better rate on the amount between $1,001 and $9,999, and the highest only on the remaining $2,000.

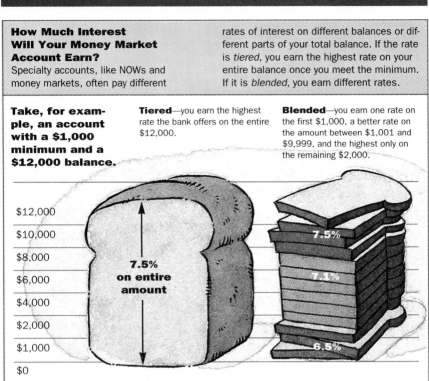

7.5% on entire amount

7.5%

7.1%

6.5%

$12,000
$10,000
$8,000
$6,000
$4,000
$2,000
$1,000
$0

Are Your Savings Safe?

Many people choose banks because their deposits are insured. The FDIC (Federal Deposit Insurance Corporation) — or state agencies or private companies in the case of some savings banks — guarantees you against losses up to $100,000, even if your bank fails. Despite a rash of savings and loan failures in recent years, and even the collapse of the FSLIC (Federal Savings and Loan Insurance Corporation) — the corporation that insured them — confidence in banks' safety continues because the vast majority of depositors have escaped any losses.

Safe Deposit Boxes

Safe deposit boxes are for keeping important papers and objects such as deeds, birth and marriage certificates, and a list of your valuable possessions. Most banks offer them for about $25 to $100, depending on the size of the box.

Boxes are kept in the bank's vault and are secured by your key and the bank's master key.

However, you only have access to the bank during regular banking hours. And the box may be sealed if you die, limiting access to valuables for your surviving family — including your spouse — until your will is legally filed.

What Amount Earns Interest?	April 1	April 29	April 30
Banks use one of three methods to determine the interest they pay. In this example, assume a 4.5% interest rate:	Begin with	Withdraw	End with
1. Day-of-deposit to day-of-withdrawal is the best method. All the money in your account earns interest every day it's there.	$2,000	$1,000	$1,000 + $9.00 interest
2. Average daily balance method pays interest only on the average balance for the period.	$2,000	$1,000	$1,000 + $9.00 interest
3. The lowest balance method pays interest only on the smallest balance during the period.	$2,000	$1,000	$1,000 + $4.50 interest

Be sure to check when interest is paid on your savings accounts. In some accounts, the interest may be credited quarterly. If you withdraw your money before the quarter ends, you currently lose all the interest for that period. But regulations expected to take effect in 1993 would require banks to pay accumulated interest for the full period the money was on deposit.

Electronic Banking

Most of the innovations in modern banking are the result of ever-more sophisticated electronic technology. Tradition keeps us doing some things that may not be necessary—or practical—like using signatures to authorize checks.

Some changes would not be possible without new technology. For instance, daily compounding of interest would be almost impossible without a computer. ATMs wouldn't work without electronic scanners. It could still take weeks to get an out-of-state check credited to your account.

Automatic Withdrawals

You can authorize automatic payments from your account for regular bills, including mortgages, insurance, college tuitions, and car loans. Usually all that's required is your signing the consent form and sending a voided check or deposit slip from your account.

However, you need to keep careful track of the withdrawal schedule so you have enough money available in your account. In selecting automatic payment, you should weigh the convenience against the risk and expense of overdrawing.

Fast Cash Costs More

Type of Transfer	Time it Takes to Reach Recipient in U.S.		Cost $250 $5...
AMERICAN EXPRESS MONEYGRAM	10 minutes	Domestic	$25
		International	$35
WESTERN UNION MONEY TRANSFER	15 minutes	Domestic	$29*
		International	$29-54*
BANK WIRE	Before noon: same day / After noon: next day	Domestic	$10-30
		International	$25-50
POSTAL MONEY ORDER	Noon next day	Domestic	$10.7
		International	$14.
ATM CARD	Instantly	Domestic/Int'l	ATM

* If a credit card is used, add a $5 credit card fee, plus any cash advance credit card companies may apply.

This chart valid as of 6/28/91

What's a Wire Transfer?

If you need to move money quickly from one account to another, you can arrange a *wire* or electronic transfer with the bank, money fund, or brokerage that holds your money. The funds are available the next business day in the account where you need them, either across town or across the country.

If you plan to move money from a mutual fund or brokerage account, you arrange wire transfer privileges by providing information about the account where the money will be sent. Since these transactions are done by telephone, you may have to verify your identity.

How About a Telephone Redemption?

Mutual funds and brokerage houses accept your telephone instructions for moving money among your accounts or sending you a check for all or part of your balance. It's their way of providing—without charge or delay—an easy withdrawal or transfer option that a local bank provides either at an ATM or with a teller.

DIRECT DEPOSITS

Direct deposit of paychecks, investment earnings, pensions, and social security payments speeds up access to your money because it eliminates any delay in checks getting to you and to your bank. The amount is credited electronically to your account on the day of payment and is available either immediately or the next day.

You sign up with your employer, broker, or the government by giving them your bank information. They handle the rest. It's also possible to have your check split between two accounts.

Problems are rare but they happen, most frequently when you change banks or your bank changes hands. Dealing with a problem means 1 contacting the source of the check and your bank to have the amount credited and 2 being sure the problem isn't the result of wrong information, which means it will happen again.

Direct deposit was originated in 1976 by the Federal government as a secure way to pay Social Security. More than half those payments are directly deposited, and today people are signed up automatically as they start to collect. Growing numbers of private and public employees use the option too.

HOME BANKING: THE NEXT WAVE?

You have the option with some banks of using your personal computer or a special telephone connection to pay bills, transfer funds, check your account balances, and sometimes even buy and sell stocks. So far customers haven't been enthusiastic.

The biggest plusses are paying bills without writing checks and programming your fixed payments so they're done automatically.

Some of the drawbacks:
• It's still relatively expensive ($5–15 per month, plus other account fees as well as a computer, the software, and the phone hook-up)
• You can't authorize payments to companies that aren't on the bank's list
• Banks can wait 5 days to pay authorized bills, while debiting your account the day you give the order

CREDIT

When you need to borrow, you use credit to get a loan from a lender, such as a bank or credit union. The amount you can borrow will depend on your worth, your income, and your credit history. But remember, it's easier to borrow than to repay. Whether you're taking a loan or using a credit card, be sure you know all the terms before you take on the debt.

Arthur Morris pioneered the installment loan. His Morris Plan, the first to make credit available to the average citizen, began in 1916 despite common wisdom that lending money to working people was doomed to failure. Less than 75 years later, it's hard to imagine how the American economy could function without credit.

What Is a Loan?

Why Lenders Lend

Lenders are willing to make loans because borrowers pay back the money—called the *principal*—plus a fee—called a *finance charge*—for using it.

Lenders have to determine your ability and willingness to repay, and protect themselves in case you don't. You have to decide whether the cost and terms of the loan make borrowing from this lender worthwhile.

Contrary to popular belief, an IOU is not a binding promise to repay a loan. American legal interpretation considers it merely an acknowledgement that money is owed.

The Interest Rate

Lenders figure the finance charge by using an *interest rate*, or percentage of the principal. Some lenders, like banks, use the *prime rate* (traditionally the rate at which banks lend money to their best commercial customers) as their base and then add percentage points. For example, if the prime rate is 7.25%, a lender might charge from 8.25% to 14% or more, depending on the type of loan. The prime rate is published daily in the Money Rates section of The Wall Street Journal.

Pawnbrokers are unconventional, but common, sources of secured loans. They hold your property and lend you a small portion of its value. If you repay the loan and the interest on time, you get your property back. If you don't, the pawnbroker sells it, although an extension can often be arranged. Pawnbrokers charge higher interest rates than other lenders, but you don't have to apply or wait for approval. Pawnbrokers' chief appeal? They rarely ask questions.

The Loan Agreement

The fine print may be off-putting, but by deciphering the loan agreement, you'll see exactly what you're getting—and getting into.

Different loans — and different

Prepayment. Most lenders allow you to prepay a loan at any time. Some charge a prepayment penalty, usually about 2% of the amount borrowed, although many states prohibit this practice.

lenders — have

Late Fee. In many cases, you may have to pay a late fee if your payment arrives after the payment due date.

different rules. But every agree-

ment (commonly called the loan

note) covers four major points:

❶ How much can you borrow?

❷ How much will it cost?

Amount Financed. This is the amount you are borrowing—or the principal. However, you may not actually get that whole amount. For example, the lender may require you to use a part of the loan amount to pay off another loan or purchase insurance to cover the loan if you die.

Preferred Customer Rate. Some lenders offer discounts on the cost of a loan if you agree to open an account with them.

❸ When do you have to repay?

❹ What if you don't repay?

You should

Co-signers. When lenders want additional assurance that you'll repay, they may require someone with good credit to co-sign (or *guarantee*) the note. This is another form of security: your co-signer guarantees to repay the loan if you can't.

Bounced Checks. Expect to be penalized if you send a payment check that bounces.

always check the key terms that

are highlighted here.

Collection Costs. Lenders may impose a stiff penalty if you default. And, if they hire a collection agency or lawyer, you'll have to pay for those services, too.

Security. Security is property (called *collateral*) which the lender can sell if you fail to repay the loan. The property used as security, such as a car, is often what's purchased with the loan. Money in an account, as well as stocks and bonds, can also be used to secure a loan.

Defaulting. Failing to live up to the agreement is called *defaulting* on the loan. The lender may have the right to repossess and sell the property you put up as security.

Set Off. Another way lenders can collect if you default is by taking (*setting off*) the amount owed from any checking or savings account you have with the lender.

The Faces of a Loan

Knowing the different kinds of loans and the special features they offer can help you negotiate a better deal with the lender. In some ways, all loans are the same: you borrow money and agree to pay it back

Installment Loans

When you take an install-ment loan, you borrow the money all at once and repay it in set amounts, or *installments,* on a regular schedule, usually once a month. Installment loans are also called *closed-end loans* because they are paid off by a specific date.

EXAMPLE

If you take a 5-year, $20,000 loan at 10% in-terest, you repay the same amount—$424.96 —every month for 5 years. The total is $25,497.60, including in-terest.

Lines of Credit

A personal line of credit is a type of revolving credit. It lets you write special checks for the amount you want to borrow, up to a limit set by the lender. The credit doesn't cost you anything until you write a check—then you begin to pay interest on the amount you borrowed. You must repay at least a minimum amount each month plus interest, but you can repay more, or even the whole loan amount, whenever you want. Whatever you repay becomes available for you to borrow again.

ADVANTAGES
• only one application
• instant access to credit
• usually no extra fees
• convenience of check writing

DISADVANTAGES
• high interest rates
• easy to over-borrow

EXAMPLE

If you have a $10,000 line of credit and borrow $6,000, your available credit becomes $4,000. If you repay $1,000 of the loan, your available credit increases to $5,000.

LOAN
REVO
ADJUS
INST
SE
FIXED

over time—with interest. But the terms of the loan—for example, whether you pay in *installments* or not, and whether the interest is *fixed* or *adjustable*—will determine how long and how much you have to repay.

"Buying on time," or paying for something while you're using it, was introduced by Isaac Singer in 1856 as a way to sell his sewing machines. At $5 down and $5 a month, the average family could afford a $125 machine—otherwise impossible on a typical $500 annual income.

Fixed Rate vs.

Most installment loans have a *fixed* rate: The interest rate and the monthly payments stay the same for the *term*, or length, of the loan.

Adjustable Rate

An adjustable rate loan has a *variable* interest rate. When the rate changes, usually every six months or once a year, the monthly payment changes also.

ADVANTAGES

- installments stay the same
- easy to budget payments
- the cost of the loan won't increase
- no surprises

- initial rate lower than fixed rate
- lower overall costs if rates drop
- annual increases usually controlled

DISADVANTAGES

- interest remains the same, even if market rates decrease
- initially higher than adjustable rate

- vulnerable to rate hikes
- hard to budget increases
- not always available

Secured Loans vs.

Your loan is secured when you put up security or collateral to guarantee it. The lender can sell the collateral if you fail to repay. Car loans and home loans are the most common types.

Unsecured Loans

An unsecured loan is made solely on your promise to repay. If the lender thinks you are a good risk, nothing but your signature is required. However, the lender may require a co-signer, who promises to repay if you don't. Since unsecured loans pose a bigger risk for lenders, they have higher interest rates and stricter conditions.

The Cost of a Loan

Many people think that the cheapest loan is the one with the lowest interest rate and the lowest payments. But that's not the whole story. The length of the loan and the fees you pay are essential in figuring the loan's real cost.

What You Learn from Ads: The Annual Percentage Rate

Lenders are required to tell you what a loan will actually cost per year, expressed as an *annual percentage rate* (APR).

8.25% APR

COMMON SEN
EQUITY LOAN

FREE CHECKING. FREE CHECKS. F
FREE CLOSING COSTS ON MOST

Get our very low fixed rate, tax deductions for your i save on fees. We pay closing costs on Equity Loans of $ for Dominion Premier® customers. When you sign up Premier, you'll also get Free Visa Gold, Free Interest/ Checks and more.

COMMON SENSE LO
FROM A COMMON S

Annual Percentage Rate (APR). Some lenders charge lower interest but add high fees; others do the reverse. The APR—annual percentage rate—allows you to compare them on equal terms. It combines the fees with a year of interest charges to give you the true annual interest rate.

For example, suppose you take out a $10,000 loan at 10% percent. You also pay an origination fee of $350, leaving you with $9,650 as the actual borrowed amount. Since you are actually getting a smaller loan, but re-paying the full $10,000 with interest, the cost is more than 10%—the APR, or **actual** *percentage rate, is closer to 10.35%.*

Periodic Interest Rate is the interest the lender will charge on the amount you borrow. If the lender also charges fees, this won't be the true interest rate.

The Cost of Taking Longer to Repay.

The term of your loan is crucial when determining cost. Shorter terms mean squeezing larger amounts into fewer payments. But they also mean paying interest for fewer years, which saves a lot of money.

Consider, for example, the interest for 3 different terms on a $13,500 car loan at 12.5%.

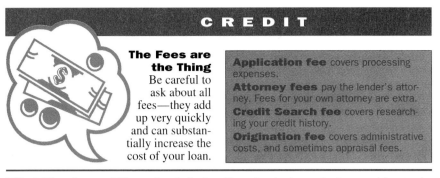

The Fees are the Thing
Be careful to ask about all fees—they add up very quickly and can substantially increase the cost of your loan.

Application fee covers processing expenses.

Attorney fees pay the lender's attorney. Fees for your own attorney are extra.

Credit Search fee covers researching your credit history.

Origination fee covers administrative costs, and sometimes appraisal fees.

What You Learn When Applying: Truth-in-Lending Disclosure

Every lender is required to provide a total cost disclosure before a loan is made. This is the only place to see in dollars and cents what the loan will actually cost you.

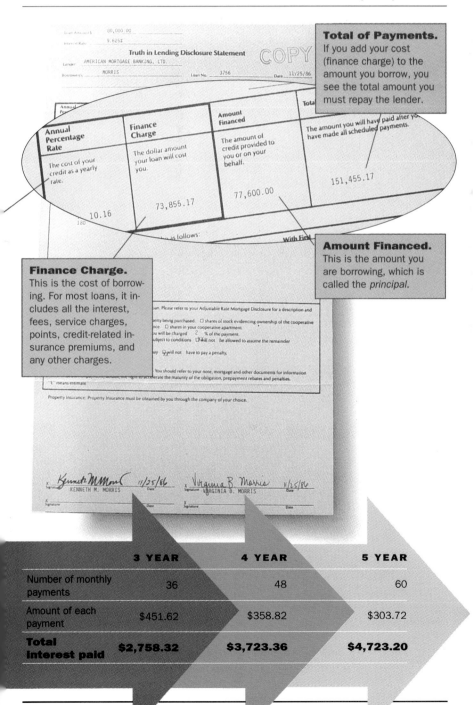

Total of Payments. If you add your cost (finance charge) to the amount you borrow, you see the total amount you must repay the lender.

Amount Financed. This is the amount you are borrowing, which is called the *principal*.

Finance Charge. This is the cost of borrowing. For most loans, it includes all the interest, fees, service charges, points, credit-related insurance premiums, and any other charges.

Annual Percentage Rate The cost of your credit as a yearly rate. 10.16

Finance Charge The dollar amount your loan will cost you. 73,855.17

Amount Financed The amount of credit provided to you or on your behalf. 77,600.00

The amount you will have paid after you have made all scheduled payments. 151,455.17

	3 YEAR	4 YEAR	5 YEAR
Number of monthly payments	36	48	60
Amount of each payment	$451.62	$358.82	$303.72
Total interest paid	**$2,758.32**	**$3,723.36**	**$4,723.20**

How Repayment Works

You may write a check for the same amount each time, but the payment always covers a different proportion of principal and interest.

From the first check you write, a certain amount goes to pay the interest, and the rest goes to repay the money you borrowed (the *principal*).

The chart below shows how $100,000 is paid off (*amortized*) over the life of a 30-year loan with a 7% interest rate. Notice how you gradually shift from paying mostly interest in the early years to paying mostly principal in the later years. That's because lenders *front-load* their interest charges to guarantee their profit. In other words, instead of spreading the interest evenly over the life of the loan, they collect most of the interest first.

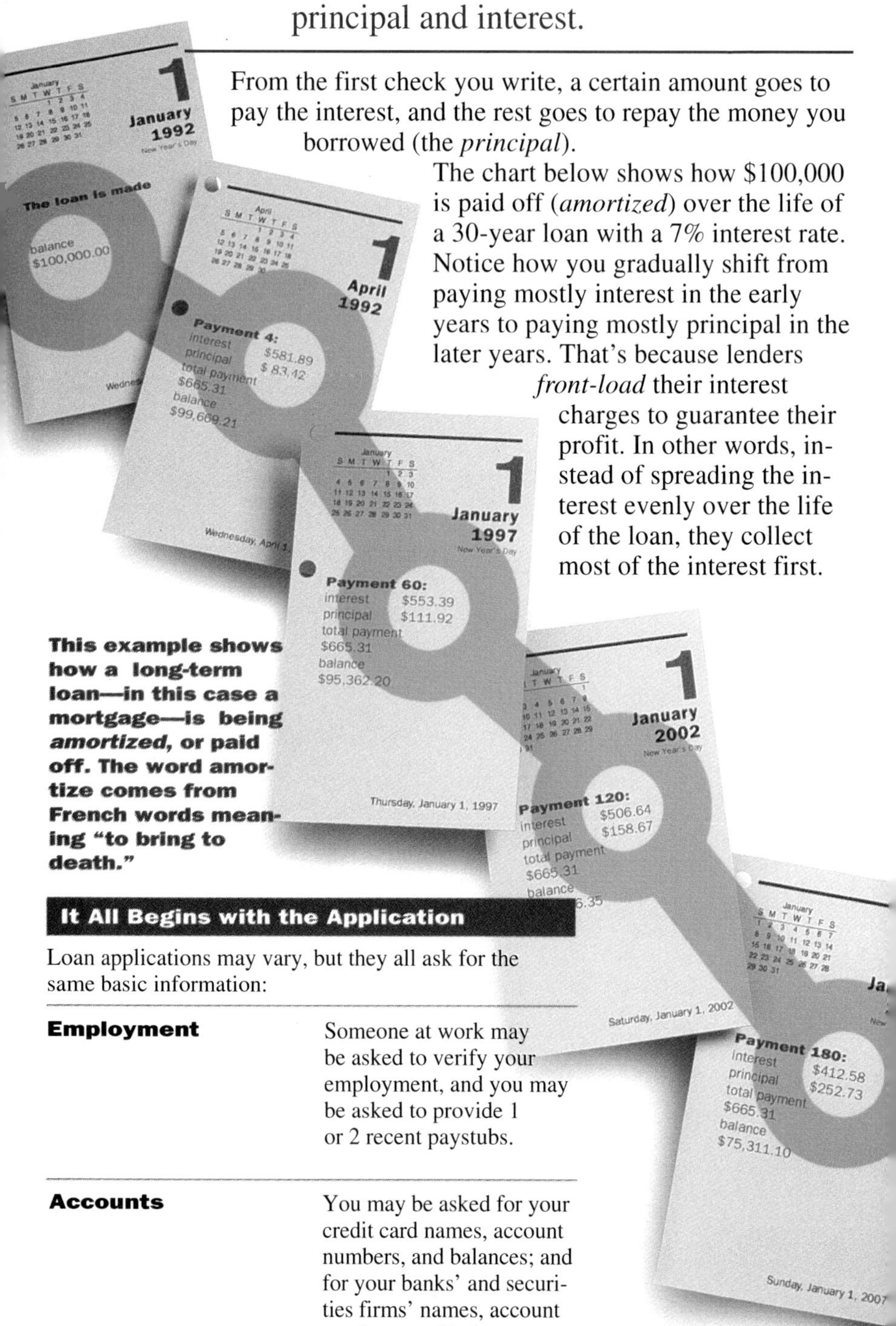

January 1992
New Year's Day

The loan is made

balance
$100,000.00

April 1 1992

Payment 4:
interest $581.89
principal $83.42
total payment $665.31
balance $99,669.21

Wednesday, April 1

January 1 1997
New Year's Day

Payment 60:
interest $553.39
principal $111.92
total payment $665.31
balance $95,362.20

Thursday, January 1, 1997

January 1 2002
New Year's Day

Payment 120:
interest $506.64
principal $158.67
total payment $665.31
balance 6.35

Saturday, January 1, 2002

Payment 180:
interest $412.58
principal $252.73
total payment $665.31
balance $75,311.10

Sunday, January 1, 2007

This example shows how a long-term loan—in this case a mortgage—is being *amortized*, or paid off. The word amortize comes from French words meaning "to bring to death."

It All Begins with the Application

Loan applications may vary, but they all ask for the same basic information:

Employment
Someone at work may be asked to verify your employment, and you may be asked to provide 1 or 2 recent paystubs.

Accounts
You may be asked for your credit card names, account numbers, and balances; and for your banks' and securities firms' names, account numbers, and balances.

References
You may need business and personal associates to supply references, if asked.

Lenders	Types of Loans	Advantages	Limitations
Commercial Banks	Home Improvement Education Personal Auto, Mobile home	Widely available locations and funds Better rates for bank customers	Higher rates than some other sources Require good credit rating
Savings & Loans	Home Improvement Education* Personal* Auto, Mobile home* *(in some states only)	Loans often cost less than at commercial banks	Require good credit rating
Savings Banks	Home improvement Personal	Some loans cost less than at commercial banks More personal service	Exist only in some states Require good credit rating
Credit Unions	Home improvement Education Personal Auto, Mobile home	Easy to arrange for members in good standing Lowest rates Better service	Membership required in organization or group
Sales Financing Companies	Auto Appliance (major) Boat Mobile home	Convenience Good terms during special promotions	High rates Since loan is secured, defaulting can mean loss of item and payments already made
Small Loan Companies (Personal Finance Companies)	Auto Personal	Easy to arrange Good credit rating not required	High rates Co-signer often required
Insurance Companies	General purpose	Easy to arrange low rates Can borrow up to 95% of policy's surrender value No obligation to repay	Outstanding loan and accumulated interest reduces payment to survivors Policy ownership is required
Brokerage Firms	Margin account General purpose loans, using investments as security	Easy to arrange Little delay in getting money Low rates (but subject to change) Flexible repayment	Changing value of investments can require payment of additional security Margin requirements can change

January
2012

New Year's Day

Payment 240:
interest $346.45
principal $318.86
total payment
$665.31
balance
$60,803.53

Monday, January 1, 2012

January
2017

New Year's Day

Payment 300:
interest $213.28
principal $452.03
total payment
$665.31
balance
$38,565.16

Tuesday, January 1,

January
2023

New Year's Day

Final Payment (360):
interest $ 3.20
principal $652.11
total payment
$665.31
balance
$00.00

Wednesday, January 1, 2023

The Auto Loan

Should you borrow the money to buy the car?

If you don't have the cash on hand to buy a new car outright—and many people don't—you might consider an auto loan to spread the payments over time. A bank or other lender will give you the money to buy the car, and you repay the loan, with interest, over a period of 3–5 years. The new car is your collateral; if you can't make your payments, the lender can repossess it.

Should You Borrow or Buy?

If you have enough money to buy the car, should you take the loan anyway? That depends. If you pay cash, you'll lose the investment interest on the amount you spend. That could be substantial if interest rates are high, or your investment is paying a good return.

But the interest you'll pay on the loan will drive up the real cost of the car. For example, if you take a 3-year loan at 8% to buy a $15,000 car, the actual cost would be about $17,000. The same loan paid back over 5 years would increase the cost to over $18,000.

Special Deals from Dealers

To promote sales, car companies periodically offer very low financing terms, sometimes as low as 2% or 3%. Provided there are no strings attached—read the agreement carefully—these loans can be very good deals. (*Zero percent financing* means you can buy the car on time without paying any interest, but check carefully for other charges.)

Loan Features

▶ You own the car.

▶ You can pay off the loan at any time.

▶ You can put as many miles on the car as you want.

▶ You are responsible for maintenance, but can get the car serviced wherever you like and keep whatever records you like.

▶ You arrange for insurance. Usually the rates drop as the car gets older.

▶ If the car is stolen or totalled, you settle with the insurance company.

▶ You can sell the car or trade it in whenever you want if you pay off the loan.

▶ Conventional wisdom says major repair costs don't occur within the first 3 years—but you may be saddled with expenses if you keep the car longer.

The Wiggly Bottom Line

Deciding whether to pay cash, borrow, or lease is not simple: money, convenience, and lifestyle are all considerations.

The following chart gives you a rough estimate of the cost factors. You can plug in your own numbers. (*Assuming the car is held for 4 years, the cost of a car for one year is the final cost divided by 4.*)

LOAN

$_____	Down payment
+$_____	Sales tax
+$_____	Monthly payment ($_____ x 48)
=$_____	Cost
–$_____	Resale value
–$_____	Interest earned on untouched investment
=$_____	**Final Cost**

Loans vs

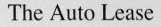

The Auto Lease

Should you borrow the car instead of the money?

Leasing is an increasingly popular way to use credit to get a car. When you lease, you never really own the car, but make monthly payments for the period of the lease — usually 3–5 years. When the lease is up, you can return the car, buy it back from the dealer for the price specified in the lease agreement, or sometimes extend the lease a month at a time.

To get the lease, you must file a credit application to establish your credit-worthiness, just as though it were a loan.

The Appeal of Leasing

Leasing's greatest appeals are upscaling — you can afford to lease a more expensive car — and exceptionally low initial costs: you pay only a leasing fee and one month's installment as security (which you get back at the end). And there's no up front sales tax — you pay a small amount of tax with each payment.

The kicker, of course, is the added cost of the car if you decide to buy it back when the lease ends. *For example, if you lease a $17,000 car for 3 years, with payments of $300 a month, you'll pay $10,800 for the lease period. But if the buy-back price is $12,000, your total cost to buy the car will then be $22,800.*

Closed vs. Open-end Leases

If you get a *closed-end lease*, the lease period and monthly payments are fixed. So is the price of the car, if you want to buy it when the lease ends. In an *open-end lease*, the lease period is variable, and the price to purchase the car varies with the market value and the car's condition.

Lease Features

▶ Leasing company owns the car.

▶ You must pay the full lease amount— even if you want to turn in the car before the lease is up. *(However if you trade your leased car in for a new one with the same dealer, you may be able to negotiate.)*

▶ There are mileage limits—usually 45,000 for 3 years and 60,000 for 4 years. If you exceed the limits, you pay a mileage charge, usually 10–15¢ each additional mile.

▶ You are responsible for maintenance. Dealers may have special plans or may provide some services free as part of the lease. You may be required to use an authorized dealer for service, and you must keep careful records to show required service was done.

▶ You arrange for insurance, though the dealer may help. However, you must insure the full value of the new car throughout the lease, so the insurance may cost more.

▶ If the leasing company doesn't agree to an insurance settlement for a loss, you may have to pay the difference.

▶ You're stuck with the car—or at least the car payments—until the lease ends.

▶ You turn in the car at the end of 3 or 4 years. Repairs after that become the dealer's—or the next owner's—problem.

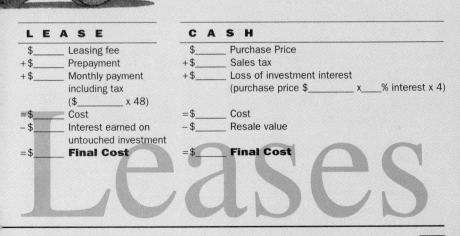

LEASE		CASH	
$_____	Leasing fee	$_____	Purchase Price
+$_____	Prepayment	+$_____	Sales tax
+$_____	Monthly payment including tax ($_____ x 48)	+$_____	Loss of investment interest (purchase price $_____ x____% interest x 4)
=$_____	Cost	=$_____	Cost
–$_____	Interest earned on untouched investment	–$_____	Resale value
=$_____	**Final Cost**	=$_____	**Final Cost**

Leases

Credit Cards

The plastic cards in your wallet may all look alike, but they definitely don't all work the same way. And chances are, at least one of them isn't even a credit card.

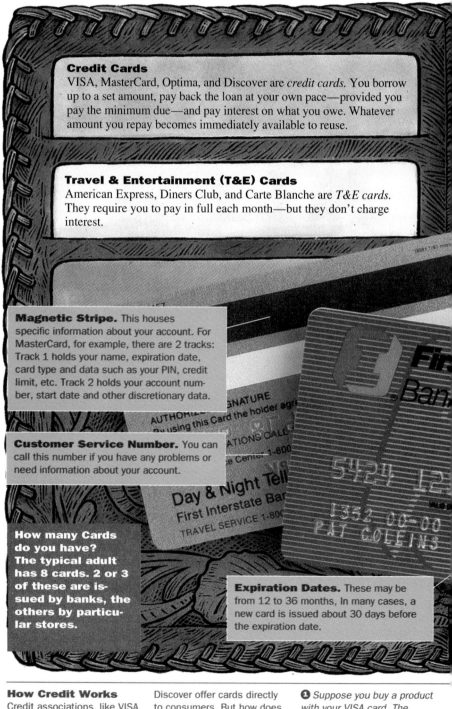

Credit Cards
VISA, MasterCard, Optima, and Discover are *credit cards*. You borrow up to a set amount, pay back the loan at your own pace—provided you pay the minimum due—and pay interest on what you owe. Whatever amount you repay becomes immediately available to reuse.

Travel & Entertainment (T&E) Cards
American Express, Diners Club, and Carte Blanche are *T&E cards*. They require you to pay in full each month—but they don't charge interest.

Magnetic Stripe. This houses specific information about your account. For MasterCard, for example, there are 2 tracks: Track 1 holds your name, expiration date, card type and data such as your PIN, credit limit, etc. Track 2 holds your account number, start date and other discretionary data.

Customer Service Number. You can call this number if you have any problems or need information about your account.

How many Cards do you have? The typical adult has 8 cards. 2 or 3 of these are issued by banks, the others by particular stores.

Expiration Dates. These may be from 12 to 36 months. In many cases, a new card is issued about 30 days before the expiration date.

How Credit Works

Credit associations, like VISA and MasterCard, sign up banks that offer cards to consumers, while companies like American Express and Discover offer cards directly to consumers. But how does the amount on your charge slip end up on your statement? And who gets paid along the way?

❶ *Suppose you buy a product with your VISA card. The store runs the card through its electronic approval machine to see if the card is valid and if you have enough*

In 1989, Sberbank became the first Soviet bank to issue VISA cards by using them to replace savings account passbooks. The cards were first issued to 2,000 of the bank's select customers, who can use them at ATMs to withdraw up to 250 rubles a week from savings.

Debit Cards

Many banks also offer debit cards, which work like checks. When you buy something, the cost is electronically deducted *(debited)* from your bank account and deposited into the seller's account.

Charge Cards

Cards from department stores and oil companies are *charge cards.* As with credit cards, you pay loans at your own pace, with interest. Ordinarily these cards can be used only to buy products from the company issuing them.

Account Number. The first 6 digits show the company that issued the card. The next 4 identify region and branch information. The next 5 are your account number. The last is attached as a check digit for extra security protection.

Holographic image. Found on many cards, it is a special design using a color foil and ultraviolet ink invisible to the naked eye. Merchants will scan the card under an ultraviolet lamp to see if the card is authentic.

credit for the purchase. You sign the receipt, which, in effect, is your agreement to repay.

❷ Within 5 business days, the store gives the receipt to VISA, which acts as a clearinghouse for all sales receipts.

What Cards Really Cost

Don't be misled by low interest rates or small annual fees. Be sure to check the *grace period*—how long you have before paying a finance charge—and how it's figured.

The cost of your credit card is spelled out in your agreement and in the terms and conditions on the back of your monthly statement. Most people don't bother with the fine print, but if they did, here's what they would find.

There's more to the cost of a card than the annual fee and the interest rate on your unpaid balances. Equally important are the grace period—the time between your purchases and when you have to pay to avoid finance charges—and how the interest is actually computed (see page 42).

Some banks that charge lower interest rates have no grace period (see the table at right.) This means you start paying interest from the day you make your purchases—even if you pay your bill on time. And that interest can add up pretty quickly.

Fees Galore

In addition to an annual fee, companies may charge extra fees for special situations. For example, if you exceed your credit line, the bank may charge an *over limit* fee, usually about $10. And if your minimum payment is overdue, there's often a late payment fee as well.

Cash Advances Can Cost

Some banks also charge *cash advance fees* for money withdrawn from an automatic teller with your credit card. And don't forget: you start paying interest on cash advances immediately—there's no grace period.

> **Interest Rate.** Lenders call this the *finance charge*. Most card lenders charge rates well above other loan rates, having raised rates in the days of high inflation and barely lowering them since. Congress considered capping rates in 1991 to keep credit card interest in line with market rates.
>
> Here's one place you may be able to cash in on your good credit. Many large banks may offer lower rates to a select number of credit-worthy customers or to those with large amounts on deposit.

Mini Charge, Maxi Interest

On many cards, even if your balance is as low as $15, you'll have to pay a *minimum finance charge* of 50¢. That's a whopping annual interest rate of 40%.

Payment Habits Affect Cost

If you "roll" your account and pay only the minimum amount due each month, you should look for a bank with the lowest finance charges, since you'll be paying interest every month. But if you pay the full amount you owe on time, then finance charges are not the issue—look for a bank with low fees and a long grace period.

Secured Credit Cards

With a secured card you have to open a savings account with the lender and keep a balance equal to your credit line. That money is the lender's security; if you don't make your payments, the lender can take what you owe from the savings account as repayment.

CARD WARS

Lenders sometimes add extra privileges to attract customers to their gold or platinum premium cards. You might be offered:
Additional Cards. Some lenders offer free cards for household members; others charge for them.

Travel insurance. Using some cards for plane, bus, or ship travel automatically covers you against accidents. Coverages range from $100,000 to upwards of $500,000.

❸ *VISA notifies the store's bank, which pays the store the sales price minus a fee (usually around 2.7%, depending on the store's monthly sales volume and other considerations). Stores can't mark up prices to customers to cover the bank's fees. But they can offer discounts to people who pay by cash or check.*

This chart was valid as of 11/14/91

Annual Fee. Many lenders charge no annual fee. Others charge from $15 to $35 for regular cards and from $75 to over $200 for premium cards. You don't owe this fee until you use the card.

How Bank Credit Cards Compare

Low-Rate Cards

Banks or savings institutions with low interest rates offering bank

INSTITUTION	INTEREST RATE	ANNUAL FEE	GRACE DAYS
Simmons First Natl, Pine Bluff, Ark.	9.50%[1]	$25	25
Arkansas Federal Savings, Little Rock	9.50[1]	35	0[2]
Wachovia Bank, Wilmington, Del.	10.40[1]	39	25
Prime Bank, Elkhart, Ind.	12.90	20	0[2]
AFBA Industrial, Alexandria, Va.	13.00[1]	0	25
Bank of New York, Newark, Del.	13.40[1]	0	0[3]
Fidelity National, Atlanta	13.70[1]	20	25
USAA Federal Savings, Tulsa, Okla.	13.75[1]	0	25
Bank of Montana, Great Falls, Mont.	13.75[1]	19	25
Bank One Wisconsin, Milwaukee	13.90	25	25

Big-Name Cards

What the 10 largest U.S. bank-card issuers are offering on their standard cards.

INSTITUTION	INTEREST RATE	ANNUAL FEE	GRACE DAYS
Citicorp	19.80%[4]	$20	30
Greenwood Trust/Discover	19.80	0	25
Chase Manhattan	19.80[4]	20[7]	30
MBNA America	19.80[4]	20	25
Bank of America	19.80[4]	18	
First Chicago	19.80[4]	20	
Centurion/Optima	16.25[1,5,6]	15	
Bank of New York	16.98[1,4]	18[7]	
Manufacturers Hanover	19.80[4]	20	
Household Bank	21.00[4]	0	

NOTE: Rates shown are for regular cards, not premium cards or cards requiring a sec
Though not listed, some cards may be through affiliate or agent banks. Temporary o
interest rates are excluded. Grace period (interest free period for cardholders paying
in full each month) is calculated from the date of billing unless footnoted.
[1]Variable rate [2]Interest charged from date of posting [3]Interest charged from date
[4]Special lower rate available on some cards [5]Higher rate charged for cash advances
[6]Relationship required [7]Fee waived under special conditions
Source: RAM Research Bankcard Update/Barometer

Grace Days. The time between billing and payment gives you a cash float. If you make a purchase right after the account closes for the month, you won't have to pay for it until the end of the next payment period, which could mean a 45 day float. However, some banks with low interest rates start charging interest from the date of your purchase.

Shopping/Travel Discounts. These give you shopping discounts and guarantee the lowest prices for hotels, cars, and planes when you use the card.
Extended Warranty. You can receive up to a year's warranty beyond the manufacturer's warranty, and even replace lost or stolen goods bought with the card.
Collision Insurance. There's often no need to buy coverage from a car rental agency; nearly all cards automatically cover you. Some cards have a hotline you can call worldwide for medical or legal help.
Year-end Statements. With some gold cards, you receive a consolidated statement of all the year's charges, designed to make tax time a little easier.

❹ Next, VISA clears the receipt from its books by charging the bank that issued you the card. Your bank immediately pays the store's bank the full amount.

❺ Your bank then sends you a statement for the full amount of the purchase and for any other purchases you made during the period.

Understanding Card Statements

Knowing how to read your statement can help you to monitor spending, reduce interest payments, catch errors, and more.

The statement is a snapshot of your account at the end of each statement period: it shows what you owed to start, what you owe now, and every charge and payment that occurred in between. Combined with your checking account ledger, it often provides a nearly complete record of your monthly expenses.

The version at the right may look different from yours, but all statements carry virtually the same information.

Your Chase Gold Visa Account

Account Nu

New Balance	Total Credit Line	Total Available Credit	Cash Advance Line	Available Cash
$41.12	$7000	$6959	$3000	$2959

Transaction Details

Post | Description

2 57TH & BWAY NEW YORK CITY

New Balance. This is the amount you owed on the day the statement was prepared. It includes any finance charges and late fees.

Credit Line. Lenders give credit lines of anywhere from $500 to $10,000 or higher, based on their assessment of your credit history and your ability to repay.

Credits. Shows any credits you received for overpayment, incorrect charges, or returned merchandise. For example, if you dispute a charge, the lender will credit you the amount until the dispute is settled. Credits are subtracted from the previous balance.

Finance Charge. This is the interest charged on the amount you owe. Two cards with the same finance charge won't necessarily cost you the same interest, even if you owe the same amount. That's because what you pay depends on how the company figures the *balance* on which they charge you interest. (See table below)

Computing Finance Charges

Example: Suppose you pay an 18% annual finance charge (1.5% per month) on amounts you owe. Your previous balance is $2,000, and you pay $1,000 on the 15th day of a 30-day period. The interest you owe will depend on the method used to calculate your finance charge.

Method	Description	Interest You Owe
Adjusted Balance	The company subtracts the amount of your payment from the beginning balance and charges you interest on the remainder. *This method costs you the least.*	$15.00
Average Daily Balance	The company charges you interest on the average of the amount you owe each day during the period. So the larger the payment you make, the lower the interest you pay.	$22.50
Previous Balance	The company does not subtract any payments you make from your previous balance. You pay interest on the total amount you owe at the beginning of the period. *This method costs you the most.*	$30.00

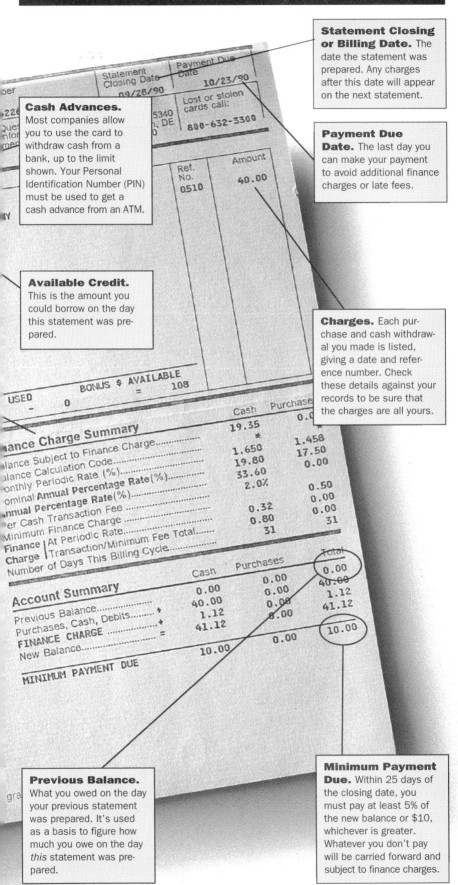

Statement Closing or Billing Date. The date the statement was prepared. Any charges after this date will appear on the next statement.

Cash Advances. Most companies allow you to use the card to withdraw cash from a bank, up to the limit shown. Your Personal Identification Number (PIN) must be used to get a cash advance from an ATM.

Payment Due Date. The last day you can make your payment to avoid additional finance charges or late fees.

Available Credit. This is the amount you could borrow on the day this statement was prepared.

Charges. Each purchase and cash withdrawal you made is listed, giving a date and reference number. Check these details against your records to be sure that the charges are all yours.

Statement Closing Date 09/28/90

Payment Due Date 10/23/90

Lost or stolen cards call: 800-632-3300

Ref. No.	Amount
0510	40.00

USED − 0   BONUS $ AVAILABLE = 108

...ance Charge Summary

	Cash	Purchase
...lance Subject to Finance Charge	19.35	0.0
...alance Calculation Code	*	*
...onthly Periodic Rate (%)	1.650	1.458
...ominal **Annual Percentage Rate** (%)	19.80	17.50
...nnual Percentage Rate (%)	33.60	0.00
...er Cash Transaction Fee	2.0%	
Minimum Finance Charge		0.50
Finance At Periodic Rate	0.32	0.00
Charge Transaction/Minimum Fee Total	0.80	0.00
Number of Days This Billing Cycle	31	31

Account Summary

	Cash	Purchases	Total
Previous Balance	0.00	0.00	0.00
Purchases, Cash, Debits +	40.00	0.00	40.00
FINANCE CHARGE =	1.12	0.00	1.12
New Balance	41.12	0.00	41.12
MINIMUM PAYMENT DUE	10.00	0.00	10.00

Previous Balance. What you owed on the day your previous statement was prepared. It's used as a basis to figure how much you owe on the day *this* statement was prepared.

Minimum Payment Due. Within 25 days of the closing date, you must pay at least 5% of the new balance or $10, whichever is greater. Whatever you don't pay will be carried forward and subject to finance charges.

Protecting Your Card Rights

Don't wait until you have a problem with your card to find out your rights. They're spelled out on the back of your statement.

A lot can go wrong with a card, even if you stay within your limits and pay promptly. It makes sense to keep your receipts, check them against your monthly statement, and notify the card company if you spot any errors.

The back of your statement may not look like the one here, but your rights will be the same.

When Charges Are Added To Your Average Daily Balance

Purchases, cash advances, and other debits, credits and payments are added to your Purchase or Cash Advance Average Daily Balance starting with:

The later of the transaction date (in the "Trans. Date" column on the front of your statement) or the first day of the billing cycle; or at our option, the posting date (in the "Post Date" column on the front of your statement). The posting date is the date that charges are processed to your Account.

How We Determine Your Finance Charges

Finance Charges on your Account are determined by applying a periodic rate to your Purchase Average Daily Balance and your Cash Advance Average Daily Balance, and adding any minimum charges and transaction fees that apply. If there is a "V" next to the "Balance Calculation Code" on the front of your statement, your Monthly Periodic Rate may vary.

Purchase Balances–Average Daily Balance (including new purchases)

To determine a portion of the Finance Charge on purchases, we apply the Monthly Periodic Rate shown on the front of your statement to the Purchase Average Daily Balance, which includes current transactions. To get the Purchase Average Daily Balance, we:
1. Take the beginning purchase balance of your Account each day;
2. Add any new purchases or other purchase debits; and
3. Subtract any purchase payments or other purchase credits.
4. This gives us the purchase daily balance for that day. We then add up all the purchase daily balances for the billing cycle; and
5. Divide the total by the number of days in the billing cycle. This gives us the Purchase Average Daily Balance.

A minimum Finance Charge may be imposed on your purchases balance.

Purchases Grace Period

The purchases grace period is 30 days on average. To avoid Finance Charges on purchases, pay the Purchases New Balance before the next Closing Date. There is no grace period for cash advances.

Cash Advance Balances

To determine a portion of the Finance Charge on cash advances, we apply the Monthly Periodic Rate shown on the front of your statement to the Cash Advance Average Daily Balance of your Account.
To get the Cash Advance Average Daily Balance, we:
1. Take the beginning cash advance balance of your Account each day;
2. Add any new cash advances or other cash advance debits; and
3. Subtract any cash advance payments or other cash advance credits.
4. This gives us the cash advance daily balance for that day. We then add up all cash advance daily balances for the billing cycle; and
5. Divide the total by the number of days in the billing cycle. This gives us the Cash Advance Average Daily Balance.

A transaction fee Finance Charge may be imposed on each cash advance.

Making Payments

You may pay all or part of your New Balance at any time. However, you must always pay at least the Minimum Payment Due by the Payment Due Date. Send your payment to the Chase address shown in the payment coupon section on the front of your Chase statement. Pay by check or money order, and be sure to allow sufficient time for your payment to reach us by the Payment Due Date. You may also pay in person to The Chase Manhattan Bank (USA) at 802 Delaware Avenue, Wilmington, Delaware 19801.

Payments received at the addresses indicated, by 12 noon, Monday through Saturday (except legal holidays in Delaware) will be credited to your Account as of that day. Payments received at the addresses indicated after 12 noon will be credited to your Account the following day which is not a Sunday or legal holiday in Delaware. If you pay elsewhere, crediting to your Account may be delayed up to 5 days.

Cancelling Your Card.

By law, you can cancel your card and avoid paying the annual fee as long as you notify the lender in writing within 40 days of receiving the bill for the fee.

SAFETY TIPS

❶ Never give your card number (or card) to anyone unless you are buying something or making a reservation. Since merchants can't charge your account if your check bounces, there's no reason to write it on your check for them. And no need to put your phone, name, or address

Lost or Stolen Cards.

If you report a missing card immediately by calling the number on the back of the statement, you aren't responsible for any charges. $50 is the most you'll owe even if you don't report losing your card.

Some companies, for a fee, keep all your card numbers on file and will report the problem for you.

If You ___

Call the ___
a day, 7 days ___

If You Have Quest___

If you see a charge on yo___
Re-check your own records ___ ___ have
forgotten. It is a good idea to k___ ___ until those
charges appear on your statemer___ ___ you've made any
telephone or mail order charges.
Ask others who have access to your ___ ___ hey made the charge.
Check to see if the amount and date of ___ charge are familiar, even if you
do not recognize the place or the merchant name. Companies may bill
under a different name or from a central location.

If you still do not recognize the transaction, if you think there is any other
error, if you have a question about a specific charge, or if you have a dispute with a merchant over the quality of merchandise or services, see the
Billing Rights Summary below. It tells you what to do to resolve your question, and how to protect your rights under the Federal Truth in Lending La___

If Your Annual Fee Is Billed On This Statement

If you close your Account within 30 days from the date this statem___
was mailed, you may avoid paying the annual fee billed on this ___
ment. You may do this by writing to us at the address or callin___
tha telephone number shown on the front of this statement u___
"Questions?". You may continue using your Account durin___
period up to the date you tell us to close your Account.

Billing Rights Summary

In Case Of Errors Or Questions About Your___
If you think your bill is wrong, or if you need mo___
transaction on your bill, write us on a separate sh___
on the front of this statement next to "Questions?" ___
We must hear from you no later than 60 days after we ___
on which the error or problem appeared. You can telepho___
so will not preserve your rights.

In your letter, give us the following information:
1. Your name and Account number.
2. The dollar amount of the suspected error.
3. Describe the error and explain, if you can, why you believe there is
   an error. If you need more information, describe the item you are
   unsure about.

You do not have to pay any amount in question while we are investigating,
but you are still obligated to pay the parts of your bill that are not in
question. While we investigate your question, we cannot report the
amount in question as delinquent ___ any action to collect the amount
you question.

Special Rule For Credi___

If you have a problem ___ ___ ices that you purchased with a cred ___ ___ h to correct the
problem with th ___ ___ aining amount
due on the ___ ___ n the
purchase ___ ___ our
nome ___

Purchases You Didn't Make and Other Billing Errors.

You have 60 days to notify the lender in writing about billing errors. This includes wrong amounts of credit extended, wrong goods or services, incorrect payments or credits, compu-tational errors or any other disputed charges.

Card companies have 30 days to respond and 90 days to resolve the problem. They can't stop you from using your card while investigat-ing the problem and can't release a bad credit report on you. And if they don't respond, they can't collect the disputed amount or finance charges.

Defective Mechandise.

You can legally refuse to pay for defec-tive merchandise if it cost more than $50 and you were unable to resolve the problem with the merchant. The purchase must be made in your home state or within 100 miles of your mail-ing address, though companies are flexible on this matter. (The price and mileage restrictions don't apply if the lender advertised the product or was in-volved in the purchase).

The *Truth in Lending Act* re-quires lenders to tell you in writing the cost of credit and the terms of repayment before you borrow. The *Fair Credit Billing Act* sets the proce-dures for resolving billing errors.

on a credit card receipt. In some states, it's ille-gal. ❷ Destroy all car-bons. Thieves can use your number to charge purchases or even order new cards.

❸ Never make your PIN available to anyone. Don't write it anywhere a thief may have access to it.

How Good Is Your Credit?

Places that give you credit want to know if you're a good risk. But the credit reporting system is enormous, complex, and sometimes flawed, so your credit history could be wrong.

Providing lenders with credit histories has spawned a $1 billion industry that has records on 150 million people. The information is collected and stored by credit bureaus, which act as clearinghouses for businesses that want to know a customer's payment history before they give credit.

Credit Bureaus.
At the center of the credit reporting system are the 3 national credit bureaus—Equifax, TRW, and Trans-Union—along with more than 1,200 local and regional bureaus. The bureaus collect and collate credit information and make it available to businesses that subscribe to their service—and to consumers who request it.

The credit bureaus issue reports—electronically or on paper—to banks, retailers and other grantors of credit.

CREDIT BU

BANKS STORES &

What Creditors Must Tell You
Anyone turning you down for credit must do the following:

❶ Send you a written rejection within 30 days of the decision.
❷ State in writing the specific reasons for rejection, or at least tell you that you can learn the reasons if you request them in writing.

WHILE BUREAUS PROVIDE A VALUABLE SERVICE TO A SOCIETY WHERE CREDIT IS A WAY OF LIFE, ERRORS DO OCCUR IN THE VAST AMOUNT OF INFORMATION THEY PROCESS — CREATING HUGE HEADACHES FOR CONSUMERS.

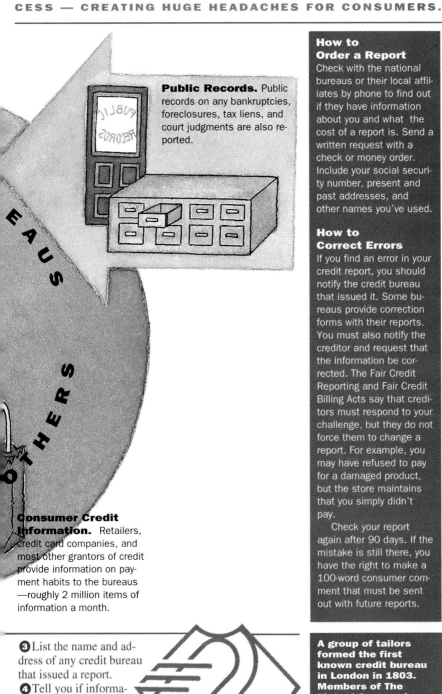

Public Records. Public records on any bankruptcies, foreclosures, tax liens, and court judgments are also reported.

Consumer Credit Information. Retailers, credit card companies, and most other grantors of credit provide information on payment habits to the bureaus —roughly 2 million items of information a month.

❸ List the name and address of any credit bureau that issued a report.
❹ Tell you if information from another source was used, and that you have the right to learn about that information if you request it in writing.

How to Order a Report

Check with the national bureaus or their local affiliates by phone to find out if they have information about you and what the cost of a report is. Send a written request with a check or money order. Include your social security number, present and past addresses, and other names you've used.

How to Correct Errors

If you find an error in your credit report, you should notify the credit bureau that issued it. Some bureaus provide correction forms with their reports. You must also notify the creditor and request that the information be corrected. The Fair Credit Reporting and Fair Credit Billing Acts say that creditors must respond to your challenge, but they do not force them to change a report. For example, you may have refused to pay for a damaged product, but the store maintains that you simply didn't pay.

Check your report again after 90 days. If the mistake is still there, you have the right to make a 100-word consumer comment that must be sent out with future reports.

A group of tailors formed the first known credit bureau in London in 1803. Members of The Mutual Communication Society of London exchanged information on bad credit risks. The first U.S. credit bureau was started in Brooklyn in 1869.

Deciphering a Credit Report

You can order a copy of your report at any time from a local or national credit bureau for a small fee, usually $5 to $20. If you've been turned down for credit or a job, you're entitled to a free report if you request it within 30 days.

The reprints issued by the major credit bureaus all look different, but contain essentially the same information. In most cases, each of them will have your credit information.

Months Reviewed.
This shows how long the account has been tracked.

.. 10024

CREDIT HIST

Company Name	Account Number	Whose Acct.	Date Opened	
		I	04/84	
CITIBK-MC		I	04/90	
AMEXTRVLSV		I	04/90	
AMEXTRVLSV		I	07/86	
CITIBNK OD		REDIT LIMIT		
AMOUNT		I	04/84	
CITIBK-MC	276	I	05/86	
EAB OD	0(03)60(01)90			
>>> PRIOR				
LINE	4724	I	10/8	
LORD & TAY	30(03)60(00)9			
>>> PRIOR		CREDIT LIMIT		
AMOU				
	9808	I	07/	
CHEM BANK	30(01)60(01)			
>>> PRIOR PAYING HISTORY - IS CREDIT LIMI				
AMOUNT IN H/C COLUMN				
ECAP PMTH	110			

Code   Meaning

This tells who is responsible for the account and who uses it.

J	Joint
I	Individual
U	Undesignated
A	Authorized user
T	Terminated
M	Maker
C	Co-maker
B	On behalf of another person
S	Shared

Is Your Credit Report Accurate?

The Wall Street Journal reports that about 3 million of the 9 million people who asked for credit reports in 1989 challenged the information they received as incorrect or outdated. Another survey found that 48% of reports it checked had errors. 19% included major mistakes.

Common Errors on Credit Reports

• Confusing you with someone else with the same name or a similar Social Security number
• Including incorrect information
• Failing to incorporate comments or changes based on information you or your creditors supply
• Failing to remove damaging information after the issue has been resolved

Credit reports don't evaluate data, though they often tell a story. They report your birthdate, address, social security number, how much you've borrowed, and how faithfully you've repaid.

Credit report information is continuously updated, but old details disappear slowly. Some states impose time limits — in New York, for example, it's 7 years in most cases. Some bankruptcy information can be reported for up to 10 years.

These reports are often hard for consumers to decipher, but credit companies came under great pressure in 1991 to make the information more accessible to consumers.

High Credit. The highest amount you've charged—or the credit limit—on a specific account. For example, the Citibank MasterCard high was for $2,100.

Balance. The amount you owed on the account at the time of the report. For example, there's nothing due on the EAB account.

Status. This shows the type of account (O = Open, R = Revolving, I = Installment) and how long it takes you to pay.

Example: R3 means a revolving account which you've been paying from 60 to 90 days after the due date.

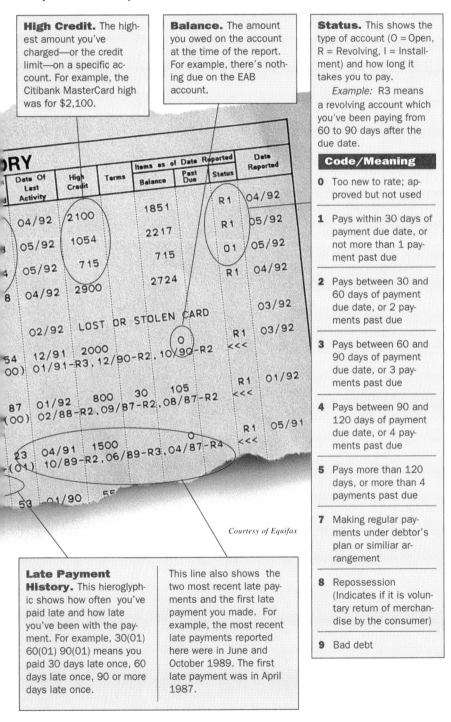

Courtesy of Equifax

Code/Meaning

0 Too new to rate; approved but not used

1 Pays within 30 days of payment due date, or not more than 1 payment past due

2 Pays between 30 and 60 days of payment due date, or 2 payments past due

3 Pays between 60 and 90 days of payment due date, or 3 payments past due

4 Pays between 90 and 120 days of payment due date, or 4 payments past due

5 Pays more than 120 days, or more than 4 payments past due

7 Making regular payments under debtor's plan or similiar arrangement

8 Repossession (Indicates if it is voluntary return of merchandise by the consumer)

9 Bad debt

Late Payment History. This hieroglyphic shows how often you've paid late and how late you've been with the payment. For example, 30(01) 60(01) 90(01) means you paid 30 days late once, 60 days late once, 90 or more days late once.

This line also shows the two most recent late payments and the first late payment you made. For example, the most recent late payments reported here were in June and October 1989. The first late payment was in April 1987.

Coping with Debt

If you're awash in red ink and can't pay your bills, you need to act quickly to rebuild your credit. There are a number of solutions, with bankruptcy as a last resort.

Restructuring Debt Without Bankruptcy

You can restructure your debts without resorting to bankruptcy. If you can't stop overspending, then you can ask for help.

Creditors. You can ask creditors to rewrite your loans to extend the time you have to pay and to change the payments so that you can afford to make them. The extensions will increase your overall cost, because the creditors will charge you interest over a longer period.

Non-profit credit counselors. These organizations have cropped up in virtually every city. For modest fees, counselors go through your debts, analyze your income, and help you work out ways to handle your debts.

Loan consolidators. These private businesses lend you money to pay off all your debts. You then owe only one creditor—them. The good news is that you pay only one check a month, you can repay over a long term,

and you can make low monthly payments. The bad news is that the interest they charge may be very high, and you may be hit with stiff fees for paying off the loan ahead of schedule.

Credit doctors. There are people who claim they can resurrect your credit. But be very careful, since they are not only expensive but are often involved in fraudulent schemes.

How Bankruptcy Works

Bankruptcy is the solution of last resort—a harsh but legal remedy for staving off financial disaster.

In general, bankruptcy is a 3-step process.

❶ You file a petition in federal or state court saying you're *insolvent* (you have no assets to pay debts).

❷ You work out a repayment plan with your creditors and the court.

❸ You *discharge* (settle) your debts, usually for less than their full amount, so that your creditors receive at least some money.

PAYING THE CONSEQUENCES

Some of the consequences of failing to repay your debts:

1. You could get a bad credit rating and be unable to borrow again.
2. Your wages may be *garnished*: a court may order your employer to pay up to 10% of your salary each pay period to people you owe.
3. Lenders may sell property you put up as security.
4. You could be sued and, if you lose, required to pay the legal costs as well.
5. You might be forced into bankruptcy.

> The National Foundation for Consumer Credit is a non-profit organization with offices in 44 states. It helps you arrange repayment plans. You can call 301-589-5600.

Types of bankruptcy.
It's always smart to consult a lawyer before filing for bankruptcy, and in some cases it's required. There are two standard ways for individuals to file for bankruptcy, each named for the section of the legal code that governs it.

Chapter 7, or "straight bankruptcy" (lawyer advisable).
You ask to be released of all your debts after selling all your assets to pay creditors. Some assets, like your home, are exempt from sale. Some debts, like taxes, fines, alimony, and student loans must still be paid. You can file for straight bankruptcy only once within a 6-year period.

Chapter 13 (lawyer required).
The purpose of Chapter 13 is to allow people to retain their property and to avoid the stigma usually associated with the term "bankruptcy."

A court approves a plan to pay out creditors over 3-5 years using your wages. Payment is not necessarily in full. The plan is supervised by a court-appointed person, called a *trustee*. Some income, like child support, is excluded from the payment plan.

> **Debts that won't be included in bankruptcy proceedings.**
> 1. Debts of more than $400 owed one creditor, if they're for purchases of luxury goods or services within 40 days of the court order for relief. 2. Cash advances totalling more than $1,000 from a revolving credit plan, if made within 20 days of the order for relief.

Bankruptcy	Pros	Cons
Here are some issues to weigh when considering bankruptcy.	• Provides legal protection from creditors • Staves off financial ruin • Resolves most debts • Prevents loss of your home • Provides chance to start again • Protects you against IRS seizing property for back taxes	• Loss of privacy • Serious harm to credit rating • Some debts remain outstanding • Involvement with courts • Loss of assets

HOME FINANCE

Seeking shelter may be an instinct, but paying for it is a long-term financial commitment. Whether you rent or buy is partly a matter of lifestyle and partly a matter of what you can afford to pay.

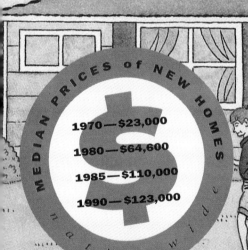

MEDIAN PRICES of NEW HOMES *nationwide*

1970 — $23,000
1980 — $64,600
1985 — $110,000
1990 — $123,000

BUYING: THE ADVANTAGES

- You build equity (or ownership) in property, which you may sell at a profit
- You can deduct mortgage interest and property taxes on your tax return

- You can often defer taxes on your profit when you sell if you buy another house
- You are protected against rent increases (though not property tax increases)

- You can rent your property to produce income
- You can often get more living space for less money
- You can borrow against home equity

The Roof over Your Head

Styles of Ownership: A Home Is Not Always a House

	You Own	Your Rights	What You Pay For
House	The building and the land on which it's built	You can rent or sell as you choose	• Real estate taxes based on assessed value of house and land • All maintenance, repairs, and renovations • Mortgage and insurance on the property
Condo	Your own private living space (the association owns the building and land)	You can rent or sell as you choose	• Real estate taxes based on assessed value of your condo unit • Monthly maintenance charge for upkeep and real estate taxes on overall condo property • Mortgage and insurance on your unit
Co-op	Shares in a corporation that owns the building and usually the land, which entitle you to live in an apartment	You can choose buyer, subject to board approval Renting may be prohibited	• Monthly maintenance charge (for real estate taxes, mortgage on the building, fuel, insurance, operating costs) based on number of shares held • Repairs paid by co-op and passed along to shareholders • Payment of loan used to finance purchase of shares (equivalent of a mortgage)

There is no simple way to determine whether it's cheaper to rent or buy. You have to balance the cost of the house—mortgage interest, property taxes, insurance, and improvements—against the potential earnings of investing your money. But interest rates—both what you pay and what you earn—may vary, as can taxes, rent increases, and the value of your house when you sell.

According to the Census Bureau, Americans spend about 28% of their income on housing.

About 36% of all Americans rent, rather than own, their homes, a percentage that has increased slightly during the last decade, especially for people under 30.

R E N T I N G :   T H E   A D V A N T A G E S

• You do not need a large amount of cash for a down payment—you may be able to invest your money more profitably

• You do not risk having to sell when prices are down
• You are not responsible for repairs and maintenance

• Heat and some utilities and services are often included
• Some rents are controlled, which can hold down your living expenses

Can You Afford to Buy?

As a rule, you can afford to buy a home that costs up to 2 ½ times your annual income. You'll usually need at least 10% of the purchase price for the down payment and will probably have to get a mortgage for the rest.

The amount you can borrow—and what you can afford to buy—is based on:

❶ How much you can pay up front. Most mortgage lenders require you to have at least 10% of the purchase price as a down payment, plus enough cash on hand for closing costs.

❷ The 28/36 qualifying ratio. Lenders usually assume you can afford to spend 28% of your total income on your mortgage, property taxes, and homeowners insurance. But even if you meet this test, you can still be turned down if your mortgage expenses and other regular debt payments—such as auto and student loans—are more than 36% of your total income.

The Other Costs of Ownership

Owning your home involves many costs you may initially overlook, including:

Insurance. You'll need enough homeowners insurance to cover the mortgage amount. The insurance company may insist that your coverage equal the house's full replacement value.

Property Taxes. Local school and property taxes vary enormously from place to place. Check before you buy.

Commuting. Communities with convenient transportation usually cost more to live in, but can save you time and money in commuting.

Schools. Paying more for a home in an area with good public schools may be cheaper in the long run than paying for private school—especially if you have several children. And houses in strong school districts often sell more easily.

Maintenance Charges. Condominium and co-op charges for monthly expenses can escalate rapidly, so anticipate them in your purchase decision.

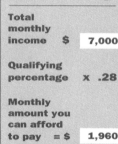

Qualifying Test 1

The following work chart will determine the monthly mortgage payments (including insurance and property taxes) you can afford.

Total monthly income	$	7,000
Qualifying percentage	x	.28
Monthly amount you can afford to pay	= $	1,960

Lenders assume that 15% of the monthly amount you can afford will cover taxes and insurance. In areas of high property taxes, you'll have less available for the mortgage itself—and so will qualify for a less expensive house.

What Can You Afford?

The following table shows the monthly payments you can expect to make on a 30-year, fixed rate mortgage. (Insurance and property taxes would add to this cost.)

Home Price	Down Payment
$ 80,000	$ 8,000
140,000	15,000
220,000	45,000

Qualifying Test 2

Lenders want to make sure that you can keep up all your regular monthly payments —insurance, loan repayments— in addition to the mortgage. So they impose a second qualification using this formula:

Total monthly income	$ **7,000**
Qualifying percentage	x **.36**
Total for regular monthly expenses	= $ **2,520**

If you have exceptionally large monthly expenses, such as high credit card interest or other outstanding debts, you may be turned down for a mortgage.

Other Routes to Ownership

If the numbers don't add up, there may be other ways to buy your home.

Employer Programs. Some companies help their employees with mortgage loans—a trend encouraged by a new FNMA program to buy or guarantee employer-assisted loans.

Rent-to-buy Option. You can often arrange with an individual owner or developer to live in a house on a rental basis, with an option to buy.

The Family Till. Some banks allow parents to buy Certificates of Deposit equal to 20% of the purchase price of their adult child's new home. The parents earn interest, but must leave the money on deposit until the child has paid off 20% of the amount borrowed.

Auctions. Arranged by sellers, auctions can be good deals for buyers too. But sellers can establish a base price, so even the highest bid may fall short. If your bid is accepted, you may need to make a substantial down payment on the spot.

The Resolution Trust Corporation, the government agency responsible for insolvent savings and loans, auctions properties it controls. The RTC has regional agency sales centers and computerized information. (Call 800-RTC-2990)

RESOLUTION TRUST CORPORATION

Mortgage Loan	Monthly Payment (including interest)		
	8%	**10%**	**12%**
$ 72,000	$ 528	$ 632	$ 741
125,000	917	1,097	1,285
175,000	1,284	1,536	1,800

Buying a House—The Initial Commitment

Buying a house is a bizarre ritual that can be astounding, unnerving and, most of all, expensive. Knowing what to expect—and how to get through the maze of paperwork—can save you time, money, and frustrating delays.

Beginning the Search

Scanning the real estate section of local newspapers has been the traditional first step in finding a new home. The electronic age is changing all that: now you can run through color videos of available homes and find out about taxes, heating costs, and other key information without ever leaving a real estate office.

Newer May Be Simpler

Buying a newly-built house is often simpler, since you deal directly with the builder—or a designated agent. Some of the advantages:
- There's usually less paperwork
- Surveys and title searches may be provided
- Interest rates may be lower
- If the builder is eager to sell, you can sometimes negotiate a *buy-down*, which means the builder pays some of your initial mortgage costs

Real Estate Agents

Most people use *a real estate agent*, who is actually paid by the seller but spends most of the time with the buyer. Agents will show you several different homes for sale in your area and price range and help you begin negotiations on those you're interested in.

Agent

Seller

Obstacles Buyers Might Face:
- House inspections that reveal serious existing or potential problems
- Limited availability of mortgages or a sharp jump in interest rates
- Changing lending rules, like requiring more money down or greater income
- A lender appraisal that is less than the purchase price so you can't borrow enough money
- Temporary living space during renovations—or the time between leaving your old home and waiting to move into the new one

The Offer. When you finally decide to buy, you make a *bid* or price offer. If the bid is accepted, you pay a fee (called a *binder*, or *earnest money*) of about $1,000 to secure your offer. Technically, once the binder is made, the seller can't accept another offer, provided you can arrange for financing. If the deal goes through, the binder amount counts toward the purchase price. If it doesn't, you get it back.

Buyer

What Is a Buyer's Agent?

Some buyers have turned to agents or brokers who represent them, rather than the seller, in finding a new home. These brokers may show a larger selection of houses, will fight for more concessions, and can often provide information about the seller that sellers' representatives cannot.

They may also ask for an up front retainer based on the purchase price to cover their commission if they have trouble collecting from the listing agent.

Do You Need an Attorney?

Buying a house is a complex process involving loads of paperwork. You may face added costs or other problems if the agreements you sign don't say what you think they do. For example, a seller may agree to make certain repairs, or there may be a *lien* (a legal claim) on the house. Real estate agents can provide some advice, but a qualified real estate lawyer is best, and may even be required by law.

The Deposit. Signing the contract requires a cash deposit, often 10% of the purchase price. This amount is held in *escrow* (or reserve) and becomes part of your down payment. You get the deposit back if the deal falls through. (But some co-op sales contracts are *non-contingent*, which means you could lose the deposit if the deal doesn't go through.)

Contract

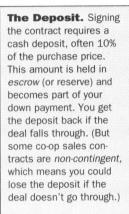

Inspection. You should arrange for a licensed building inspector to examine the property. If there are any serious problems, like cracks in the foundation, water damage, or a leaky roof, you may lower your offer or withdraw it altogether.

Negotiating. Real estate agents sometimes agree to a reduced commission to close a sale that has gotten stalled over price. The chances of negotiating a reduction are better if the agent works for the broker that listed the property, so the commission won't have to be split.

Real estate agents are licensed to sell property. They work for brokers, who operate real estate companies. Brokers are known as Realtors if they belong to the National Associaton of Realtors.

The Contract. This is the first legal document you and the seller sign. Contracts are standard, but are modified to reflect the details of your purchase—price, date of sale, items included in the sale (like appliances), and the conditions of the sale, such as:
• a *free and clear title*, which means no one else has any legal claim to the property
• a *mortgage contingency*, which means the sale depends on your getting the mortgage loan you need
• a *termite-free certificate* from a pest inspector

Shopping for a Mortgage

Interest rates may not seem to vary much, but even ¼% difference can translate into thousands of dollars in savings—or extra expenses—over the term of the loan. You may also qualify for special government-subsidized mortgages. So it pays to shop around.

Virtually everyone who buys a home needs a mortgage—a special type of installment loan (see page 30) that makes a home affordable by spreading monthly payments over a 15- to 30-year period.

Where to Look

To get started, you can check local ads or banks, or you can buy a computer-generated list of lenders and the going mortgage rates in your area from HSH Associates at 800-873-2837.

What Are VA and FHA Mortgages?

VA (Veterans Administration) mortgages enable qualifying veterans to borrow up to $144,000, sometimes with little or no down payment. For more information, call the VA's toll-free number (under U.S. Government in your local phone book).

FHA (Federal Housing Administration) mortgages let you borrow up to 95% of the price of a house, but only if the total cost is within their guidelines. Income is not a factor, but in many parts of the country few houses may qualify. Also, new rules limit payments for closing costs. You can get the information from your lender or directly from FHA.

What's an Assumable Mortgage?

VA and *FHA* mortgages can sometimes be *assumed* by (or passed on to) a buyer. This eliminates closing costs and often preserves a low interest rate. However, the buyer needs enough down payment to cover the seller's equity (the percentage of the house the seller owns). And the seller may be liable for the loan if the buyer defaults. New conventional loans are never assumable, but some older ones may be.

State-Sponsored Programs

Many states provide mortgages at below-market rates for first-time buyers, provided your income and the price of the house meet their guidelines. Check with your state government for information about its program.

Who Are Fannie Mae and Freddie Mac?

National standards for mortgage loans are set by *Fannie Mae* (or FNMA), the Federal National Mortgage Association. Together with *Freddie Mac*, the Federal Home Loan Mortgage Corporation, they buy mortgages from banks for resale in the *secondary market*. As a result, the banks conform strictly to their guidelines.

What's a Wraparound Mortgage?

It's a special mortgage deal that may save you money if you can *assume* or take over the seller's existing, low rate mortgage. The new mortgage "wraps around" the old one, so you can continue to pay it off at the old rate. But the lender will charge you current rates for the extra money you need to pay off the seller.

The oldest recorded mortgages were in Egypt during the time of the Pharaohs—mortgages of various kinds were used throughout history. They took on their modern forms of paying principal interest in the 1500s, but the conventional mortgages as we know them today were first offered in the 1930s.

The average mortgage is held for 7 years before it's paid off—usually because the house is sold.

Who Provides Mortgages?

Virtually all financial service companies, including brokerage firms, have entered the mortgage market.

• **Banks**, savings banks, S&Ls, and credit unions may offer better rates if you're already a customer.

• **Mortgage Companies** may offer lower rates or make qualifying easier than banks do. They often sell the mortgages they negotiate.

• **Mortgage brokers** act as middlemen. They help you find the best deal or get a mortgage when you're having difficulty.

• **Sellers** may give you a mortgage if:
1. they don't need the cash up front,
2. they're satisfied you'll repay, or
3. the sale has been stalled because you can't get a mortgage and they're eager to sell. Sellers might also agree to a *write down*, which means they pay some of the costs during the first years of your regular mortgage.

• **Developers** also make arrangements with lenders to get you financing if you're interested in their properties.

Electronic mortgage information, now in its infancy, will revolutionize the mortgage business. Programs that combine rates and charges with loan advice — and even computerized programs — are already in use.

Dealing with the Lender

Most lenders require you to complete a mortgage application—a comprehensive financial statement that determines whether you qualify for a mortgage and how much you can borrow. It all depends on: ❶ what you earn ❷ other regular income ❸ your current debts.

The Mortgage Application Form

The mortgage application—usually the standard FNMA (Federal National Mortgage Association) form or a variation—asks for very detailed financial information. The more you can provide at the start, the speedier the process.

What Else Does the Lender Require?

Besides the application, you'll need to pay for:

• A *survey*, or official surveyor's drawing, of the property and the buildings on it. A survey costs about $500.

• An *application fee* and an *origination fee* to cover the costs of processing the application. This includes an appraisal of the house by the lender to make sure it's worth the mortgage loan. Plan to spend $250 to apply, plus 1% of the mortgage amount.

If your down payment is less than 20%, the lender may require *private mortgage insurance* (PMI) to guarantee payment if you default on the loan. You may also have to increase your down payment to reduce the amount you're borrowing.

Monthly housing expenses shows what you are spending now and what you expect to spend in the new house, including taxes, utilities, and homeowners insurance.

Job information focuses on regular employment—you'll need verification from your employer. If you're self-employed, you often have to provide more information, including income tax returns, credit reports, and profit and loss statements for your business.

MARINE MIDLAND MORTGAGE CORPORATION

Uniform Resi

This application is designed to be completed by the Borrower(s) with ... must be completed and the appropriate box(es) checked if ... another relying on income from alimony, child support or separate maintenance ... or ☐ the Borrower is married and resides in, or the property is located ...

Freddie Mac Form 65/Rev. ...
(Amended)

MARINE

The Commitment Letter

If your mortgage is approved, you'll receive a commitment letter spelling out how much you can borrow and how long the offer is good for. It may also state the interest rate, which you can *lock-in*, or fix. Otherwise the rate is determined when the final loan documents are prepared.

What if a Lender Turns You Down?

Try another one. All lenders use the same basic information, but they may evaluate it differently. Your real estate agent or a mortgage broker can help you find mortgage sources. You can also ask if the seller is willing to reduce the price or lend you a portion of the money required.

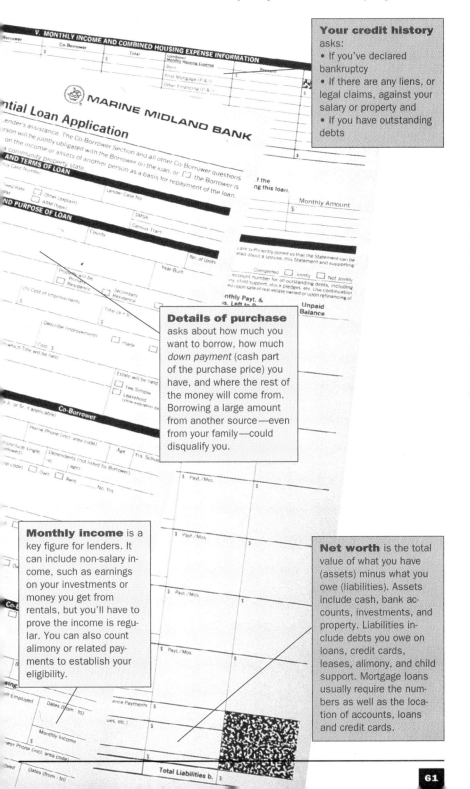

Your credit history asks:
• If you've declared bankruptcy
• If there are any liens, or legal claims, against your salary or property and
• If you have outstanding debts

Details of purchase asks about how much you want to borrow, how much *down payment* (cash part of the purchase price) you have, and where the rest of the money will come from. Borrowing a large amount from another source—even from your family—could disqualify you.

Monthly income is a key figure for lenders. It can include non-salary income, such as earnings on your investments or money you get from rentals, but you'll have to prove the income is regular. You can also count alimony or related payments to establish your eligibility.

Net worth is the total value of what you have (assets) minus what you owe (liabilities). Assets include cash, bank accounts, investments, and property. Liabilities include debts you owe on loans, credit cards, leases, alimony, and child support. Mortgage loans usually require the numbers as well as the location of accounts, loans and credit cards.

Surviving the Closing

You'll write many checks, sign your name countless times, and sift through mounds of paper—but in the end, you'll walk away with the keys to your new house.

At the closing, or *settlement,* the buyer and seller, the lender, all the attorneys, a representative of the title company, the real estate agent, and assorted others meet to sign the papers and pay the costs that legally complete the deal.

To help prepare you for this ritual, the lender will provide a *good faith written estimate* of the closing costs you can expect to pay—usually from 5 to 10% of the loan amount. You can get a HUD guide called *Settlement Costs* from your lender, or by calling the local HUD office.

The title attests that there are no claims against the property that might jeopardize your ownership.

Title insurance, which many lenders require, guarantees those findings. Title insurance for yourself, called *fee insurance,* is available for an additional charge. You'll spend several hundred dollars for title search and insurance.

The Truth-in-Lending Statement shows the real cost of the mortgage loan, including:
• The amount of the loan
• The *finance charge* (the interest you'll owe over the term of the loan)
• The *annual percentage rate (APR),* which is the actual interest rate you'll pay on the loan amount, plus fees and points (See page 32 for more information on APR.)

The mortgage is a standard legal document that describes your agreement with the lender, the property itself, and the amount of the mortgage.

The certificate of occupancy is issued by the local authority and attests that the house is safe and habitable.

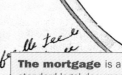

Proof of insurance is often required by your lender. If your policy also covers your car and other possessions, ask the company to break out the house insurance separately. This will lower the amount on which your escrow is calculated.

The loan note spells out the terms of your mortgage loan: what's due, when it's due, and what happens if you *default* (don't pay) or pay late.

The closing statement itemizes all the costs you'll need to pay at the closing, including:
• **Balance** of the down payment you still owe the seller for the purchase price.
• **Points,** an up-front interest charge paid to the lender. A point is 1% of the mortgage amount, and paying 2–3 points is typical. The amount is either deducted from the mortgage loan, or you may write a separate check, which is preferable for tax purposes. Since points are fully deductible on an original purchase, you'll need a record of the payment.
• **Filing fee** and other fees required for recording the transfer of ownership with local authorities.
• **Mortgage tax** paid to the state where the sale occurs (the amount is not tax deductible).
• **Attorney's fees** for both your lawyer and the lender's as well. To save money, you can use the lender's lawyer or even represent yourself, but this is risky if there are any hitches. Lawyer's fees can be a flat fee or a percentage of the mortgage amount.
• **Real estate taxes** paid to seller to cover the portion of taxes the seller has already paid for the year. For example, if you bought the house April 1, and the seller had paid school taxes in September and town taxes in January, you would pay:

6 months (or $6/12$) of total school taxes

and 9 months (or $9/12$) of the town taxes

• **Escrow**, a kind of enforced savings paid into a reserve account. It covers your real estate taxes and home insurance when they come due. That's good for lenders, who want to protect their interest, but not good for you, since you must prepay these costs ahead of time. And most lenders pay little or no interest on your escrow account.

How Escrow Works

The escrow statement below assumes a closing date of 1/1/92.

Payments	Due Date	Months Collected	Amount Paid at Closing	Estimated Monthly Payment
County Tax	1/1/92	0		$ 92
School Tax	9/1/92	4	$ 736	184
Town Tax	6/1/92	7	735	105
Insurance Premium	4/1/92	9	1,377	153
	Total Paid at Closing		**$2,848**	
	Total Monthly Escrow Payment			**$534**

Escrow Overcharges The law says that at least one month a year your escrow account should hold no more than $1/6$ of your total tax and insurance bills. For example, if that total is $3600, there must be at least one month when your account has no more than $600. A good month to check is the one after your biggest payment is due.

Call the lender if you think you're paying too much escrow. If you can't resolve your differences, call the state Attorney General.

You may be eligible to stop paying escrow if you've paid off 20% of your mortgage and have never been late with a payment. You may be able to avoid escrow altogether if you put down more than 20% of the purchase price and have an excellent credit history.

The Cost of a Mortgage

The cost of a mortgage depends on  **five** key numbers: the amount you borrow, the interest rate, and how long it takes to repay. But don't overlook up-front interest —or *points*—and other fees.

Since monthly payments are modest, it's easy to forget the total cost of a mortgage. For example, if you borrow $100,000 for 30 years at an 8.5% interest rate, your total repayment will be around $277,000, more than $2 \frac{1}{2}$ times the original loan.

Minor differences in the interest rate —8.75% vs. 8.25% — can add up to a lot of money over 30 years.

1 Loan Amount (Principal)

The amount you actually borrow after fees and points are deducted. It's the basis for figuring the real interest, or APR (annual percentage rate), on the money you're borrowing.

2 Term (Length of the Loan)

The length of time you want to borrow the money. The longer the term, the lower the monthly payments, but the more you'll pay in the end.

3 Interest Rate

The interest rate may be fixed for the length of the loan or adjusted periodically to reflect prevailing interest rates. Over time, a lower interest rate will have the greatest impact on overall cost.

4 Points (Prepaid Interest)

Interest that you prepay at the closing. Each point is 1% of the loan amount. For example, on a $90,000 loan with 3 points, you'd prepay $2,700.

5 Fees

Fees include application fees, loan origination fees, and other initial costs imposed by the lender.

Bottom Line: any of the factors will increase the overall cost, but a higher interest rate and longer term will have the greatest impact.

Cutting Mortgage Expenses

You can reduce the cost several ways.

❶ Consider a Shorter-term Mortgage. With a shorter term, you'll pay less interest overall, and your monthly payments will be somewhat larger. A 15-year mortgage, as opposed to 30-year mortgage for the same amount, can cut your costs by more than 55%.

Some banks also offer 20-year mortgages, which reduce the overall interest cost without significantly raising monthly payments.

❷ Consider Amortizing (paying off) the Loan Faster. You can pay your mortgage bi-weekly instead of monthly, or you can make an additional payment each month.

• **Biweekly payments.** You make 26 regular payments instead of 12 every year. The mortgage is paid off in a little more than half the time, and you pay a little more than half the interest.

• **Extra payments.** An additional payment each month reduces your principal. With a fixed rate mortgage, you pay off the loan quicker, but regular monthly payments remain the same. With an ARM, interest is figured on a smaller principal each time the rate is adjusted, so your monthly payments become lower.

Be sure the lender knows you want the extra payments credited toward the principal. Your mortgage bill should have a line for entering the additional amount, and you can send a separate check. Also, you can change the amount or stop anytime.

The catch to additional payments: you may come out ahead by investing your extra cash elsewhere. This is especially true in the last years of a fixed rate loan, when you're paying off mostly principal so you can't reduce the interest cost much.

The effect of the term on a $100,000 mortgage.

	Monthly Amount at Different Interest Rates			
Term	8.5%	9.0%	9.5%	10%
15 year	$ 985	1014	1044	1075
30 year	$ 769	805	841	878
	Total Payment			
Term	8.5%	9.0%	9.5%	10%
15 year	$ 177,300	182,520	187,920	193,500
30 year	$ 276,840	289,800	302,760	316,080

A Point Well Taken

Lenders might be willing to raise the rate by a fraction (say an ⅛% or ¼%) and lower the points—or the reverse—as long as they make the same profit.

The advantages of fewer points are lower closing costs and laying out less money when you're apt to need it most. But if you plan to keep the house longer than 5 to 7 years, paying more points to get a lower interest rate will reduce your long-term cost.

The following chart shows the effect of points and interest on a 30-year, $100,000 mortgage.

	Loan A	Loan B
Interest rate	8.75%	8.5%
Number of points	1	2
Cost of points	$1000	$2000
Year 1 total	10,441	11,227
Year 2 total	19,881	20.454
Year 3 total	29,321	29,681
Year 4 total	38,762	38,908
Year 5 total	48,202	48,135
Year 10 total	95,405	94,270
Year 30 total	284,215	278,811

Years 1-4: Loan A (higher interest rate but fewer points) costs less.
Year 5: Loan B's lower interest rate compensates for the higher initial points, and begins to cost less.
The longer you have the mortgage, the cheaper Loan B becomes compared to Loan A.

Fixed Rate Mortgages

Mortgages are *fixed rate* or *adjustable rate*, or sometimes a hybrid of the two. Your choice will depend on available cash, how frequently you move, and most important of all—whether you think interest rates will go up or down.

Fixed rate or *conventional* mortgages have been around since the 1930s. The total interest and monthly payments are set at the closing. You repay the principal and interest in equal (usually monthly) installments over a 15-, 20- or 30-year period. You'll always know what you'll pay and for how long.

Although ARMs are very common, there have been wide-spread problems in figuring the changes in interest and payments. Audits of lenders' records have revealed both undercharges and overcharges. It's hard to do your own computation or verify the accuracy of your lenders' figures because the calculations are very convoluted. But you can question unexpected changes.

P L U S S E S

1. You always know your housing costs, so you can budget more easily.
2. Your mortgage won't increase if interest rates go up.

M I N U S E S

1. Initial rates and closing costs are higher than for ARMs.
2. Your monthly payments may be larger than with ARMs.
3. You won't benefit if interest rates drop—you'll have to refinance to get the lower rates.

Hybrid Mortgages: Fixed vs. adjustable rate is not a black-and-white issue: there are a variety of blends to choose from.

Type	How It Works
Graduated Payment Mortgage (GPM)	Your initial payments are small, with gradual increases over a 5- or 10-year period until a preset, fixed rate is reached.
Growing Equity Mortgage (GEM)	Your payments increase on a fixed schedule, so you pay off the mortgage more quickly—usually after 18 years on a 30-year mortgage.
Balloon Mortgage	You make a down payment, borrow the balance—often from the seller—and pay interest only for a period of 3, 5, or 7 years. Then you pay principal in a lump sum or refinance.
Seven Year ARM or 7/23	You have one rate for 7 years, and just 1 adjustment for the rest of the 30-year term.

Adjustable Rate Mortgages

Adjustable Rate Mortgages (ARM) were introduced in the 1980s to help more buyers qualify for mortgages, and to protect lenders by letting them pass along higher interest costs to borrowers.

How Do ARMs Work? An ARM has a variable interest rate: the rate changes on a regular schedule—such as once a year—to reflect fluctuations in the cost of borrowing. Unlike fixed rate mortgages, the total cost can't be figured in advance, and monthly payments may rise or fall over the term of the loan.

Lenders determine the new rate using two measures: ❶ **The index**, which is often a published figure, like the rate on one-year U.S. Treasury securities or the cost of funds indexes from the Office of Thrift Supervision. Be sure to check the index: some fluctuate more, and change more rapidly, than others. ❷ **The Margin,** which is the hundredths of a percentage point added to the index to determine the new rate.

How Do Caps Work? All ARMs have *caps*, or limits, on the amount the interest rate can be changed.

ARMs declined from 61% of the home mortgage market in 1984 to 31% in 1986 to less than 25% in 1990.

An *annual cap* limits the rate change each year (usually by 2 percentage points), while a *lifetime* cap limits the change (typically, by 5 or 6 points) over the life of the loan.

Be careful: lifetime caps are often based on the actual cost and not on the introductory rate. For example, with a 7.25% teaser rate and 9.50% actual interest cost, your rate could go as high as 15.50% —even with a 6 point lifetime cap.

What Is Negative Amortization?
It means you still owe money when the mortgage is up, because interest rates have gone higher than your cap.

Put simply, if interest rates rise 5% one year, but your annual cap is 1%, you still owe the 4% difference. The additional interest is added to the amount of your loan.

Eventually, the term of the loan may be extended, creating extra payments to cover the extra money you owe.

Not all ARMs allow negative amortization. If they do, the most they can accumulate is 125% of the original loan amount. Then some resolution must be arranged, such as a lump sum payment or loan extension.

Chopping off Your ARM
Qualifying for ARMs has become much more difficult. Fannie Mae now uses 7% as the base rate for determining qualification—even if you can get a lower rate initially. This way, lenders feel you're less likely to default if interest rates rise.

ADJUSTABLE

P L U S S E S	M I N U S E S
1. Low initial rates (sometimes called *teaser rates*) reduce your closing costs and beginning monthly payments. **2.** Your interest rate will drop if interest rates go down.	**1.** It's hard to budget housing costs, since monthly payments can change yearly. **2.** Interest costs may jump after the teaser rate expires. **3.** You may have to pay more interest if rates go up.

Refinancing

When interest rates go down, you may want to refinance a fixed rate loan to get a lower rate. But remember, you may have to pay hefty closing costs and up-front fees again, even if your mortgage is only a few years old.

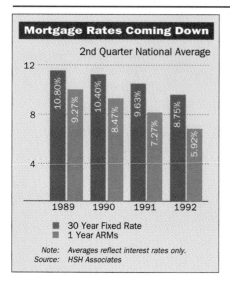

Mortgage Rates Coming Down

2nd Quarter National Average

- 30 Year Fixed Rate
- 1 Year ARMs

Note: Averages reflect interest rates only.
Source: HSH Associates

Why Refinance?

You may want to refinance your mortgage for several reasons:
- You can get a lower interest rate, which will reduce your monthly payment and the overall cost of the mortgage
- You may want to consolidate outstanding debt—for example, by combining a first and second mortgage into a single new one
- You may want to reduce the term of your loan; while this may increase your monthly payment, it will dramatically reduce your total cost

For example, a California condo owner traded his 10 ¼% 30-year fixed rate mortgage for a 15-year fixed-rate at 8 ¼%. His monthly payments will increase $74, but he plans to save some $175,000 in interest.

When to Refinance

The rule of thumb is that it pays to refinance if you can get interest rates at least *2 percentage points* lower than you're currently paying.

But every situation is different. To figure out whether you can save money, you need to consider: ❶ how much lower your monthly payments will be ❷ what refinancing costs you must pay and ❸ how long you plan to stay put.

Your best bet is to tell the lender what you paid for the house, what you still owe, and how much you're paying each month. Have the lender itemize all the expenses involved and estimate your new payments. Then you can figure when you will break even.

For example, if you save $1,600 a year by refinancing, but it costs you $4,800 to do it, you'll have to stay put more than three years to realize any savings.

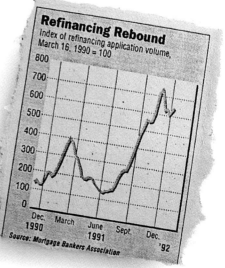

Refinancing Rebound
Index of refinancing application volume,
March 16, 1990 = 100

Source: Mortgage Bankers Association

Refinancing is often like reliving the closing on your first mortgage. It requires an application and credit check, new survey, title search and insurance, an appraisal and inspection, and of course, attorneys. If the lender is the same or the original mortgage has been recently approved, you may be able to negotiate these costs.

THE MORTGAGE BANKERS ASSOCIATION ESTIMATES THAT REFINANCINGS, COUPLED WITH LOWER ADJUSTABLE RATE MORTGAGES, SAVED HOMEOWNERS $10– $12 BILLION IN 1991.

When Does It Pay to Refinance?

People who refinance their mortgages should be planning to stay in their homes at least long enough to recover the costs. This worksheet can help estimate how long it will take before refinancing begins paying off. (The example shows the estimated payback period for refinancing a $100,000 mortgage if an existing loan at 10.25% is replaced with an 8.5% loan; amounts shown are typical, but will vary by bank and by area.)

ITEMIZED COSTS OF REFINANCING		EXAMPLE
Discount Points	$	$2,000
Origination Points (if any)		0
Application Fee		350
Credit Check		70
Attorney Review fee (yours)		200
Attorney Review fee (lender's)		200
Title Search Fee		50
Title Insurance Fee		400
Appraisal Fee		250
Inspections		350
Local Fees (taxes, transfers)		1,000[1]
Other Fees		0
Estimate for other costs		250
Prepayment penalty on your existing mortgage (if any)		0
Total of all fees on your new mortgage		5,120
Current mortgage's monthly payment[2]		896
New mortgage's monthly payment[2]		769
Difference between the two payments		127
Number of months to recoup costs: (Total of all fees, divided by the difference in monthly payments)		40 months

[1] Varies by area, from 0% to about 2.5%
[2] Principal and interest only

Source: HSH Associates

What if You Fall Behind in Your Mortgage Payments?

Although lenders can *foreclose on* (repossess) your house if you're 90 days behind in your payments, most will agree to less drastic measures. Some solutions:

- Add the amount you're behind to the end of the mortgage, which extends the term and cost of the loan
- Renegotiate with the lender to reduce each monthly payment. Then pay the difference, plus the amount you're behind, at the end of the mortgage
- Temporarily reduce payments and increase later ones, or make a *balloon* (one time) payment to catch up
- Increase future payments slightly until you've paid up the amount you're behind

If you sometimes feel you're a slave to your mortgage, consider the ancient Romans. They DID become slaves if they defaulted on a mortgage—at least before 326 BC.

Your Home as Investment

Your house may have emotional, aesthetic, and historical value, but it has financial value as well. Some people even buy houses as investments, fix them up, and sell them at a profit. Since a lot of your money is probably invested in your house, it's important to keep an eye on its value.

What Is the Value of Your House?

That depends on whether you're talking to the seller, the appraiser or the tax collector.

▶ *Market value* is the price you pay when you buy a house—it's what the market will bear. A house built in a certain style, or in a prestigious neighborhood, will often command a higher price. And a house in a booming area may sell for tens of thousands of dollars more than essentially the same house in a depressed or undesirable location.

▶ *Appraised value* (sometimes called *fair market value*) is what a real estate appraiser says your house is worth. The appraisal is based on the selling prices of similar houses in the area, as well as subjective judgment. So two appraisers may value the same house differently.

The appraised value doesn't dictate the market value. But many appraisers are also real estate agents, so there's usually a strong correlation.

▶ *Assessed value* is assigned by the local tax assessor and is the basis for your real estate taxes. There can be a large difference between assessed and appraised value, depending on how recently the assessment was done and the standards used in your community.

Often a house is reassessed when it is sold or remodeled. If you consider the assessment too high, you can appeal it on *grievance day*. Be prepared to show the assessments of comparable houses and to point out shortcomings the assessor might have overlooked that reduce its value.

If you purchased your house for $200,000 and you put $100,000 down and have a $100,000 mortage, your equity is 50%.

EQUITY

50%

Your Equity Painter

What Is Equity?

When you make a down payment on a house, the amount of the payment determines your *equity*. The more you put down, the greater your equity.

As you pay off the principal on your mortgage, your equity in the house increases. When your mortgage is fully paid, your equity is 100%. The house is yours free and clear, and you get the *deed* (or legal title) to it.

Equity Can Change

The value of a house changes continually—and so does your equity for as long as you have a mortgage.

If your house later is reappraised at $250,000, your equity increases to $150,000 or 60%.

Does It Pay to Make Improvements?

Improvements can be a real asset when you want to sell. Modern kitchens and bathrooms usually pay for themselves by increasing the market value of your house. So does a fireplace. But you may have a harder time getting back the cost of a swimming pool, sauna, or converted garage.

And if improvements make your house overpriced for the neighborhood, it may be hard to sell.

Local governments and condo and co-op associations often have strict rules about additions and renovations. There may be a fee, based on the estimated cost of improvements. And you'll have to get approvals and permits, schedule inspections for electrical and plumbing work, and get a certificate of occupancy.

Renting Your Home

You can make money by renting your home. The rent is taxable income, but you can deduct the cost of improvements up to certain limits. You can also rent out a second home, but special tax rules apply to how much you can use it if you want to deduct expenses.

And if your house is reappraised to $150,000, your equity will decrease to $50,000 or 33%.

E Q U I T Y

60%

E Q U I T Y

33%

Borrowing on Your Home

You can use the equity in your home to borrow money for major improvements or for other needs. Under current tax laws, this is one of the few loans with tax-deductible interest.

> The **interest rate** varies by the lender. The APR (Annual Percentage Rate) the lender quotes does not include closing costs, which are considered extra expenses. That makes it more difficult to calculate your total costs.

Home equity *lines of credit* let you borrow up to a fixed amount (or credit limit) without reapplying each time you need cash. Lenders issue special checks or credit cards to give you immediate access to your funds.

Usually, you repay the loan in regular installments, which you can change as long as you repay the required minimum. With some home equity loans, you pay only the interest in installments; you then pay off the principal in a lump sum on a specific date.

What Is a Reverse Mortgage?

It's a loan designed to help elderly people get cash by borrowing against the equity in their homes. It's *reverse* because the lender pays *the borrower* for a fixed period of time, usually 3 to 7 years. Since it's a loan, the money is also tax-free. When the people move or die, the house is sold to repay the loan.

Reverse mortages have many pitfalls, however, including high interest rates, losing equity in the home, and having nothing to leave heirs.

How Much Can You Borrow?

The more equity you have in your house, the more you can borrow against it. For example, if you owe $15,000 on a house appraised at $125,000, you can probably borrow up to $88,000 (or 80% of your equity) using your house as collateral.

How Do the Loans Work?

Most home equity loans are *adjustable rate* loans. The rate is adjusted periodically and is based on an *index*, which is either public—like the prime rate or the U.S. Treasury Bill rate—or established by the lender.

Public indexes are better because you can check the rates—whether they go up or down—against the index.

You may also be charged an annual fee, and a usage fee each time you borrow. Some lenders allow you to take a minimum amount only, while others make you activate your loan as soon as you get it. Federal rules now require lenders to make the terms clear.

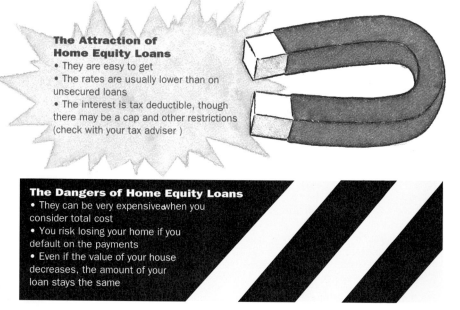

The Attraction of Home Equity Loans
- They are easy to get
- The rates are usually lower than on unsecured loans
- The interest is tax deductible, though there may be a cap and other restrictions (check with your tax adviser)

The Dangers of Home Equity Loans
- They can be very expensive when you consider total cost
- You risk losing your home if you default on the payments
- Even if the value of your house decreases, the amount of your loan stays the same

Bank	%Rate	%Above Prime	Promotional Rate	Access Period	Repayment Period
Apple	11.25	1.75	(None)	5 years	20 years
Barclays	11.00	1.50	Prime, 1st 2 years	5 years	20 years
Chase	11.40	1.40	Prime 1st year	10 years	30 years
Chemical	11.25	1.75	(None)	10 years	15 years
Citibank	10.65	0.90	(None)	10 years	30 years
Dime	11.25	1.75	Intro rate: 9.00%	10 years	20 years
LISB	11.50	1.75	7.25%: 1st 3 months	10 years	25 years
Marine Midland	11.25	1.25	(None)	5 years	20 years
Nat'l Westminster	11.75	2.25	(None)	10 years	20 years

The **margin,** or percentage points, when added to the index, determines the new interest rate each time it is adjusted. In this case, the index being used is the prime rate, which is reported daily in The Wall Street Journal.

For illustration only: rates may have changed.

The **teaser rate,** or *promotional rate,* can be significantly lower for a short period of time to attract customers. Check the regular interest rate and initial fees to figure your actual costs.

The **access period** is the time during which you can borrow money. You can often renegotiate a new line of credit when the period ends.

Long term **repayments** make home equity loans very expensive. Borrowing $5,000 at 11.25% for 20 years will cost you $11,250 in interest. The same loan repaid in 5 years would cost only $2,812.

Where to Get the Loans

Banks and thrift institutions offer home equity loans. So do credit unions, brokerage houses, retirement plans, and insurance companies.

To apply, you'll need to provide the lender with details about your property and personal finances. You may also have to pay fees and closing costs as though you were taking a mortgage. Some lenders waive these fees to get your business.

Other Ways You Can Borrow against Your Home

▶ *Second Mortgages* are more traditional, and often cheaper, ways of borrowing against your equity. You apply the same way you do for a mortgage; the closing costs are usually less and the interest rates usually more. You get a lump sum, which you repay in monthly installments over a 5-to 15-year term. Most second mortgages now have adjustable interest rates.
▶ *Title One,* an FHA (Federal Housing Administration) program, insures home improvement or home repair loans that resemble second mortgages. If you own a 1 to 4 family house, look for a participating lender or get in touch with the Federal Housing Administration.

▶ *Homeowner or home improvement loans* are actually personal loans that use your house as collateral. You get the money in a lump sum and repay it on a fixed schedule for a specific term—usually 1-to-7 years.

The interest rate may be higher than on home equity loans, but the fees are often smaller, so the total cost may be less. You may be able to get lower rates if you're using the money for home improvements, or if you have other accounts with the lender.

Can You Really Lose Your House if You Can't Pay?

Yes, you certainly can. Because your house is the collateral for the loan, the lender has a right to *foreclose* (take your house) if you don't keep up your payments or default on a lump sum or *balloon* payment.

Even if you pay your mortgage on time, you may lose your house if you default on your home equity loan. And if your house is sold at auction for less than what you owe, you are responsible for the outstanding debt.

Insuring Your Home

Insurance protects your investment in your home. It can also protect you if you are sued for damages or injury you cause. But be sure you have the right amount and type of coverage, so you can collect when there's a loss.

Homeowners insurance covers your house and its contents—including your personal possessions and valuable articles —against damage or loss. If you rent, you can get insurance just for your home's contents. There are also special policies for condos and co-ops.

Benjamin Franklin organized the first fire insurance company in North America in 1752. It's still doing business in Philadelphia.

What's Covered?

Policies vary in the kinds of *perils* or *hazards* they cover, and how they compensate you for a loss.

A standard, or *named perils,* policy provides limited protection—it lists the specific perils (for example, fire, theft) that are covered. Broad coverage gives you insurance for all types of losses except those excluded from the policy.

You can also get special insurance for valuable articles—jewelry, art work, collectibles—for which you pay a separate premium.

The insurance industry codes Homeowners policies from HO 1 to HO 8 to reflect the range of coverages. The broader the policy, the higher the premium you'll pay.

What's Excluded?

Virtually no basic policy covers losses resulting from war, riots, police actions, nuclear explosion, or "acts of God." You can sometimes get a rider or endorsement to your policy to cover situations that are normally excluded, such as floods and earthquakes, but you'll pay an extra premium for this coverage.

What's Liability Coverage?

This coverage can protect you if you're sued for causing property damage or injuring someone. Extra or *excess liability* increases the amount of coverage and may give you added protection for a wider range of activities, such as your role in community or government organizations.

What's a Deductible?

Every policy has a *deductible*, an amount you pay for a loss before the coverage kicks in. Deductibles may vary from a few hundred to a few thousand dollars. You can reduce the cost of your insurance by taking a larger deductible, but you'll have to pay the amount of any loss up to the deductible.

How Much Coverage Do You Need?

You should insure your house for at least 80% of its *replacement value*—what it would cost to repair or rebuild the house at today's prices. But it probably makes better sense to insure your house for its full replacement value. Most companies will automatically increase your coverage and raise your premium each year to cover rising costs. It often pays to get replacement cost coverage for the contents of your home.

What Do You Get after a Loss?

That depends on the policy terms (the fine print) which you should read carefully, or discuss with your insurance agent, when you get the policy. Learning how much— or how little—you'll get paid after a loss can be an unpleasant surprise.

Some policies require you to replace the damaged or stolen property, and then reimburse you for the expense. Others give you the money for the agreed-upon value, but don't require the replacement; you can spend the money as you see fit.

Selling Your House

On average, people live in a house for five to seven years before selling it and moving on. So buying is only half the story: the other half is getting a good deal when you sell.

Using an Agent vs. Selling It Yourself

Using a real estate agent costs money—sometimes up to 7% of your selling price in commissions or fees.

Agents generally know the local market, can help you determine a fair selling price, and can screen potential buyers. It pays to invite several agents to suggest an asking price and explain their commission structure. Realtors ordinarily do this for free: they want your business.

Selling on your own requires more time. You must always be available to show the house, and you'll have to make more decisions about everything from setting a price to accepting an offer. You'll also have to judge if potential buyers are serious, and whether they'll be able to get a mortgage.

What if Nothing Happens?
The seller's nightmare is a house that won't sell. If it's the economy—national or local—you can't do much about it. But you can consider:
- lowering your asking price
- changing agents—or using one if you haven't already
- offering to finance all or part of the purchase price yourself

Does Fixing-up Pay?

Opinion is divided. Some believe that buyers want to do their own fixing up, so it isn't worth the trouble. Others argue that buyers respond better to places that look good: minor repairs and cosmetic touch-ups don't hurt, and they don't cost much. Neither does cleanliness.

And if there are major problems—like a leaky roof—that you don't repair, you may have to lower your price in negotiating the final contract.

What's a Fair Price?

Realistically, it's whatever you can get. To judge if your price is fair, check local sales records of *comparables*—similar homes that have sold in your community recently. Charts available in real estate agents' offices tell you the asking price, time on the market, and selling price of other houses.

Don't be misled by the *asking price* for houses in your area: it's what they actually sell for that counts.

Statistics from Realtors and lenders show that agents (and brokers) account for nearly 90% of all house sales.

Sellers' Headaches
• Getting the price you want
• Deciding how much fix-up to do before selling
• Selling in a slow market
• Lowering the price or having to provide financing yourself

• Paying extra costs for needed repairs identified during inspections
• Avoiding unacceptable contract terms, like long delays or zoning approvals
• Discovering unexpected liens against your property, like unpaid contractor bills or court costs

Bridge loans—sometimes called swing loans or turnarounds—let you buy a new house if the sale of your old one hasn't been completed. You borrow the amount you need, pay only interest while you have the loan, and repay the lump sum when your sale closes. A signed contract can make a bridge loan easier to get.

Negotiating a Contract

When you get a good offer, you'll need a real estate lawyer to be sure the terms of the contract don't tie your hands if the buyer delays or drops out.

The sale usually depends on the buyer's being able to get a mortgage and a free and clear title to the property. But any unusual contingencies—like dependence on inheritance or insurance money—should have a time limit. The contract should also spell out who pays specific closing costs, since these practices vary.

The Closing

Though there's a lot of paperwork, it all comes down to paying off what you owe and settling with the buyer. Here's what you can expect to pay:
• The balance of your mortgage, plus fees
• The real estate agent—usually 5 to 7% of the selling price
• Pro-rated real estate taxes
• Transfer taxes
• Your lawyer
• Other costs specified in the contract

If you're providing some of the financing, you'll also get a copy of the loan agreement. Be sure to record it with the local government to secure your claim if the buyer defaults.

Paying Taxes on Profits

Whether you have a profit (or loss) when you sell your house, you must report the sale on your tax return for that year. But you can usually defer the tax if you buy another house, or you may be entitled to a one time exclusion on the profits.

Since property values tend to rise over time, you'll probably sell your house at a profit. But in hard-pressed areas, and down economic times, you may sell at a loss. In either case, you must report the sale on IRS Form 2119.

Deferring Taxes on Your Profit.
You can postpone paying tax on your profit if you buy another house that costs more than the one you just sold—provided you meet these conditions:
- You buy within two years
- The property is your primary residence
- You haven't deferred taxes on profit from the sale of another home within the last two years

You can keep buying and selling houses at a profit—and deferring taxes—indefinitely, as long as you meet these conditions.

What If You Pay Less for a New House?
If you move to a less expensive area, you may pay less for a new home than you got from selling the old one. In that case, you

may owe tax on the difference between the adjusted sales price and the cost of the new home. However, you have two years to improve your new house to bring its cost above the amount you sold the old one for.

Age 55 Exclusion
If you are 55 or over when you sell, you can exclude tax on profits from the sale of your primary residence. You can exclude up to $125,000 ($62,500 if you're single or were married on the date of sale and file separate returns). But you can do this only once in a lifetime, and married couples can take only one exclusion between them.

Keeping Records
When you sell, you can reduce the tax on any profit by adding to the basis the cost of permanent improvements, such as replacing the roof, installing hardwood floors, and landscaping your yard. But you'll need to document the costs with detailed

Figuring Your Profit (or loss)

To figure the profit or loss on the sale of your house, you can use the following formula:			
Selling price	**Selling Price**		**$239,000**
— Original purchase price	Original purchase price	$156,000	
— Cost of improvements	Improvements		
	replaced the roof	3,500	
	remodeled the bathroom	4,000	
	converted the attic	3,900	
	added kitchen cabinets	1,700	
	Cost Basis		**— $169,100**
	Title insurance and transfer taxes	1,500	
	Legal fees	450	
	Real estate commission (6%)	14,340	
— Cost of selling	**Total Selling Costs**		**— $16,290**
= Profit (or loss)	**Total Profit (Adjusted selling price)**		**= $53,610**

records, including: architect fees; contractor payments; receipts for construction materials, appliances, and installation costs; building and zoning permit fees.

Routine upkeep, like painting, cannot be deducted from the selling price.

IRS rules on deferring and excluding taxes on real estate profits are specific. You can find them in IRS *Publication 523*. Whether you owe, defer, or exclude the taxes, you have to report the sale of your primary residence on Form 2119. Sales of vacation and rental property go on Schedule D.

Form 2119

Department of the Treasury
Internal Revenue Service

Sale of Your Home

▶ Attach to Form 1040 for year of sale.
▶ See separate instructions. ▶ Please print or type.

OMB No. 1545-0072

1991

Attachment Sequence No. 20

Your first name and initial. (If joint return, also give spouse's name and initial.) — Theodore and Dorathea
Last name — Taxpayer

Fill in Your Address Only If You Are Filing This Form by Itself and Not With Your Tax Return

Present address (no., street, and apt. no., rural route, or P.O. box no. if mail is not delivered to street address) — 222 Elm Street

City, town or post office, state, and ZIP code — Anytown, USA

Your social security number — 123 45 6789

Spouse's social security number — 123 45 6789

Caution: *If the home sold was financed (in whole or part) from a mortgage credit certificate or the proceeds of a tax-exempt qualified mortgage bond, you may owe additional tax. Get Form 8828, Recapture of Federal Mortgage Subsidy, for details.*

Part I General Information

1a Date your former main home was sold (month, day, year) . . . . ▶ | 1a | 9/19/92

b Face amount of any mortgage, note (e.g., second trust), or other financial instrument on which you will get periodic payments of principal or interest from this sale (see instructions) . . . | 1b |

2 Have you bought or built a new main home? . . . . | ☑ Yes ☐ No

3 Is or was any part of either main home rented out or used for business? (If "Yes," see instructions.) | ☐ Yes ☑ No

Part II Gain on Sale (Do not include amounts you deduct as moving expenses.)

4 Selling price of home. (Do not include personal property items that you sold with your home.) | 4 | 239,000

5 Expense of sale. (Include sales commissions, advertising, legal, etc.) . . . . | 5 | 16,290

6 Amount realized. Subtract line 5 from line 4 . . . . | 6 | 222,710

7 Basis of home sold (see instructions) . . . . | 7 | 169,100

8a Gain on sale. Subtract line 7 from line 6 . . . . | 8a | 53,610

● If line 8a is zero or less, stop here and attach this form to your return.
● If line 2 is "Yes," you **must** go to Part III or Part IV, whichever applies.
If you haven't replaced your home, do you plan to do so within the replacement period (see instructions)? . . ☐ Yes ☐ No
● If "Yes," stop here, attach this form to your return, and see *Additional Filing Requirements* in the instructions.
● If "No," you **must** go to Part III or Part IV, whichever applies.

Part III One-Time Exclusion of Gain for People Age 55 or Older (If you are not taking the exclusion, go to Part IV now.)

5 Who was age 55 or older on date of sale? . . . . ☐ You ☐ Your spouse ☑ Both of you

6 Did the person who was age 55 or older own and use the property as his or her main home for a total of at least 3 years (except for short absences) of the 5-year period before the sale? (If "No," go to Part IV now.) | ☑ Yes ☐ No

7 If line 9b is "Yes," do you elect to take the one-time exclusion? (If "No," go to Part IV now.) . . | ☐ Yes ☑ No

8 At time of sale, who owned the home? . . . . ☐ You ☐ Your spouse ☐ Both of you

9 Social security number of spouse at time of sale if you had a different spouse from the one above at time of sale. (If you were not married at time of sale, enter "None.") . . . . . . ▶ | 9e |

10 Exclusion. Enter the smaller of line 8a or $125,000 ($62,500, if married filing separate return) . . ▶ | 9f |

Part IV Adjusted Sales Price, Taxable Gain, and Adjusted Basis of New Home

11 Subtract line 9f from line 8a . . . . | 10 |

● If line 10 is zero, stop here and attach this form to your return.
● If line 2 is "Yes," go to line 11 now.

[...] method, stop here and see the line 1b instructions.

[...] line 10 on Schedule D, line 2 or line 9.

[...] b Cost of new home . . . | 11 | 13b |

[...] or less, enter -0- | 14a |
[...] 4b . . | 14b |
[...] rm to your return. | 14c |

[...] see the line 1b instructions and go to line 15.
[...] edule D, line 2 or line 9, and go to line 15.

[...] line 13b . . . . . | 15 |
[...] ined this form, including attachments, and to the best of my knowledge and belief, it is true. | 16 |

Date — Spouse's signature — Date

▶

Cat. No. 11710J

Form **2119** (1991)

*U.S. Government Printing Office: 1991 — 285-286

Cost Basis

The original purchase price and cost of improvements together are called the *cost basis*.

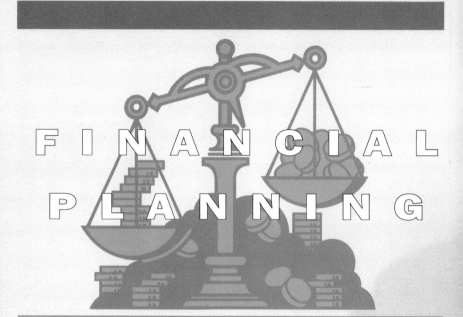

FINANCIAL PLANNING

A financial plan is a blueprint that evaluates your current assets and debts, identifies the things you want (or need) to provide for, and lays out a strategy to pay for them. Developing the plan is one thing; sticking to it is another.

The Financial Planning Process

Examining your current situation and understanding your needs	Gathering information	Setting your objectives: • Gaining wealth • Providing protection • Minimizing taxes • Preserving wealth

R E V

Financial Planning

Financial planning is directed at the future. The idea is to evaluate your current financial situation, estimate the cost of life-long goals, and establish strategies to meet them.

Why Have a Plan?

Without planning, you run certain financial risks. For example, you may not have enough in reserve to meet large costs, such as college tuition or a down payment on a home, or you may have to scale back expected vacations and special purchases.

Six out of ten Americans rate a steady source of retirement income as their primary financial goal.

WHAT A SUCCESSFUL FINANCIAL PLAN CAN DO

Beat Inflation

Helps your money earn more than the rate of inflation. (Money saved, rather than money invested, doesn't grow.)

Minimize Taxes

Uses tax-free investments to avoid income taxes, and tax-deferred investments to postpone income taxes. Sets up trusts to reduce the taxes your heirs will owe later.

Manage the Unexpected

Provides a cash fund plus adequate health and life insurance as a hedge against unexpected expenses and illness.

Provide Money for Special Expenses

Lets you afford things that are important to you, like college expenses, a vacation home, or travel and leisure activities.

Enrich Your Retirement

Supplements pensions and Social Security so you can maintain your lifestyle when you retire.

REVISIONS | BY

HOW

FINANCIAL PLANNING

A

Developing a plan

Proposing solutions

Implementing the plan

Based on a model from IDS Financial Services Inc.

I   E   W

Financial Plans—and Planners

Financial planning gets a standing ovation, but financial planners get mixed reviews.

A professional financial plan begins with a *profile*—a questionnaire that a planner completes in an initial interview. You'll need to provide some basic documents—recent tax forms, insurance policies and retirement plans—and be prepared to discuss your financial goals.

Profiles vary in level of detail and sophistication. The more elaborate they are, the more customized information they provide. The cost is more as well.

1. Your current financial situation and net worth
2. Planning assumptions
3. Financial goals, and timetable to meet them
4. Insurance
5. Retirement planning
6. Tax strategies
7. Estate planning, wills and trusts
8. Recommended actions

What's in a Financial Plan?

The plan itself—also called a *personal financial analysis*—is typically a computer-generated document that summarizes the information you've provided, explains financial planning strategies, and recommends specific steps you should take to achieve your objectives.

Ownership: One of the Keys to Planning

The kind of ownership you select for property and other assets determines what you can do with them, how vulnerable they are to creditors, and what happens to them after you die. Laws are complicated and vary from state-to-state, so you should get professional advice.

Type	Features
Individual (or sole)	• You own the asset outright *(but see Community Property, below)*
Joint Tenants with Rights of Survivorship	• You share the asset equally with one or more joint owners • At your death, the assets automatically transfer to joint owner(s) • You generally can't sell property without consent of joint owners
Tenants in Common	• Each owner owns a part which can be deeded, sold, or given away without other owners' consent
Tenants by the Entirety	• You must be married • Mutual consent is needed to divide or sell the property
Community Property	• In the nine states with community property laws, most property acquired after marriage is owned equally by both partners. Once property becomes community property, it remains such even if you move out of the state.

Look Before You Leap

Financial planning is a big investment of time and money, so look into it carefully. In evaluating planners, check their qualifications, their rates, and how they are paid.

Fee-only planners charge a flat rate or by the hour for their advice. (NAPFA—the National Association of Personal Financial Planners is a source for names. You can contact NAPFA at 1130 Lake Cook Road, Suite 105, Buffalo Grove, IL 60089.)

Other planners get a commission on products they sell, so they may have an interest in selling you specific investments. Still others *offset* their fees by the amount of commission they receive.

The financial planning profession is not regulated, so it's hard to judge a planner's qualifications. "Certified" financial planners (CFPs) have passed a qualifying exam, and the International Association of Financial Planners lists 810 (of its 11,500 members) who have met six quality control tests. Contact the IAFP at 2 Concourse Parkway, Atlanta, GA 30328.

Before signing on with a financial planner, ask these questions:
• How are you paid?
• How do you set your fees?
• Which products do you make commissions on?
• What are your other sources of professional income?

How Much Will Your Money Be Worth?

The following chart, taken from The Wall Street Journal, will help you figure out what your money—savings or investments—will be worth in the future. Example: What will $1,000 be worth 15 years from now, assuming an 8% growth rate, using this chart?

Year @	5%	8%	10%
5	1.28	1.47	1.61
10	1.63	2.16	2.59
15	2.08	**3.17**	4.18
20	2.65	4.66	6.73
25	3.39	6.85	10.83

Investment x **MULTIPLIER** = Future Worth

$1000 x **3.17** = $3,170

Use this space to make some estimates of your own.

$_____ x _____ = $_____

Your financial plan should be updated periodically, especially if there is a major change in your family or financial situation. Major changes in the economy, such as the rise and fall of interest rates, or new tax laws, should also trigger a review.

Financial Planning Sources

Independent financial planners	Provide individual attention. Fee-only planners charge by the hour; commission-based planners earn commissions on the investments they sell. They may have a bias for investments that provide commissions.
Employer provided planners	May provide helpful advice because they understand the benefits you already have. But many also sell investments, so may have conflict of interest.
Certified Public Accountants	They charge hourly fees, but don't usually recommend investments. They are banned in most states from accepting commissions.
Banks	Financial planning advice is often tied to the sale of annuities, insurance, and mutual funds.
Money management firms	Provide planning information to affluent clients. The annual fees are typically 1% to 2% of assets under management.

Your Net Worth

A financial plan begins with a personal balance sheet, a snapshot of your net worth, showing what you have and what you owe at a given time.

Your balance sheet shows your net worth: your *assets* — the value of what you own or have invested — minus your *liabilities* — the money you owe. If your assets out-weigh your liabilities, you are said to have a *positive* net worth; if your liabilities are larger, you have a *negative* net worth.

Assets are what you own.

• *Cash reserve assets* are cash, or the equivalent of cash, that you can use on short notice to cover an emergency or make an investment. They include the money in your checking, savings, and money market accounts; CDs; Treasury bills; and the cash value of your life insurance policy.
• *Investment assets* like stocks, bonds and mutual funds produce income and growth. Retirement plans and annuities are also long term investments.
• *Personal assets* are your possessions. Some—like antiques, stamp collections, and art—may *appreciate* (increase in value), making them investments as well. Others—like cars, boats, and electronic equipment—*depreciate* (decrease in value) over time.
• *Real Estate* is a special asset because you can use it yourself, rent it, or perhaps sell it for a profit.

Assets	
Current Estimated Value	
Cash in Banks & Money Market Accounts	
Amounts Owed to Me	
Stocks/Bonds	
Other Investments	
Life Insurance (cash surrender value)	
IRA & Keogh Accounts	
Pension & Profit Sharing (vested interest)	
Real Estate home	
other	
Business Interests	
Personal Property*	
Total Assets	
Net Worth	

* *Include furnishings, jewelry, collections, cars, security deposit on rent, etc.*

When Do You Need to Figure Your Net Worth?

Figuring your net worth is not only a critical first step in financial planning; it will come in handy in many financial situations.

For example:
• Banks and other lenders may require a statement of your assets and liabilities as part of your mortgage application

• College Financial Aid is based on your net worth, so you'll have to report your assets and liabilities when you apply
• Certain high risk investments may require that you have a minimum net worth—say $1 million or more
   It's a good idea to do a personal balance sheet periodically, just to see where you stand.

Assets

Liabilities are what you owe both currently and long-term.

• *Short-term debts* are your current bills: credit card charges, installment and personal loans, income and real estate taxes, and insurance. Your present credit card balances are often included, even if you regularly pay your entire bill each month.

• *Long-term debts* are mortgages and other loans that you repay in installments over several years.

Liabilities

	Amount
Mortgages	_____
Bank Loans	_____
Car Loans	_____
Lines of Credit	_____
Charge Accounts	_____
Margin Loans	_____
Alimony	_____
Taxes Owed: income	_____
real estate	_____
other	_____
Other Liabilities	
_____	_____
_____	_____
_____	_____
_____	_____
_____	_____
Total Liabilities	_____

(subtract liabilities from assets for net worth)

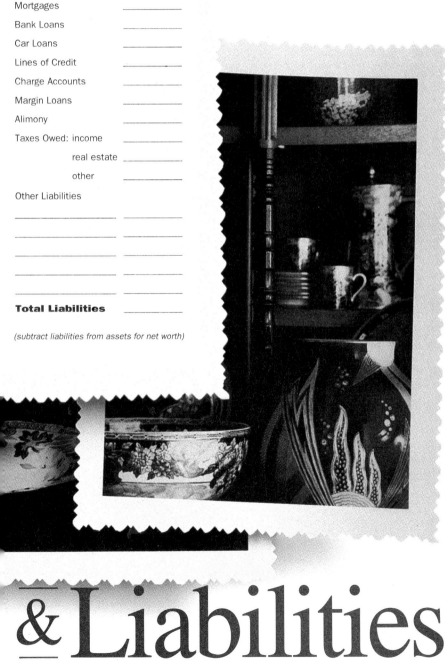

&Liabilities

Managing Your Cash Flow

A cash flow statement shows how you're spending your money. By planning, you can adjust your expenses to cover immediate needs, and still invest for long-term goals.

Your finances are in constant motion. Even as money comes in from employment, investment, and other sources, it goes out for regular living expenses, like food and shelter, and periodic bills like taxes and insurance. This in-and-out movement is called your *cash flow*.

One way to improve cash flow is to use direct deposit: the amount of your paycheck will be available sooner than if you deposit the check yourself.

What Is a Household Budget?

A budget is a plan that helps you set spending goals and monitor how well you're meeting them. Using last year's expenses as a base, you allocate how much you will spend this year for housing, food, transportation, and so forth—including the large bills like insurance that you pay quarterly or annually.

If your expenses are too high or you want to invest more, review your budget to see where you can cut back. The simpler and more realistic your budget, the more you're likely to stick to it.

What Kinds of Expenses Do You Have to Plan For?

Weekly:	food, transportation, household supplies, childcare
Monthly:	housing, utilities, phone, loan repayments
Quarterly/ Annually:	insurance, taxes
Other:	medical and dental expenses, repairs, entertainment

If you're serious about financial planning, you should invest between 5% and 10% of your employment income regularly—like each time you get paid. If you reinvest your dividends, interest, and other investment income instead of spending it, you'll build your net worth more quickly.

How Much Should You Keep on Hand?

Irregular income, unexpected repair bills, medical expenses, or loss of your job can pose special cash flow problems. It pays to have a safety net—2 to 6 months take-home pay set aside in cash reserves—to meet sudden expenses. You can put the money in savings accounts, money market funds, short-term CDs, or Treasury bills.

Using the Cash Float

A *cash float* is the time you have between buying something and actually parting with the cash to pay for it. If you charge something, you wait for the bill before paying. When you write a check, it takes time to clear your account (see page 10). Understanding cash float lets you plan deposits to your checking account to cover your payments.

For example, suppose you buy a television with your credit card on July 10 and get the bill on August 5. The due date is August 25. You write a check on August 20, which doesn't clear your bank until August 27. You've had a cash float of almost 7 weeks. (But be careful—some credit cards charge you interest from the day of purchase. See page 41.)

If you pay cash or use a *debit card*—which deducts the amount of your purchase from your checking account instantly—you have no cash float.

Annual Expenditures of U.S. Population		
Income before Taxes		**$28,540**
	Amount	**%**
Total expenditures, excluding taxes	$25,892	100
Housing (inclusive)	8,078	31
Food, including alcoholic beverages	4,017	16
Clothing	1,489	6
Transportation	5,093	20
Health Care	1,298	5
Pensions and Social Security	1,935	7
Other expenses	3,982	15

(Bureau of Labor Statistics, 1988) *Latest data available*

The Cost of a College Education

Going to college is the norm for many Americans. But paying for it can be an extraordinary expense.

Next to your home, one of the biggest expenses you may face is college tuition. If you send your children to private or prep school as well, the price tag for education can be very hefty indeed.

Since these costs keep going up—college and private school tuitions consistently exceed the rate of inflation and rise even in a down economy—planning ahead is essential.

How Much Will You Have to Save?

Four-year college costs, including tuition, room and board, books and transportation, and the monthly investments required to finance them. Table assumes 8% annual increase in college costs and 6% annual after-tax investment return, and no additional investments or earnings on balance invested once the child starts college.

YEARS UNTIL CHILD STARTS COLLEGE	PROJECTED COST OF 4-YEAR PROGRAM		MONTHLY INVESTMENT FOR 4-YEAR COST	
	PUBLIC	PRIVATE	PUBLIC	PRIVATE
1	$34,022	$74,547	$2,744	$6,013
3	39,684	86,951	1,004	2,199
6	49,990	109,533	576	1,261
9	62,973	137,981	439	962
12	79,328	173,816	376	823
15	99,930	218,958	342	749
18	125,884	275,824	323	709

Source: T. Rowe Price Associates Inc.

The Growing Cost of Education

Tuition at private colleges and universities has increased more than 154% since 1980. What cost $8,000 a year then, costs $20,320 now—and could cost $32,000 in 2002, when 1990s first graders start college. Tuition at public institutions has also increased, sometimes dramatically, reflecting the crunch of tighter state budgets and decreasing federal aid.

Average annual cost for
PUBLIC EDUCATION: $11,876

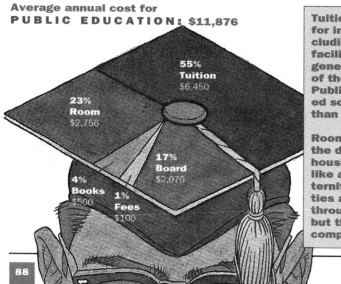

55% Tuition $6,450

23% Room $2,756

17% Board $2,070

4% Books $500

1% Fees $100

Tuition: the charge for instruction, including salaries, facilities, and the general operations of the institution. Public, tax-supported schools cost less than private ones.

Room: housing in the dorms. Other housing options, like apartments, fraternities, and sororities aren't billed through the college, but the costs are comparable.

Investing for a College Education

Putting away money for education calls for special investment strategies, such as:
· Timing when your investments will come due
· Minimizing or deferring taxes
· Deciding how much risk to take to get higher returns

Smart planning means starting early and adding regularly.

Strategy	Advantages
Zero-coupon bonds	Bonds can be scheduled to come due on a staggered basis during the years you need the money, so you can calculate the amount you will have available. Some bonds are tax-free.
Mutual funds	Growth funds emphasize long-term gains. You can transfer profits from riskier funds into safer ones as your child gets closer to college age. Regular contributions are convenient, and may even be arranged as a payroll deduction.
CDs	Return on investment is guaranteed, so you'll know what's available, but yield may be low. Reinvestment rates change, so your long-term yield is unpredictable.
U.S. Savings Bonds	Interest is completely tax-free if you use the money to pay for education—provided your income is less than $60,000 a year (or $40,000 if you're a single parent).

Saving in Your Child's Name

You can save for college by opening a custodial account in your child's name. The advantage is that the earnings will probably be taxed at a lower rate once the child reaches age 14. (Before then, some of a child's earnings are taxed at your rate.)

But the tax savings can be marginal, and you lose control of the money when your child turns 18 or 21, depending on the state.

What's more, the strategy can backfire if your child applies for financial aid. That's because most financial aid formulas require students to contribute 35% of their savings, while parents are required to supply only 5.6% of theirs.

Borrowing is another source of college funds. You can take out a home equity loan (see page 72), or borrow from your profit sharing or 401(k) plan. You can also borrow most of the cash value of your life insurance policy.

The more prestigious the school, the higher the cost. The exception: top-flight state universities. Compare the 1991–92 tuition bill at Yale for $16,300 to the $9,564 at the University of Virginia ($12,867 for an out-of-state student).

Board: dining hall meals. Most schools offer several different plans, at different costs. Students who don't live in college housing pay for food individually.

Activity Fees: extra money for clubs, the yearbook, school newspaper, and graduation. Everybody pays them.

Average annual cost for
PRIVATE EDUCATION: $22,495

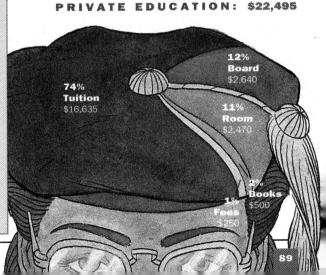

74% Tuition $16,635

12% Board $2,640

11% Room $2,470

2% Books $500

1% Fees $250

Financial Aid

Tuition: $19,500

Over 5 million students nationwide receive some form of financial aid, and over half of all families borrow some of the cost of education.

Providers of financial aid assume that parents have primary responsibility for their children's higher education. Aid is considered a supplement, not a replacement.

How much you can afford to pay determines whether your child will qualify for financial aid, including federally guaranteed loans. This amount is computed by either the College Scholarship Service of the College Board or the American College Test using a process called *Congressional Methodology*.

Tuition: $12,000

The Amount You're Responsible for is Fixed. Your child is eligible for the difference between what a college costs and the amount you're responsible for.

Assume You're Responsible for $9,500

Available Aid: $2,500

Available Aid: $10,000

COLLEGE **A**

COLLEGE **B**

Factors That Determine Eligibility for Aid:
• Income
• Family assets, including all savings and investments
• Number of other persons in the family also paying tuition
• Family expenses, both ordinary and unusual

Factors That Influence What You Get:
• Financial resources of the college or university
• Needs of other students
• Special interest in your child (some colleges offer aid to diversify their student body)

What if You're Turned Down for Aid?
You can appeal, especially if your financial situation has changed since you applied, or you can show that numbers alone don't give an accurate picture of your situation. About 10% of the aid applicants for the 1991–92 school year appealed, and about half got extra help.

What Kinds of Aid Are Available from Schools?

Even if you haven't been able to put aside all the money you need for college education, there are a number of sources you may be able to tap. Schools may offer a package of aid including:

Scholarships or grants. This money does not have to be repaid.

Loans. The loans must be repaid, but usually not until after graduation. Working in certain jobs or locations can reduce the loan or delay repayment.

Work/study grants. Colleges may offer jobs on campus to students. Sometimes their earnings are deducted from tuition; other times the student earns a salary.

Paying Off Loans

People who borrow large amounts for undergraduate and graduate education can be burdened with debts of $50,000 or more. Repayments can run up to several hundred dollars a month over a 10-year period. Failing to repay can hurt your credit rating, making it difficult to borrow money later if you need it.

Who Is Sallie Mae?

The Student Loan Marketing Association helps graduates repay their loans by consolidating them into a single debt and extending the repayment period. For example, using the Smart Loan Account

CREATIVE FINANCING

Most colleges and universities offer one or more of these options:

❶ Spread out a year's cost over 10 or 12 months for a modest fee—usually $25 to $35. A typical plan divides your total bill into 10 equal payments, with the first due in June, and the last in March.

❷ Prepay four years' tuition at the freshman rate. That means a significant outlay, but projected savings of 18% or more. If your child doesn't finish, you get a refund but lose interest earnings.

❸ Prepay your child's tuition to a specific college now—even if she's in the first grade. You pay at the present rate, and if she goes, you've saved a bundle. You get a refund if she doesn't attend, but you'll lose a lot of interest. The college that started this program—Duquesne—has dropped it because it wasn't profitable.

❹ Investigate national and state prepayment plans. Florida and Wyoming offer this option already, and at least one private company has tried developing a nationwide system of prepayment that could be used for any of the participating schools.

you can repay student loans at 9% interest instead of the current 11.49%. The phone number is 800-524-9100.

Government Sources of Money

Stafford Loans	• U.S. provides money for direct loans or guarantees loans from other lenders • Total amount of loan can be up to $17,125 over 4 years • When family income is less than $70,000, no interest or repayment is due until student leaves school • Loans are available regardless of family income
Parent Loan for Undergraduate Students (PLUS)	• Federally funded and guaranteed loans are provided through local banks, credit unions, and S&Ls • Interest rates are capped at 12%; loan insurance is required • Repayment begins immediately • Loans are available regardless of family income
Pell Grants	• U.S. authorizes grants of up to $3,700 a year to students whose family income is less than $42,000 • Grants may be less than authorized amounts because program is not fully funded

Where To Go For More Information

• Books about college costs and financial aid are available in libraries, high school guidance offices, and bookstores.
• Financial Aid Offices publicize their own programs as well as government loan and work/study programs.
• The U.S. Department of Education has regional offices—listed in the phone book—for information on state scholarships, grants, and work programs.
• High school guidance offices should know about local scholarships, and your employer, service club, or religious organization about the ones they sponsor.

Planning for Retirement

The rule of thumb is that you need 80% of your salary, adjusted for inflation, to live comfortably when you retire. Retirement plans can provide a large chunk of this income—or a pittance.

How Do Retirement Plans Work?

With a traditional pension plan, your employer makes contributions in your name while you work there. With other plans, you make the contribution. (The different plans are discussed in more detail on the opposite page.)

When you retire or leave the company, the money is paid out either as:
- a *distribution* (a lump sum payment); or
- a *pension*—regular periodic payments for a specific period or for the rest of your life. With some plans, your spouse or your heirs receive *survivor benefits* after you die.

One advantage of the distribution is having the money to do with as you please. But you'll have to pay taxes on it unless you transfer the money into a qualified plan or IRA.

If you receive a check and then *roll* it into an IRA, 20% will be withheld. But you can get a refund after filing your tax return as long as you roll over the amount within 60 days.

You should check with your retirement plan adviser, accountant, or financial planner to select the best payout option for you.

> Federal efforts to make setting up pension programs easier may encourage small employers to offer them. In 1991, only 8% of businesses with fewer than 100 employees offered plans, in contrast to 90% of businesses with more than 250 employees.

Retirement Plan Distribution Basics

Taking charge of money from a company retirement plan doesn't have to be a daunting experience, if you keep a few things in mind.

- A person can keep money distributed from a retirement plan and pay taxes on it or roll it into another qualified plan within 60 days.

- If you don't roll over the money, taxes and penalties will take a big bite—perhaps 40% or more for people under age 59 1/2.

- Individual retirement accounts get most rollover money because of their flexibility, but sometimes there are other options:
  - Some companies allow employees to continue keeping their retirement money in an existing plan after they leave the company.
  - Some companies allow a new employee to roll over money into their retirement plans.

- Keeping rollover money in a separate individual retirement account—and not adding to it—preserves your ability to roll the money into a new company plan at a later date.

Staying Longer Can Pay Off—

If you change jobs often, your retirement benefits will be less. According to The Wall Street Journal, if you work for 4 different employers for 10 years apiece, you'll get about half the pension you'd have if you worked for the same company for 40 years.

Pension Points—

Most pensions are not adjusted for inflation, which means the fixed amount you receive each year will buy less. And some pension plans reduce the amount of your pension by the Social Security you get.

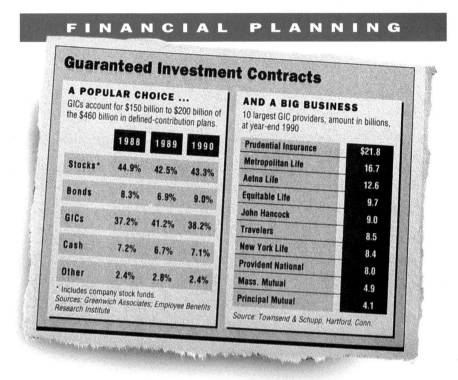

Guaranteed Investment Contracts

A POPULAR CHOICE ...
GICs account for $150 billion to $200 billion of the $460 billion in defined-contribution plans.

	1988	1989	1990
Stocks*	44.9%	42.5%	43.3%
Bonds	8.3%	6.9%	9.0%
GICs	37.2%	41.2%	38.2%
Cash	7.2%	6.7%	7.1%
Other	2.4%	2.8%	2.4%

* Includes company stock funds.
Sources: Greenwich Associates; Employee Benefits Research Institute

AND A BIG BUSINESS
10 largest GIC providers, amount in billions, at year-end 1990

Prudential Insurance	$21.8
Metropolitan Life	16.7
Aetna Life	12.6
Equitable Life	9.7
John Hancock	9.0
Travelers	8.5
New York Life	8.4
Provident National	8.0
Mass. Mutual	4.9
Principal Mutual	4.1

Source: Townsend & Schupp, Hartford, Conn.

How Are Contributions Invested?

Pension funds usually have a plan manager who invests in stocks, bonds, or other financial products.

Many funds have been invested in *Guaranteed Investment Contracts* (GICs) offered by insurance companies. Their appeal is that they pay a guaranteed fixed rate of return for a fixed period. The potential problem is the solvency of the insurance company offering them.

The newest versions try to minimize that risk by backing GICs with securities like Treasury notes and giving fund managers more control over where the money is invested.

Defined-benefits vs. Defined-contribution Plans

Retirement plans differ in the way they're funded.

A *defined-benefits plan* guarantees you a specific dollar amount when you retire. It's based on your salary or length of service, or a combination of the two. Your employer contributes enough to meet that amount.

In a *defined-contributions plan*, you elect to contribute a certain percentage of your pre-tax earnings to the plan each year. The benefits, however, are *not* guaranteed—they depend on the amount contributed, the management of the plan, and changing economic conditions.

Profit-sharing retirement plans are funded by the company, often based on annual profits. The company determines the rate of contributions each year. In lean years, there may be none at all.

Corporate *defined-benefit plans* have federal insurance through the Pension Benefit Guaranty Corporation. The major threats to pension plans are underfunding, bankruptcy and corporate take-overs.

What Is Long-term Care Insurance?

Long term care insurance provides coverage for chronic illness and long term disability not covered by Medicaid. It generally covers the cost of nursing homes, as well as certain agency services such as visiting nurses, home health aides, and respite care.

Your age, financial situation, and overall health will determine if this coverage makes sense for you. For example, it can help you preserve assets for family members if you don't want to "spend down" your savings to qualify for Medicaid.

You can get individual coverage from most life insurance companies. You may also be able to get group coverage for yourself—and possibly your parents—through your employer or other associations. As with all insurance, you should carefully check the costs, as well as the type and amount of coverage.

For more information, you can write the National Associations of Insurance Commissioners (NAIC) at 120 W. 12th Street, Suite 1100, Kansas City, Missouri 64105, or Health Insurance Association of America (HIAA), 1025 Connecticut Avenue, NW, Washington, DC 20036-3988.

Individual Retirement Arrangements

A convenient way to prepare for retirement is to invest in an IRA. You can make periodic deposits, and your earnings aren't taxed until you make withdrawals, so your money grows faster. But there are several restrictions to be aware of before you invest.

Individual Retirement Arrangements, or IRAs, were established by the Federal government in 1981 as an inducement for people to save money for retirement.

The concept was relatively simple: individuals with income from employment could deposit up to 10% of their earnings ($2000 maximum) each year into a special account set up by banks, brokerages, or mutual funds.

The Benefits of IRAs

Tax deferral. IRAs allow you to defer or postpone paying taxes on your earnings until you begin making withdrawals at age 59 ½. The tax-deferral can make a big difference in what your investment is worth. For example, suppose you invest $2,000 a year for 30 years, at an 8% return. Assuming you're in the 28% tax bracket, here's the return you can expect:

Earnings with taxes	$160,326
Tax-deferred earnings	$244,692

Investment options. IRAs are self-directed, which means you choose how the money is invested— CDs, stocks, bonds or mutual funds, for example. Tax-free bonds are poor IRA investments because you end up paying taxes on the interest.

Tax deduction. Originally, people who invested in an IRA could deduct the contribution on their tax return. Changes in the law have phased out the deduction for people who have qualified plans where they work if their incomes are over $25,000 if single, and $40,000 if married.

However, the laws keep changing, and the tax deduction may again become more available.

Contribution options. You can make one lump sum annual payment, pay in small amounts during the year, or make no contribution at all. You have until April 15 to make your contribution for the previous year.

Individual Retirement Account
August 29 - September 30, 1988
Account number 111-00011-19 415 SALLY SEP

SHEARSON
LEHMAN HUTTON

An American Express company

IRA activity summary

Amounts added to your IRA

The IRS requires Shearson Lehman Hutton to report only the total amount contributed to your IRA during the calendar year. It is your responsibility to determine which contributions, if any, are deductible when you calculate your income tax. The designations shown below are based on information you provided to your financial consultant.

Employer's contributions

	Total
	$ 30.00
Description	
Contributions made in past prior calendar year	30.00
Contributions made in prior calendar year	30.00
Contributions made in current calendar year	

Employee's voluntary contributions

	Deductible portion	Non-deductible portion	Unspecified	Total
				$ 90.00
	$ 30.00	$ 30.00	$ 30.00	90.00
Description		30.00	30.00	90.00
Contributions for prior tax year made in prior year		30.00	30.00	
Contributions for prior tax year made in current tax year				$ 30.00
Contributions for current tax year				30.00

Employee's elective deferral (salary reduction) contributions

Contributions made in prior year	$ 30.00
Contributions made in current year	

Rollovers

Amounts rolled over from IRAs and other qualified plans	$ 30.00

Transfers in

Cash transferred directly into your Shearson Lehman Hutton IRA from other financial institutions (Not including value of securities)	$ 30.00
	30.00

Amounts withdrawn from your IRA

Distributions

Amounts paid to you since Jan 1 of current year	$ 30.00
Federal taxes withheld	

Transfers out

Cash transferred directly from your Shearson Lehman Hutton IRA to other financial institutions (Not including value of securities)

IF YOU ADD $2,000 PER YEAR TO YOUR IRA EACH JANUARY 1 RATHER THAN WAITING UNTIL THE FOLLOWING APRIL 15, YOU'LL HAVE ALMOST $6,000 MORE IN 10 YEARS AND $16,000 MORE AFTER 20 YEARS.

What Are IRA Limitations?

Despite the many advantages, IRAs have their drawbacks:
• If you withdraw money before reaching 59 ½ you pay a stiff 10% penalty, plus the taxes owed
• You must begin withdrawing by age 70 ½ or pay a substantial tax on the money
• You have to keep track of the contributions you make for each tax year and know the maximum you can contribute. If you contribute more than the limit, you are subject to a penalty

The Tax on Withdrawals

Contributions you made before 1987 were made with pre-tax dollars, so you'll owe tax on both the earnings and the contribution when you begin to withdraw.

If you make non-deductible contributions, you owe tax only on the earnings. Since all your IRA accounts are treated as one when you begin to withdraw, the taxes on different parts of the withdrawal will vary.

For people who can no longer make tax deductible contributions, it may pay to invest in tax-free bonds instead. See the chart from The Wall Street Journal below.

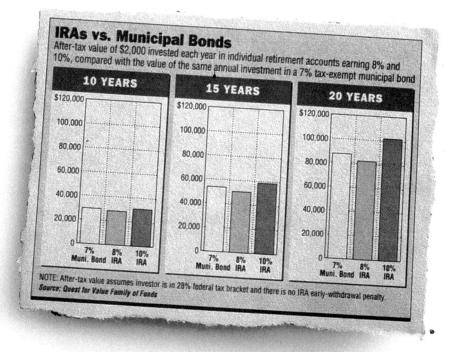

IRAs vs. Municipal Bonds
After-tax value of $2,000 invested each year in individual retirement accounts earning 8% and 10%, compared with the value of the same annual investment in a 7% tax-exempt municipal bond

NOTE: After-tax value assumes investor is in 28% federal tax bracket and there is no IRA early-withdrawal penalty.
Source: Quest for Value Family of Funds

Transferring Your IRAs

If you are unhappy with the return on your IRA investment, you can transfer the account to another institution. All companies that provide IRAs have special forms for this purpose. You can also put lump sum payments from other qualified retirement plans into an IRA.

What Is a SEP?

A Simplified Employee Pension Plan (SEP) is designed for owners of small businesses and the self-employed. Your contributions are tax-deductible and your earnings tax-deferred.

You can contribute a fixed percentage of your earned net income (up to $30,000 maximum annually). SEPs are more flexible than Keogh Plans, easier to set up, and simpler to administer.

401(k) Plans

Named after an obscure section of the IRS code, the 401(k) is often considered the blue ribbon of retirement plans. You can salt away a lot of money, defer taxes on the earnings, and reduce your taxable income as well.

For simplicity, convenience, and tax savings, it's hard to find a better deal than a 401(k), or a 403(b) in government and tax-exempt organizations.

The plan allows you to defer taxes on part of your salary by contributing it to a special account set up by your company. You don't pay taxes on the earnings until the money is withdrawn, usually at retirement.

The amount you contribute is not reported on your W-2 to the IRS, reducing your taxable income for the year. For example, if you contributed $4,000 of your $60,000 salary to a 401(k) plan, only $56,000 would be reported as income.

Also, you may receive periodic statements showing the amounts you have in each investment option and how each one performed. It will also show your contributions and any matching contributions made by your company.

Pre-tax Contributions. You may be able to contribute a percentage of your pre-tax salary up to a pre-set dollar limit—$8,728 for 1992. The cap on 403(b)s is 25% of your salary, up to a limit of $9,500. The limits on 401(k)s are increased each year to keep pace with inflation.

Post-tax Contributions. Some plans allow you to make after-tax contributions as well. Though you enjoy tax-deferred earnings, your money is tied up. There may be better investments that provide more flexibility and access to your money.

Matching Contributions. Many companies kick in 50¢ for every $1 put in by the employee. The matching contribution may be even higher.

Savings Plan—401(K) Statement

Period: 6/1–9/30/92

	Company Stock (25%)	Equity (50%
Account To Date		
Employer contributions	$21,312.50	$42,625.0
Pre-tax	$0.00	$0.0
After-tax	$2,664.00	$5,328.0
Company match	$0	$0.
Rollovers		
Totals	$23,976.50	$47,953.
Activity This Period		
Employee contributions	$1,375.00	$2,75C
Pre-tax	$4,000.00	$C
After-tax	$343.75	$68
Company match	$0.00	$
Withdrawals	– $500.00	$
Loans	1,000.00	
Transfers in	0.00	– 1,0
Transfers out		
Totals	$6,218.75	$2,4
Current Totals	$30,195.25	$50,39

Borrowing from the Plan. You can take out loans against your plan if your company allows loans. The loan has to be paid back on a regular basis, usually at market rates. Since you're repaying the money, it's not considered a withdrawal and isn't taxed.

Early Withdrawals. You'll pay tax on withdrawals, plus a 10% penalty, and will not be allowed to make contributions for a period of time. The IRS has softened these rules to allow withdrawals in "hardship" cases—such as paying for medical emergencies, college tuition or a principal residence. But you can only withdraw what you need, and have to prove you need it.

When Do You Get Your Money?

You can start making withdrawals without penalty after age 59 ½, or when you retire or are permanently disabled. You can also initiate periodic withdrawals based on a life expectancy formula, for at least five years or until age 59 ½, whichever is later. You must start withdrawing by age 70 ½.

You can take a lump sum distribution, but it must be put into an IRA to preserve tax-deferral. You can also buy an immediate annuity (see page 99) or receive installment payments if your plan provides them.

Keogh Plans: Tax-deferred Savings for the Self-employed

If you work for yourself full-or part–time, it may pay to set up a Keogh plan.

A Keogh lets you make tax-deductible contributions—in some cases, as much as 25% of your net income, up to a limit of $30,000 per year. Earnings from the plan are tax-deferred.

There are different versions of the plan, which determine how much you can contribute. In some cases, you *must* contribute to the plan each year, regardless of your profitability. In others, the contribution is optional, but the cap on contributions is lower. If you have employees, you must contribute the same percentage of income for them as you do for yourself.

While Keoghs provide substantial tax savings, they can be complicated to set up. You may need professional advice.

Balanced (0%)	Fixed (25%)	Totals
		$85,250.00
$0.00	$21,312.50	$0.00
$0.00	$0.00	$10,656.00
$0.00	$2,664.00	$0.00
$0.00	$0.00	
$0.00	$23,976.50	$95,906.00
		$5,500.00
$0.00	$1,375.00	$4,000.00
$0.00	$0.00	$1,375.00
$0.00	$343.75	$0.00
$0.00	$0.00	
$0.00	$0.00	– $500.00
0.00	0.00	1,000.00
0.00	0.00	– 1,000.00
$0.00	$1,718.75	$11,375.00
$0.00	$25,695.25	$106,281.00

INVESTMENT OPTIONS

Companies typically provide at least four investment options: ❶ company stock ❷ an equity fund (a stock mutual fund) ❸ a balanced fund of stocks and bonds, and ❹ a fixed fund based on GICs (guaranteed investment contracts—see page 93).

Most plans let you shift your investment mix from time to time. For example, you may switch from 100% fixed, to 25% company stock, 50% equity, and 25% fixed.

You Can Take It with You. If you leave for another job, your 401(k) balance can be transferred to your new employer's plan, if the plan allows it. Or you can put it into an IRA or leave it with your old employer.

401(k)	vs.	IRAs	
➕ Contribution of 10% of salary up to set limit		➖ Maximum tax-deferred contribution of $2,000 a year	
➕ Matching contributions by company		➖ No matching contributions	
➕ Available to all qualified employees regardless of salary		➖ Not tax-deductible for employees with higher income (see page 94)	
➕ Convenient contributions through employer		➖ Individuals responsible for heeding contribution limits	
➖ Limited to investment options offered by plan		➕ Diversity of investment options	

Annuities

Under an annuity contract, you make an up-front payment —or series of payments—in return for a stream of income in the future, often after retirement. What's more, your earnings are tax-deferred until you take the money out. But annuities are not simple, and they're not for everybody.

What's a Deferred Annuity?

With a deferred annuity, your earnings grow tax-free during an *accumulation period*. You can buy the annuity contract with one big payment—this is called a *single premium annuity*—or you can invest smaller amounts over time. There are no limits on how much you invest.

You can start collecting your annuity during the *payout period*. If you're 59$\frac{1}{2}$, you'll owe tax on your earnings, but no penalty. If you're younger, you'll pay an additional 10% penalty on the earnings you withdraw.

You can get regular monthly payments for as long as you live or for a set period of time. Or you can transfer the money to another annuity. You may lose money if your plan imposes a penalty for early withdrawal.

SOME ADVANTAGES OF DEFERRED ANNUITIES

Tax-deferred earnings on interest

No caps on the amount you can invest each year

Postpones initial withdrawals beyond age 70 $\frac{1}{2}$

THE DISADVANTAGES OF DEFERRED ANNUITIES

Variable annuities may have large fees, which can offset the advantages of tax-deferral

Stiff penalties if you withdraw early

Little control over how the fixed annuities are invested

Investment made with post-tax dollars

Fixed or Variable?

A *fixed* annuity earns a set rate of interest during an initial period. But the rates can change dramatically, substantially reducing your projected earnings.

A *variable* annuity lets you choose how your money is invested, though usually from a limited selection of investments. The advantage is the chance to put your money in better paying investments; but you can lose more if the market declines.

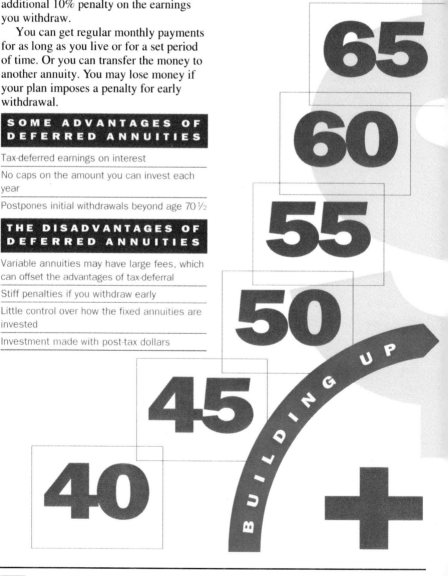

What's an Immediate Annuity?

You buy an *immediate annuity* with a single payment and begin the payout period right away or within the first year. Annuity payments on the same investment can vary greatly—sometimes 30% or more—so it pays to shop around.

The most common payout options for immediate annuities are:

Single life	Pays a set sum per month as long as you live. When you die, the payments stop
Life or period certain	Covers your lifetime or a set number of years, whichever is longer. Your heirs get the balance if you die before the term is up
Joint and several	Makes payments for your lifetime and the lifetime of a beneficiary

Are Immediate Annuities a Smart Move?

Immediate annuities provide the security of a regular income for people who are uncomfortable managing their investments. But they have some serious drawbacks:

• If you choose a single life annuity and die within a few years, the company keeps the balance of your money and your heirs get nothing
• Your annuity income may not keep pace with inflation
• The seller, usually an insurance company, may not stay solvent

C H E C K L I S T
FOR ANNUITY INVESTORS

• Consider annuities only if you're investing for the long haul. Withdrawals before age 59 ½ face a 10% penalty tax, plus income tax

• Buy only from top-rated insurers

• Compare surrender periods. Most annuities have surrender charges in the first seven years or so. Avoid annuities with surrender charges that never go away

• If buying an annuity paying a fixed rate, look beyond the initial rate. Approach unusually high rates with caution

• Look for maximum flexibility on getting your money out. Avoid annuities that don't let you take your money out in a lump sum or give you a lower interest rate if you do

• Generally avoid variable annuities with total fees higher than about 2%; stick with contracts that offer at least five different investment accounts

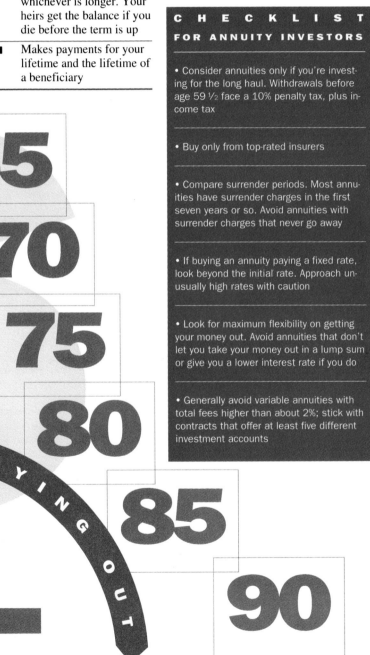

65 70 75 80 85 90

PAYING OUT

Social Security

For many workers, Social Security is a regular (and sometimes irksome) deduction from their paycheck. But for those who are retired—and for their spouses and dependents—it is often a primary source of income.

Begun during the Depression in 1935 to provide funds for retired workers, Social Security has become one of the major sources of retirement income for millions of people.

Some estimates show that Social Security will provide 60% of the retirement needs for minimum wage earners, but only 28% for those who earned the maximum Social Security wage (in 1992, $55,500) or more. So the higher your salary over time, the less Social Security will figure in your retirement planning.

How Much Will You Get?

You can check Social Security records of your earnings and get a statement of your estimated benefits. Call your local Social Security office or 800-772-1213 and ask for the "Request for Statement of Earnings" card, form SSA-7004.

If you think the record is wrong, you can contact your local office. You can use W-2 tax-report forms or pay stubs to support your claim.

SOCIAL SECURITY ADMINISTRATION
Request for Earnings and Benefit Estimate Statement

The Social Security program belongs to you and you can count on it to be there for you. Social Security can protect you in many ways. It can help support your family in the event of your death and provide monthly payments and health insurance when you retire or if you become disabled.

To help you learn how Social Security is a part of your life, we are pleased to offer you a free Personal Earnings and Benefit Estimate Statement.

The Personal Earnings and Benefit Estimate Statement shows your Social Security earnings history and estimates how much you have paid in Social Security taxes. It also estimates your future benefits and tells you how you can qualify for benefits. When you receive your earnings statement, we hope you will use it to start planning for a strong financial future.

To receive your statement, please fill out the form on the reverse and mail it to us. You should receive your statement in 6 weeks or less. We look forward to sending it to you.

Gwendolyn S. King

GWENDOLYN S. KING
Commissioner of Social Security

How Does Social Security Work?

During your working years, you and your employer pay a fixed percentage of your salary into the system for retirement, disability, and Medicare. (For 1992, deductions from salaries over $55,500 fund only Medicare.)

'92 Salary	Your Contribution
The first $55,500	7.65% ($4,245.75 maximum)
Amount from $55,501–$130,200	1.45% ($1,083.14 maximum)

You can earn up to 4 credits each year you contribute, and become eligible for benefits when you've accumulated 40 credits.

The benefit you receive when you retire is based on *the average of your 35 highest salary years.* It's then adjusted annually to reflect the increased cost of living. Because the rules have changed in recent years, you should check with the Social Security Administration about your contributions and projected benefits.

SOCIAL SECURITY FACTS

- **16% of the population (about 43 million people) receive benefits**
- **92% of the people over age 65 receive benefits**
- **More than 50% of the people claiming retirement benefits each year are younger than 65**
- **Social Security paid over $248.6 billion in benefits in 1990**

> Almost everybody is registered with Social Security. Your 9-digit number stays the same for life, even if you change your name.
> • To get the benefits, you must contribute to the system or be the spouse or dependent of someone who does.
> • Divorced people can collect on their ex-spouse's benefit if they were married 10 years or more.

When Can You Start Collecting?

You can collect full Social Security benefits when you turn 65. This age will increase gradually every year until it reaches 66 in 2009, and 67 in 2027.

You can collect 80% of your benefit if you retire at 62. But if you work beyond the full retirement age and keep on contributing, you increase your benefits.

When you die, your surviving spouse is entitled to your benefits, though the exact amount will depend on your spouse's age.

Is Social Security Taxable?

It is, if your income is more than the base amount set by Social Security. You'll owe Federal (and in some places state) taxes on up to half your benefit amount if the following applies:

	your adjusted gross income
+	your tax-exempt interest
+	$\frac{1}{2}$ your Social Security benefit
=	more than $32,000 ($25,000 if single).

Can You Earn Money while Collecting Social Security?	Yes you can, but there's a penalty attached, depending on your age and the amount of money you earn.	
Age	**Limit You Can Earn Without Penalty**	**Impact on Social Security Payment**
Over 70	No limit on earnings	None
65–70	$10,200	For every $3 you earn over the limit, your payment is reduced by $1
62–65	$7,740	For every $2 you earn over the limit, your payment is reduced by $1

For Example: *If you earn $15,000 when you're age 66, your Social Security benefit will be reduced by $1,600. (That's $15,000 – $10,200 limit = $4,800. Divide this by 3—you lose $1 for every $3 over the limit—to get $1,600.)*

Life Insurance

Evaluating your life insurance needs is a key part of financial planning. But how much you need, and what type you should buy, is less clear-cut.

Does Everyone Need Life Insurance?

If you support a family, keep a household running, have a mortgage, or expect the kids to go to college, insurance can fill the financial gap left by your death or disability. But if you don't have dependents, or they don't need your money to live on, you may be better off investing your money elsewhere.

How Much Do You Need?

The simple answer is, enough money to cover your dependents' immediate cash needs and living expenses. In general, older people need less insurance because their financial obligations have been met—mortgages and college tuition are paid—and their investments are producing income. Experts disagree on how much coverage is enough. An old rule of thumb says that you need 5 to 7 times (or even 10 times) your annual salary. But a lot depends on your lifestyle, number of dependents, and other sources of income.

Roughing Out Your Life Insurance Needs

Estimated coverage, expressed as multiples of annual salary, needed to replace 75% of take-home pay until insured would have reached age 65.*

Annual pay (before taxes)	Current Age of Person Insured						
	25	30	35	40	45	50	55
$20,000	14	13	12	10	9	7	6
$30,000	14	13	12	10	9	7	5
$40,000	13	12	11	10	9	7	5
$60,000	12	12	11	9	8	6	5
$80,000	12	11	10	9	8	6	4
$100,000	11	10	9	8	7	5	4
$150,000	10	10	9	8	7	5	4
$200,000	9	9	8	7	6	5	5

*Doesn't take into account any income survivors can expect from Social Security, investments, or other sources. More or less coverage may be needed, depending on individual family circumstances. Source: Principal Financial Group

UNDERWRITING is the process insurance companies use to assess you as a risk and decide if they will sell you insurance. It's based on the information you provide in the application. If you don't tell the truth, your insurance may be cancelled, or the company may refuse to pay a claim.

Life Insurance Workchart

You need enough life insurance to cover your dependents' living expenses. Use this chart to estimate that amount. Numbers are provided to show how the calculation is made.

A. Dependents Annual Living Costs (including mortgage payments and other loans) — **$65,000**

B. Dependents Sources of Income

Salary	35,500
Investment Income	3,500
Social Security	
Pensions and Other	5,000

— **44,000**

C. Additional Income Needed (subtract A from B) = **21,000**

D. Divide Line C by the Prevailing Interest Rate ÷ **7 %**

E. Face Value of the Policy You Need = **300,000**

To provide money for educational expenses, you can increase your coverage.

A Few Things a Fee-only Insurance Adviser Can Do

- Provide second opinions about policies you're planning to buy
- Tell you whether your existing insurer is healthy
- Evaluate whether your existing policy or annuity is appropriate
- Help you buy policies and choose options and riders
- Negotiate lower commissions from your agent

What Does Insurance Cost?

The cost varies enormously, depending on the type of insurance you buy, the company you buy it from, the size of the commission the insurance agent gets, and how long the company thinks you are likely to live.

You also have to consider the total cost. This can be tricky, since the *premium,* or amount you pay for the insurance, may increase over time. There may also be hidden fees and other charges that only surface after you purchase the policy.

As a rule, *group* life insurance provided by your employer is the least expensive.

One way to begin is to use a fee-only consultant, who can help you sift among the many options and select the one that's best for you. There's no commission, but the services aren't cheap.

Risk vs. Cost

The cost of insurance is largely determined by the *risk* you pose to the insurance company, as shown on an *actuarial table.* These tables project your life expectancy based on age, gender, health, and lifestyle.

If you're considered a high risk—for example, you smoke, are overweight, or have a dangerous occupation or hobby—the company may charge you a higher premium than others of the same age or gender, or refuse to insure you at all.

However, if you are a *preferred* risk—generally a non-smoker whose health and lifestyle make you likely to live longer—you may qualify for lower rates that significantly reduce your premium.

Term Insurance

You can buy life insurance that protects you for a limited period of time, or stays in effect until you die. Certain policies also let you accumulate tax-free earnings—but there may be better ways to invest your money.

All life insurance policies work on the same basic premise: you make payments—called *premiums*—to the insurance company, which promises to pay your beneficiaries a *death benefit* when you die.

But there are major differences between *term* and *cash value* policies. What you buy will depend on how much you can afford, how long you need the coverage, whether you want only pure protection or an investment as well, and how much effort you want to spend shopping around.

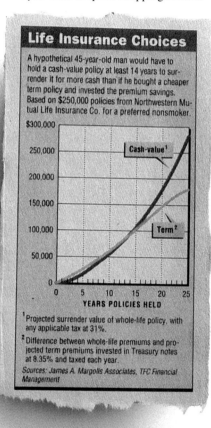

Life Insurance Choices

A hypothetical 45-year-old man would have to hold a cash-value policy at least 14 years to surrender it for more cash than if he bought a cheaper term policy and invested the premium savings. Based on $250,000 policies from Northwestern Mutual Life Insurance Co. for a preferred nonsmoker.

[1] Projected surrender value of whole-life policy, with any applicable tax at 31%.

[2] Difference between whole-life premiums and projected term premiums invested in Treasury notes at 8.35% and taxed each year.

Sources: James A. Margolis Associates, TFC Financial Management

The most straightforward and often least expensive type of coverage is term insurance. You can buy it one year at a time, or for a specific period—say 5 or 10 years. If you die during the term, your beneficiaries collect. But if you're alive when the policy expires, the coverage ends and there's no payout.

With a *decreasing* term policy, the face amount diminishes each year. This gives you the most protection at the beginning and very little towards the end, when you may need less protection anyway.

What Is Term and Invest?

If you need life insurance for 10 years or less, term insurance is almost always your best bet. Because initial premiums for term policies are lower than those for cash value policies—sometimes as much as 10 times less—you may want to "buy term and invest the difference," getting a better return and more control of your money.

But unlike cash value policies, term policies don't accumulate any cash savings that you can get back or borrow against.

Renewable vs. Level Term

All term insurance isn't the same. *Annual renewable* policies can be renewed year after year, but with ever-higher premiums. With *level premium* policies, your payments are fixed for the entire term, say 5 or 10 years: though your initial premiums are higher, they don't rise during the term, which can mean substantial savings over time.

WHAT COSTS MORE: RENEWABLE OR LEVEL TERM?

Consider a 45 year old man who wants $250,000 of coverage for the next 10 years. A company offers a renewable policy with premiums starting at $432 a year, and projected to reach $920 in the 10th year.

Or he could get a level premium policy for the same period, for $513 a year. Adding up the premiums for both policies, the level premium would be cheaper than the renewable policy by some $1,500.

Cash Value...and Countless Variations

According to The Wall Street Journal, fully half the cash reserve policies written are dropped within 7 years. This means the coverage has been very expensive because high commissions and other fees have limited the amount of cash that could accumulate during that time.

What Is Cash Value Insurance?

In contrast to term policies, cash value policies—such as *whole life* and *universal life*—combine a death benefit with tax-deferred savings. Part of the premiums you pay forms a cash reserve, which accumulates tax-deferred. If you surrender the policy, you get the cash reserve back. When you die, your beneficiaries get the death benefit provided by the policy.

If you drop the policy, you get to keep some of the savings—this is the *cash surrender value*—but you'll owe tax on it. When the policy is held until death, however, your beneficiaries owe no tax on the payment they receive.

Are All Cash Value Policies the Same?

Despite the seemingly endless varieties there are three basic types:

❶ *Whole Life* is the more traditional policy. The premiums stay the same for the length of the policy—this is sometimes called *straight life*. Once you've paid all the premiums, the policy remains in effect until you die. You accumulate a cash reserve, but you have no say over how the money is invested—that's left to the insurer to decide.

❷ *Universal Life* offers a certain flexibility. You can vary the amount of the premium by applying a portion of the accumulated savings to cover the cost. You can also increase or decrease the amount of the death benefit while the policy is in force. But you pay for this flexibility with higher fees and administrative costs.

Typically, there's a guaranteed rate of return for the first year, and a minimum, or floor, for the life of the policy.

❸ *Variable life* is a form of cash value insurance designed for investment growth. You can choose where to invest your cash value from the choices the insurance company offers. The value of your policy at any point reflects how well the investments are doing.

Can You Borrow Against Your Insurance Policy?

It depends on the type of policy you have. You can't borrow against a term policy. But with a cash value policy you can borrow against your cash reserve: if you don't repay, the amount of the loan is deducted from the benefit paid at your death. Loan rates on cash value policies are generally lower than prevailing market rates, but you risk leaving less for your dependents.

Who Sells Insurance?

If you don't get life insurance coverage as part of your employee benefits, and you can't buy it through a group, you can contact an *insurance agent* or *broker*, or speak with a financial planner.

An agent represents one insurance company, while a broker can offer policies provided by several different insurers. Some companies also sell insurance through the mail, but you should check carefully into these companies before making any purchase.

You can have any policies an agent proposes evaluated, for a modest fee, by the National Insurance Consumer Organization (NICO), 121 N. Payne Street, Alexandria, VA 22314.

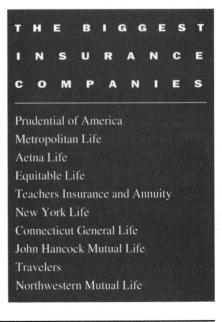

THE BIGGEST INSURANCE COMPANIES

Prudential of America
Metropolitan Life
Aetna Life
Equitable Life
Teachers Insurance and Annuity
New York Life
Connecticut General Life
John Hancock Mutual Life
Travelers
Northwestern Mutual Life

Planning for Your Heirs

Part of financial planning should include a strategy to protect your assets for your family and heirs. But be prepared: the tax collector, the courts, and federal and state governments all may want a piece of the pie.

There are many ways to protect what you own after you die. A will can be relatively simple; a trust, surprisingly complex. With so much at stake, it pays to consult a lawyer or qualified professional in preparing any document that affects your *estate.*

What Is a Will?

One of the simplest strategies is to make a *will*—a legal document that transfers what you own to others—your *beneficiaries*—when you die. It also names the people—the *executors*—whom you want to carry out your wishes.

You should make a will as soon as you have sizeable assets or get married—certainly by the time you have children. A will clarifies your intent and may save your heirs hefty legal and court fees.

What Is a Trust?

Trusts are legal entities—they actually function like corporations—that you can set up solely to shelter income for your heirs. Trusts may let you:
• avoid some estate taxes
• save on taxes by paying at a lower rate
• control the assets you leave your heirs
• specify how the trust money can be spent
• provide for minors and others who are unable to manage their finances

What Is Estate Planning?

If you have substantial wealth, it makes sense to have a comprehensive plan involving gifts, trusts, and other strategies. The more you have, the more estate planning can preserve for your heirs—sometimes to the tune of several hundred thousand dollars. Estate planning requires a long-term strategy and professional help.

Your Estate

Your Estate

Ingredients

Anything you own in your own name, including life insurance and retirement benefits

Half of what you own jointly with your spouse—for example, your home or joint accounts

Your share of anything you own in common, such as property you own with business partners

Assets in trusts and custodial accounts for which you are the trustee or custodian

Everything you own jointly with anyone except your spouse, unless there's proof the other person helped pay for it.

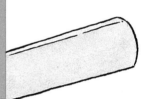

Inheritance Taxes—These are state taxes paid by your heirs—those who inherit your assets. The tax is based on their share of the inheritance and their relationship to you.

Federal Estate Taxes—If your assets are over $600,000 after certain deductions and expenses (see page 112), the estate will owe federal tax. The larger the estate the greater the tax rate—up to 55%. The top rate will drop to 49% in 1993.

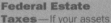

Legal and Court Fees—If someone contests the will, or makes a claim against your estate which is disputed (for unpaid debts, for example), your heirs can anticipate court costs and legal fees, in addition to long delays in settling the estate.

Making a Will

Two out of three Americans die *intestate*—without a will.
If you do, and have no relatives, your assets go
to the state where you live. The
legal term is "escheated"—
which is how your friends may feel.

A 184—Will with extra spa

What's in a *Will*

A statement that it's your will.

What Makes a Will Legal?

Your signature and those of two witnesses make the
will authentic. Witnesses don't have to know what
the will says, but they must watch you sign it and you
must watch them witness it. Hand-written wills—
called *holographs*—are legal in about half the states,
but most wills are typed and follow a standard format.

Changing Your Will

There are many reasons to change a will—the birth of a
child, the death of a beneficiary, a new marriage or a di-
vorce, increased personal wealth, or new tax laws.

Major changes require a new will that clearly states it
supercedes the old one. Minor changes are handled with a
codicil, or written amendment, that you sign and date, with
witnesses.

What About Leaving People Out?

You can disinherit anybody except your spouse, and in some
community property states you can even do that. If you want to
disinherit some or all of your children, say so specifically—it's
harder to contest. Other people you can just omit. Or you might
leave them $1. It makes your point.

Timing Is an Issue

You can require that a beneficiary must survive you by a certain
length of time—often 45 days—in order to inherit. This provision
saves double taxes and court costs if the beneficiary should die
shortly after you do, and it lets you determine who gets your property next.

Timing is also critical when a married couple die at the same
time. A *simultaneous death clause* in your will passes your property directly to your surviving heirs.

▶ A **guardian** to take responsibility for your minor
children and possibly a
trustee to manage the
children's assets in coop-
eration with the guardian.

What If You Don't Have a Will?

Without a will, you die *intestate*. The law of your state then
determines what happens to your estate and your minor
children. This process, called *administration*, is governed
by the probate court and is notoriously slow, often expensive, and subject to some surprising state laws.

For example, in some states, if you remarried and have
children only from your first marriage, your spouse could get
your entire estate and your children nothing. If you are unmarried and childless, your estate will be divided among relatives. Friends, partners, and charities will not share.

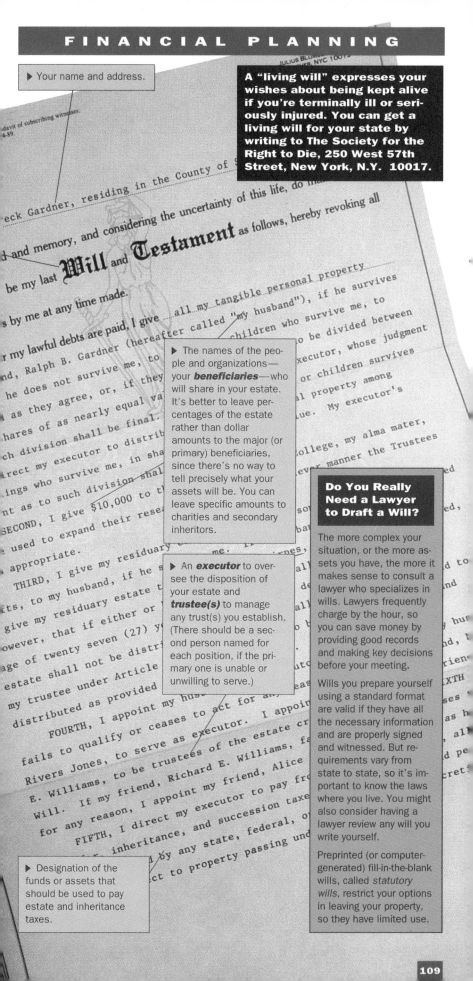

▶ Your name and address.

A "living will" expresses your wishes about being kept alive if you're terminally ill or seriously injured. You can get a living will for your state by writing to The Society for the Right to Die, 250 West 57th Street, New York, N.Y. 10017.

▶ The names of the people and organizations—your **beneficiaries**—who will share in your estate. It's better to leave percentages of the estate rather than dollar amounts to the major (or primary) beneficiaries, since there's no way to tell precisely what your assets will be. You can leave specific amounts to charities and secondary inheritors.

▶ An **executor** to oversee the disposition of your estate and **trustee(s)** to manage any trust(s) you establish. (There should be a second person named for each position, if the primary one is unable or unwilling to serve.)

▶ Designation of the funds or assets that should be used to pay estate and inheritance taxes.

Do You Really Need a Lawyer to Draft a Will?

The more complex your situation, or the more assets you have, the more it makes sense to consult a lawyer who specializes in wills. Lawyers frequently charge by the hour, so you can save money by providing good records and making key decisions before your meeting.

Wills you prepare yourself using a standard format are valid if they have all the necessary information and are properly signed and witnessed. But requirements vary from state to state, so it's important to know the laws where you live. You might also consider having a lawyer review any will you write yourself.

Preprinted (or computer-generated) fill-in-the-blank wills, called *statutory wills*, restrict your options in leaving your property, so they have limited use.

Trusts

Despite what many people think, trusts are not just for the very rich. The size of the trust may be different, but the purpose is the same: sheltering money for your heirs and providing for those who can't fend for themselves.

WHO Is a Trust For?
Anyone you want to provide income for: your spouse, elderly parents, your children, or a close friend. For example, the trust might last for your parent's lifetime, until your children reach 28, or until your grandchildren finish college.

Types of Trusts

There are two major types of trusts:

❶ *Testamentary trusts* are created by your will when you die and are funded by your estate. They are administered by trustees, whom you name in your will.

❷ *Inter vivos* or *living trusts* are set up while you are alive. You can often serve as the trustee yourself, or you can name someone else. When you die, the trust's assets are distributed directly to your beneficiaries.

You can set up your own living trust using a standard form, but there are legal pitfalls. Poorly executed trusts can foil your best intentions for avoiding the hassle and costs of probate.

Pour-over trusts combine aspects of both types: they are established while you are alive to receive assets, like life insurance benefits, through your will.

HOW Do Trusts Work?
Trusts are legal entities—like corporations—that earn income, pay taxes, and distribute earnings. The trustee administers the trust, making investment decisions, paying taxes, and distributing the income. You can give the trustee the authority to match the distributions to the specific needs of your heirs; for example, you might restrict funds for those unable to manage their financial affairs.

The trust can make regular distributions, or be set up as an *accumulation trust* to retain and reinvest the income it earns for future distribution.

WHAT Should You Consider When Setting Up a Trust?
Before you see your lawyer or bank trust officer, you should consider:

- The type of trust you want to set up
- Who will benefit from the trust
- Who the trustee will be
- How long it should last
- What assets are included
- Whether income should be distributed or reinvested
- The tax benefits

Can You Change a Trust?

A trust can be *irrevocable*—which means you can't make changes once it's set up, or *revocable,* meaning you can modify the terms over time. Their features are:

Irrevocable Trusts

- You can't make any changes
- You lose control over the assets
- You cannot benefit from the assets
- The trust pays the taxes
- Gifts are limited to $10,000 annually
- You may be able to avoid estate taxes

Revocable Trusts

- You can modify them until you die
- You control assets and pay the taxes
- You can transfer assets in and out easily with no annual limits
- They will be taxed as part of your estate

Trusts for Special Purposes

By–pass Trust	Provides income for two generations of beneficiaries. It avoids estate taxes at the first beneficiary's death by automatically passing income and principal to other beneficiaries.
Exemption–equivalent Trust	Pays your surviving spouse the income from the trust, but the trust itself is not taxed as part of your spouse's estate, which makes it particularly useful for married people with estates over $600,000.
Qualified Terminable Interest Property (QTIP) Trust	Leaves your estate to your spouse in trust, but lets you control its disposition after your spouse's death. Your spouse receives the trust income, but cannot use the principal or change the beneficiaries you have designated.
Charitable Remainder Trust	Benefits a specific charity—eventually. It has the double advantage of a lifetime income from the trust's investments for you (or your beneficiary) and tax deductions each year you contribute to the trust. At your (or your beneficiary's) death, the principal goes to the charity.
Life Insurance Trusts	Set up while you are alive to own your life insurance policy. Your death benefit is paid to the trust, avoiding estate taxes and probate.
Children's Trusts	Living trusts for minor children. The money must be used for their benefit—such as paying tuition—and becomes theirs at age 18 or 21. A trustee controls the money until then, and the trust pays its own taxes. If established early, the trust could cover a large portion of the beneficiary's education expenses.

What Is the Crummey Doctrine?

This strategy lets you take annual gift exclusions for money you contribute to create or fund a trust. It works if the beneficiary—even a minor child without a guardian—has the power to withdraw the gift within a fixed time period—often 30–60 days from when the gift was made.

The beneficiary must be notified of that right, and the money must be on hand to be withdrawn if the option is exercised. Including this option in a trust document is known as "using Crummey powers."

A *blind trust* means you have no information about or influence on the decisions the trustee makes. Political figures use them to protect themselves from charges of conflicts of interest.

Certain trusts are designed to let you qualify for Medicaid if you need long-term nursing home care. The law says you can have no more than $2,000 in countable assets to qualify for help in paying nursing home bills. Your spouse may keep half of your joint property, up to a limit of $66,480, plus your home, household goods, and one car. You must spend all the rest before you qualify for help.

One option is to put your assets in an irrevocable trust which provides income but no access to principal. If you enter a nursing home, the income goes to your spouse. But be prepared for the 30-month waiting period between the creation of the trust and your eligibility for Medicaid.

The ABCs of Estate Planning

Your estate is what you leave behind when you die: cash, investments, real estate, personal property, life insurance, and retirement benefits. Estate planning, especially where substantial assets are involved, can save your heirs lots of money—and headaches.

A You can leave your heirs up to $600,000 free of estate taxes.

If you're married, you have an unlimited marital deduction. You can leave everything to your spouse without estate tax at your death.

Both you and your spouse can make annual tax-free gifts of $10,000 to anyone you want. For example, by giving each of your three children a gift of $10,000 a year for 7 years ($210,000), you could reduce an $800,000 estate to less than $600,000.

B You can set up one or more trusts in your will. When your spouse dies, the trust exists independently and is not subject to tax. For example, if your estate were worth $800,000, you could leave $200,000 to your spouse tax-free and establish a $600,000 trust, which would escape estate taxes entirely.

C Don't own your own life insurance policy. If you do, the insurance benefit becomes part of your estate. You can assign ownership to someone else, have them buy the policy, or set up a trust to own the policy.

D Leave money and property to charity. The value of those gifts decreases your taxable estate.

What Is the Unified Tax Credit?

Every person gets a Federal unified tax credit of $192,800, the tax that would be due on assets of $600,000. That's how much you can leave your heirs free of Federal estate taxes (though there still may be state taxes).

The unified tax credit is cumulative and includes the taxes due on *taxable* gifts you've made throughout your life. Non-taxable gifts of $10,000 or less per person per year don't count against this credit. For example, if you gave your daughter a house assessed at $250,000, you'd owe taxes of about $70,000. At your death, the $70,000 would be subtracted from your tax credit, reducing the estate you could leave tax free.

FAMILY TRUST FUND

GIFT TO ALMA MATER

CHARITABLE TRUST

GIFTS TO EMPLOYEES

What Is Probate?

Probate derives from the Latin word *probare,* which means to prove. It is a legal process that validates your will and authorizes the person you've named in your will as the executor to carry out your wishes. Everything transferred by your will is subject to probate.

Can You Avoid Probate?

Any assets that aren't covered by your will avoid probate including:
• Insurance benefits paid directly to a beneficiary instead of to your estate
• Anything you hold jointly with rights of survivorship, such as bank accounts, investments, real estate
• Death benefits from retirement plans or annuities payable to a surviving beneficiary
• Assets distributed to your beneficiary from a living trust

But remember: avoiding probate does not mean you avoid estate taxes.

Cutting Estate Taxes

Possible federal estate tax savings from transferring a $500,000 life insurance policy into an irrevocable trust.

SIZE OF ESTATE (excluding life insurance)	ESTATE TAX SAVINGS*
$ 250,000	$ 55,000
500,000	153,000
1,000,000	210,000
1,500,000	225,000
2,000,000	245,000
3,000,000	275,000

* Examples assume no prior use of the $600,000 lifetime gift tax exemption; no gift tax on annual insurance premiums; and person lives at least three years after the policy is transferred to the trust.
Source: Arthur Andersen & Co.

Don't Give 'Til It Hurts.

Providing for yourself and your family is as important as avoiding estate taxes. But don't leave yourself short by giving away money you might need.

Give It or Will It?

One way to reduce taxes on your estate is to make outright gifts during your lifetime. The people receiving the money will be able to enjoy it sooner, and the government will receive less in taxes.

If you're unsure about making a gift or leaving it in your will, consider the following:

	Outright Gift	Inheritance
Value for income tax purposes	Value is what you paid for it originally.	Value is what the property is worth at the time of inheritance.
What taxes are due	No income taxes are due until the property is sold. Gift taxes are due only if the value of the gift is more than $10,000.	Inheritance or estate taxes are due shortly after you die. No income tax is due until the property is sold.

What is UGMA?

The Uniform Gifts to Minors Account is a way of giving minor children tax-free gifts. The advantage is simplicity: it's easy to set up a UGMA with most financial institutions—no complicated legal documents are required. You, as the custodian, control the investment.

But remember, the gifts are irrevocable—you can't get the money back once it's given. And the child has the right to take control of the money at age 18 or age 21, depending on the laws of your state.

DOLLAR GIFTS

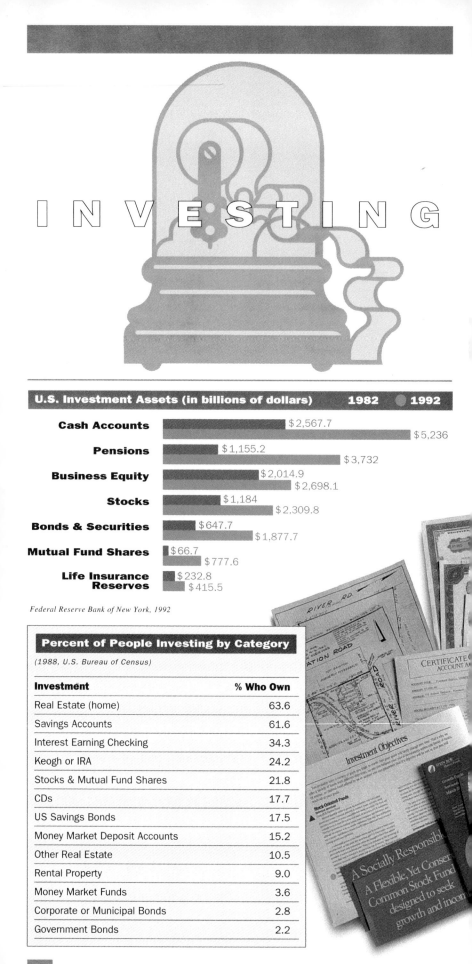

INVESTING

U.S. Investment Assets (in billions of dollars)   1982 1992

Category	1982	1992
Cash Accounts	$2,567.7	$5,236
Pensions	$1,155.2	$3,732
Business Equity	$2,014.9	$2,698.1
Stocks	$1,184	$2,309.8
Bonds & Securities	$647.7	$1,877.7
Mutual Fund Shares	$66.7	$777.6
Life Insurance Reserves	$232.8	$415.5

Federal Reserve Bank of New York, 1992

Percent of People Investing by Category

(1988, U.S. Bureau of Census)

Investment	% Who Own
Real Estate (home)	63.6
Savings Accounts	61.6
Interest Earning Checking	34.3
Keogh or IRA	24.2
Stocks & Mutual Fund Shares	21.8
CDs	17.7
US Savings Bonds	17.5
Money Market Deposit Accounts	15.2
Other Real Estate	10.5
Rental Property	9.0
Money Market Funds	3.6
Corporate or Municipal Bonds	2.8
Government Bonds	2.2

What's the Right Investment?

Selecting the right investment will depend on your personal circumstances as well as general market conditions. For example, a good investment for retirement may be a poor choice for a college savings plan. In each case, the "right" investment is a balance of three things: *liquidity*, *safety*, and *return*.

❶ Liquidity — *How accessible is your money?* If your money must be available to cover unexpected costs, you'll be concerned about *liquidity*, or how easily it can be converted to cash. Money market funds and savings accounts are very liquid; real estate is not. If you need cash, you may want to avoid long term investments that tie up your money or charge a penalty if you withdraw it too soon.

❷ Safety — *What's the risk involved?* Generally, the more liquid your investments, the safer they are. Safe investments like savings accounts, CDs, and Treasury Bills usually have a smaller return, especially if they are insured by the government. Stock in big companies with a long history of profitability is considered fairly safe, but the return is not guaranteed.

❸ Return — *What can you expect to earn?* Safe investments promise a specific, though limited, return. Others offer the opportunity to make—or lose—a lot. The kind of investments you make, the amount you can afford to invest, and the degree of risk you are willing to take will all determine your return.

> *Securities*, by definition, are written proofs of ownership, like stock certificates. But as electronic records replace paper ones, the term survives, describing investments that are secured only in the computer.

Whether you start with a little money or a lot, you can choose from a wide range of investments both in the U.S. and around the world. You can buy stocks in a Japanese computer company, bonds from the U.S. government, or a fund that invests exclusively in Mexico. What you decide to do depends on your goals, the amount you have to invest, and your willingness to take risks.

> The range of investments can be overwhelming. Besides traditional stocks, bonds, and savings accounts, there are spin-offs being introduced all the time.
> For relatively little money you can invest in exotica, gold, real estate, or commodities—as well as most overseas markets. Knowing what to choose—and when to choose it—is the key to sound investing.

Risk vs. Reward

Risk is the chance you take of making or losing money on your investment. The greater the risk, the more you stand to gain or lose.

INVESTMENT PYRAMID

Your range of investment choices —and their relative risk factors— are often described as a pyramid. Most experts recommend that you have a solid cash base (enough to cover 3–6 months of living expenses), a spread of other investments, and a small percentage of your total *portfolio* in the highest risk category.

FUTURES
OPTIONS
SPECULATIVE STOCKS
JUNK BONDS

high risk

MUTUAL FUNDS
GROWTH STOCKS
CORPORATE BONDS
RENTAL REAL ESTATE

moderate risk

BLUE CHIP STOCKS
TREASURY BONDS
HIGH-RATED MUNICIPAL BONDS
ZERO-COUPON BONDS

limited risk

SAVINGS ACCOUNTS
MONEY MARKET FUNDS
CDs

low risk

Investment Strategies:
• **Conservative:** take only limited risk by concentrating on liquid, secure stock and fixed income investments
• **Aggressive:** take risks by putting money into growth stocks
• **Speculative:** take major risks on investments with unpredictable results

Levels of Risk
Low risk investments, like government bonds, guarantee that you'll get your money back, plus interest. *High risk* investments, like stock in a new company, aren't guaranteed. But if the company succeeds, your investment could someday be worth lots of money.

There's no such thing as *zero risk*. There are always factors you can't control—like an oil embargo or high inflation. Or you may have to sell when prices are down if you need the cash.

What Causes Risk?
❶ **Volatility** means sudden swings in value—from high to low, or the reverse. The more volatile an investment is, the more profit you can make since there's a bigger spread between what you paid and what you sell it for. But if the price drops by the same amount, you can lose big, too.
❷ **Demanding High Yield**—When the economy is down and interest earnings decline, many investors seek investments with the same returns they got in better times. The risk is buying lower quality, often unfamiliar, investments that promise big returns, as junk bonds did in the 1980s. But the search for higher returns can result in higher losses as well.
❸ **Playing It Too Safe**—If you take no chances, you run the risk of coming out short. The more you have in the safest investments like CDs, bank accounts, and Treasury bills, the smaller your chance of substantial reward. There's also the risk of outliving your assets because they won't keep up with inflation.

What Is a Risk Ratio?

One way to measure the relationship of risk vs. reward in the stock market is to balance how much you think a stock is likely to rise against how far it could fall from its current price. If a stock selling for $20 could go up to $50 or fall to $10, its ratio is 3:1 (or 30 up /10 down). If the price does go up to $45 but could still fall to $10, the ratio is 1:7 (or 5 up/35 down) which may make it too risky.

Risk vs. Return: What's the Trade-off?

When it comes to investing, trying to weigh risk and reward can seem like throwing darts blindfolded: Investors don't know the actual returns that securities will deliver, or the ups and downs that will occur along the way.

Looking to the past can provide some clues. Over several decades, for instance, investors who put up with the stock market's gyrations earned returns far in excess of bonds and "cash" investments like Treasury bills.

	Compound Annual Return[1]				
	Over years 1926–1988	Over years 1984–1988	Jan–June 1989[2]	Best year	Worst year
Stocks (S&P 500)	10.0%	15.4%	16.4%	54.0% ('33)	–43.3% ('31)
Long-term U.S. Bonds	4.4	15.0	13.1	40.4 ('82)	–9.2 ('67)
Cash (Treasury bills)	3.5	7.1	4.1	14.7 ('81)	0.0 ('38)
Equal Mix of Stocks Bonds & Cash	6.5	12.8	11.2	24.1 ('81)	–15.9 ('38)
Price Inflation	3.1	3.5	3.0		

[1] Price changes of securities plus dividends and interest income
[2] Actual performance, not annualized

Figuring Your Return

Figuring out how well your investments are doing is as important as deciding what to buy in the first place. What you're looking for is the total return on the money you've invested.

Profit vs. Annual Return

Your *profit* on an investment is the dollar amount you gain (or lose) when you sell it. *Annual return* is the average percentage that you earn on the investment over a series of one-year periods.

For example, if you buy a share for $15 and sell it for $20, your profit is $5. If that happens within a year, your rate of return is an impressive 33%. If it takes five years, your return will be closer to 6%, since the profit is spread over a 5-year period.

Sell at	Profit	Return
Year 1	$5	33%
Year 3	$5	11%
Year 5	$5	6.6%

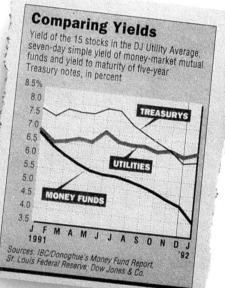

Comparing Yields

Yield of the 15 stocks in the DJ Utility Average, seven-day simple yield of money-market mutual funds and yield to maturity of five-year Treasury notes, in percent

Sources: IBC/Donoghue's Money Fund Report, St. Louis Federal Reserve; Dow Jones & Co.

Measuring Total Return

In addition to yield—which is generally the amount of income on your investment—total return also includes how much your investment gains (or loses) in value. For example, your total return on stock is not just the dividends it pays, but how much you gain or lose when you sell it.

	YIELD
+/-	CHANGE IN VALUE
—	INVESTMENT COSTS
=	**TOTAL RETURN**

What's a Good Return?
Experts say your overall return should top inflation by at least 3%. For example, during a period of 5% inflation, your return should be 8% or more. An investment mix of 60% stocks, 30% bonds, and 10% in cash—the standard asset mix of many pension funds—has historically earned 4% more than inflation.

The Wall Street Journal's MARKETS DIARY reports past and current activity in various financial markets.

The **STOCKS** section shows the movement of the Dow Jones Industrial Average for the previous 18 months, and for the previous week. It also summarizes the activity of several major domestic and foreign indexes on the most recent trading day, as well as from the beginning of the current year, and during the previous 12 months.

The **BONDS** section shows the Lehman Brothers T-Bond Index for the same periods and compares the price and yield of five different bond indexes for the previous two trading days and for the most recent 12 months.

The **INTEREST** section shows the interest rate charged on Federal funds, which is the money banks lend each other for short periods, often overnight. There's also a comparison of interest paid on T-bills, new CDs, and other issues.

Figuring the Return on Your Investment Is Not That Simple

Figuring out the actual return on your investments is hard because:

• The amount of your investment changes. Most investment portfolios are active, with money moving in and out.

• The time you hold specific investments varies. *When* you buy or sell can have a dramatic effect on overall return.

• The return on some other investments— like limited partnerships, real estate investments, and zero-coupon bonds—is difficult to pin down, partly because they're more difficult to liquidate easily. You have to evaluate them by different standards, including their tax advantages.

• The method of computing return can vary. For example, performance can be *averaged* or *compounded*, which changes the rate of return dramatically, as this chart from The Wall Street Journal shows.

Compound vs. Average Rate of Return

Here are 6 sets of investment returns totaling 27% over 3 years. While the average return in each case is 9%, compound annual returns vary.

Investment	1	2	3	4	5	6
Year 1	9%	5%	0%	0%	-1%	-5%
Year 2	9%	10%	7%	0%	-1%	8%
Year 3	9%	12%	20%	27%	29%	40%
Average return	9.00%	9.00%	9.00%	9.00%	9.00%	9.00%
Compound return	9.00%	8.96%	8.69%	8.29%	8.13%	6.96%

MEASURING PERFORMANCE

MARKETS DIARY 6/23/92

You also judge how your investments are doing by comparing them to standard benchmarks, or *indexes*. The Dow Jones Averages, the Wilshire 4,500, the Standard & Poors Indexes, the NASDAQ National Market System Composite Index and a half-dozen others show the movement of investments for the previous day, month, and year. Long-term patterns are more revealing than changes within a relatively short period.

What Investment Has Averaged the Best Return Since 1926?

Stock	10%
Long-term bonds	4.4%
Treasury bills	3.5%
Equal blend	6.5%
Inflation	3.1%

Diversifying Your Portfolio

Even if you find risk exciting, you'll probably sleep better if you've got your investment nest eggs in different baskets.

Your best protection against risk is *diversification*—spreading your investments around instead of investing in only one thing. For example, you can balance cash investments like CDs and money market funds with bonds and mutual funds.

You can speculate on stocks of small *growth companies* while also investing in *blue-chips*, or large, well-established companies. Usually when the return is down in one area, it's up in others.

Diversification also means regularly evaluating your assets and realigning the mix. For example, if your stocks increase in value, they will make up a larger percentage of your portfolio. To keep the balance, you may want to increase your fixed-income holdings.

The Benefits of Diversification

Well-diversified portfolios—containing various mixes of stocks, bonds, cash equivalents like Treasury bills or money funds, and sometimes other types of investments—can iron out a lot of the ups and downs in investing. And studies show that over lengthy periods, investors don't have to sacrifice much in the way of returns to get that reduced volatility. Finding the right portfolio mix depends on your assets, your age, and your risk tolerance.

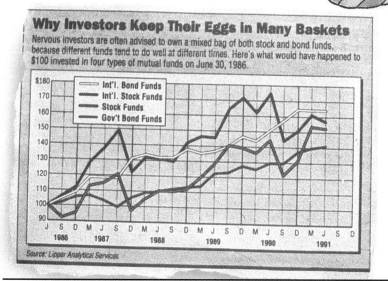

Why Investors Keep Their Eggs in Many Baskets

Nervous investors are often advised to own a mixed bag of both stock and bond funds, because different funds tend to do well at different times. Here's what would have happened to $100 invested in four types of mutual funds on June 30, 1986.

Legend:
- Int'l. Bond Funds
- Int'l. Stock Funds
- Stock Funds
- Gov't Bond Funds

Source: Lipper Analytical Services

Stocks, Bonds or Cash?

What's the 'Right' Mix?

Recommendations from different asset-allocation services may vary, as shown by these suggestions from some major investment firms for four individual investors.

THE BREADWINNER

Early-30s, nonearner spouse, two kids; "moderate" risk taker, with investment assets of $726,200 (41.6% cash, 6.8% fixed income, 51.6% growth).

	SHEARSON	PRUDENTIAL	PAINEWEBBER	DREYFUS
CASH	5.8%	11.5%	12.6%	6 – 25%
FIXED INCOME	32.5	39.7	25.0	19 – 37
GROWTH	61.7	48.8	62.4	61 – 84

THE DINKS

Double income, no kids, late-20s, "moderate" risk takers with investment assets of $182,000 (11.5% cash, 66.5% fixed income, 22% growth).

	SHEARSON	PRUDENTIAL	PAINEWEBBER	DREYFUS
CASH	7.5%	12.4%	27.0%	18 – 34%
FIXED INCOME	33.0	47.2	25.4	33 – 53
GROWTH	59.5	40.4	47.6	25 – 41

THE SINGLE PARENT

Late-30s, one child; "moderate to aggressive" risk taker; investment assets of $95,300 (10.8% cash, 20.7% fixed income, 68.5% growth).

	SHEARSON	PRUDENTIAL	PAINEWEBBER	DREYFUS
CASH	3.8%	14.9%	29.0%	39 – 51%
FIXED INCOME	29.9	36.4	37.4	24 – 40
GROWTH	66.3	48.7	33.6	18 – 31

THE YOUNG ACHIEVER

Single, mid-20s; "aggressive" risk taker; investment assets of $14,000 (60.7% cash, 39.3% growth).

	SHEARSON	PRUDENTIAL	PAINEWEBBER	DREYFUS
CASH	2.7%*	17.2%	45.4%	100%
FIXED INCOME	10.9*	26.4	23.0	0
GROWTH	86.4*	56.4	31.6	0

*Broker would override allocation model to put this investor 45.5% in cash, 54.5% in growth.

This chart valid as of 11/25/91

What Is Asset Allocation?

Many brokerage and mutual fund statements will show your asset allocation. This is the percentage of your portfolio invested in different categories, typically cash, equities (stocks and stock mutual funds), and fixed income (like bonds). Some companies even recommend what your asset allocation should be, given their assessment of the market.

Investing in Stocks

When you buy stock, you buy part of a company. If the company does well, you receive dividends, which are your part of the profits. And if the share price goes up, you can sell your stock at a profit.

More than 47 million people—about 20% of the population—own stocks, with an average portfolio worth about $6,000.

You can buy stock in more than 34,000 publicly held companies, though chances are your portfolio will have only a tiny fraction of what's available. If you know what your goals are, both short- and long-term, you can make rational decisions about what to buy.

How Do Investors Make Money?

Investors buy stock to make money:
• Through dividend payments while they own the stock
• By selling the stock for more than they paid

As a rule, the more profit a company makes, the better its stockholders do.

Many companies pay out part of their annual profits to stockholders as *dividends*.

The amount of the dividend varies from company to company and from year to year, but some companies, like General Electric and Pfizer, have paid dividends for 50 or more consecutive years.

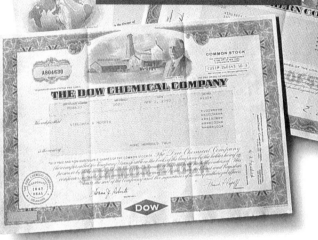

Stock certificates may become relics of the past, as they already have in Europe. They're being replaced with electronic records, just as bond certificates have been. Some brokerages now charge to send you a stock certificate.

Bulls and Bears

The stock market goes through cycles, heading up for a time and then correcting itself by reversing and heading down. A rising period is known as a *bull market*—bulls being the market optimists who drive prices up. A *bear market* is a falling market, where stock prices fall by 15% or more. Between 1960 and 1990, there were 6 bear markets.

Changing market direction doesn't always mirror the state of the economy. The crash of 1987 occurred in a period of economic growth, and the bull market of late 1990–early 1991 roared along despite a recession.

The Wall Street Journal reports that since 1926, the odds of losing money in the stock market over one year have been about 30%, but over 10 years the risk is just 4%.

If your goals are long-term, like college tuition for your baby or your own retirement, time and risk are on your side if you buy stock. But if you're investing to buy a house or reach some other short-term goal, the stock market may be too chancy.

Q. What Do Stocks Cost?

A. A stock can cost 50¢ or $185, or any amount from a penny up. A stock's price reflects its market value—what investors are willing to pay for it because of how well it is doing currently, its track record, and how well they expect it to do in the future.

Q. What Affects a Stock's Price?

A. The financial situation of the company, including its assets, earning power and debt—its *book value,* or net worth (see page 131) and:
- The number of issued shares
- Changes in interest rates
- The state of the market in general and of the stock's industry in particular
- Whether Wall Street likes it—that is, whether it is popular

Q. What Is a Stock Worth?

A. While a stock does not have a fixed objective worth, its value can be measured by the *return* you get—the difference between what you paid and what you sold it for, plus any dividends you earned.

Some stocks are *undervalued*, which means that they are selling for less than analysts think they're worth, while others are *overvalued*.

Figuring a Stock's One-Year Return

$$\frac{\text{Current Price} + \text{Dividends}}{\text{Purchase Price} + \text{Commissions/Fees}} - 1 \times 100 = \text{Return}$$

Assume, for example, you own for one year 100 shares of a stock that is trading at $40 a share, and has paid dividends of $1.60 a year. The purchase price was $32 a share, and the commission $125.

$$\frac{4000 + 160}{3200 + 125} = \frac{4160}{3325} = 1.25 \ -1 \times 100 = 25\%$$

The World of Stocks

Understanding the wide variety of stocks you can purchase—and the ones to select—is a key to successful investing.

Income vs. Growth Stocks

Stocks with consistent histories of paying high dividends are known as *income stocks*. Investors buy them for current income and regular dividends.

Growth stocks, in contrast, are shares in companies that reinvest most of their profits to expand and strengthen the business. Although they pay little if any dividend, investors buy them because they expect the price to go up as the company grows.

Growth stocks appeal to investors with long-term goals who want to postpone tax on their profits.

Penny vs. Blue Chip Stocks

Stocks that sell for less then $5 a share are generally known as *penny stocks* (a solid example of the influence of inflation!). Though cheap, they may not be worth the money, since the companies offering them may never be profitable. Worse, they are sometimes scams sold over the phone by clever salespeople to unwary investors.

However, some penny stocks have increased substantially in value, providing hefty returns for astute investors.

Stocks in the largest, best established and consistently profitable companies are often called *blue chips*, like the most valuable poker chip. They tend to be income stocks, and they tend to be expensive.

Small vs. Large Companies

Another stock choice is between large and small companies. Size is determined by *capitalization*, or the number of outstanding shares multiplied by the price of one share.

Small company stocks are usually bought as growth stocks, but low-priced stocks in profitable small companies can provide income as well. Small companies have fewer resources to fall back on in tough economic times, so declining profitability can hurt the value of your investment.

The minimum number of shares and market value vary for the major exchanges.

Exchange	Minimum # of Shares	Minimum Market Value
New York Stock Exchange	1.1 million	$18 million
American Stock Exchange	500,000	$3 million
	250,000*	$2.5 million*
NASDAQ-Listed Over-the-Counter	100,000	$ 1 million

For companies listed on the Exchanges' Merging Company Marketplace, a new market started in 1992 for smaller emerging companies.

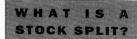

WHAT IS A STOCK SPLIT?

If a company thinks the price of its stock is too high to attract investors, it can split its stock—that is, give stockholders more shares at a lower price.

If the stock is split 2 for 1, the price is cut in half and the number of shares is doubled. Initially, the total value of your stock is the same—like getting two nickels for a dime. But if the price climbs back toward its pre-split price, the value increases.

Stocks can split 3 for 1, 3 for 2, 10 for 1, or any other combination. There can even be a reverse split, where you exchange 10 shares for 5, with each new share worth twice as much as the old one. Reverse splits can make a stock attractive to many institutional investors who will not buy stocks under $5 per share.

Common vs. Preferred Stock

Some companies offer different classes of stock to appeal to different types of investors. If you have *common stock*, you share directly in the success or failure of the business. If it has large profits, your return increases; If it has a bad year, so does your investment.

With *preferred stock*, the dividends are fixed, regardless of how the company is doing. You may get some of your investment back even if the company goes out of business. The down side is that your dividends stay the same even if company profits jump.

Defensive vs. Cyclical Stocks

Defensive stocks in industries like utilities, drugs, health care, food, tobacco, and alcohol are more resilient in recessions and stock market slides—at least theoretically—because product demand continues. Many investors include them in their portfolios as a hedge against sharp losses in other stocks.

Cyclical stocks, on the other hand, flourish in good times and suffer when the economy dips. Airlines, for example, lose money when business and pleasure travel are cut back. If you buy in as the economy rebounds, the cycle works in your favor.

Buying and Selling Stocks

People who want to trade stock generally have to use a brokerage firm. Brokers' track records and commissions can vary greatly, so comparison shopping pays.

Choosing a Broker

Full-service brokerages maintain a research department of analysts and employ people who specialize in various kinds of stock. Their stockbrokers can provide you with advice on what and when to buy and sell.

Discount brokerages act as your agent when you tell them what to buy or sell, but offer no advice. Like full-service brokers, many discounters also provide market information and financial services, including money-market accounts.

The *confirmation* you get from your broker spells out the details of a trade. The terms and conditions are on the back. You should keep all buy and sell confirmations as part of your tax records.

5. The **price per share** reports the price you paid or received. You can buy or sell either at the current market price, or you can authorize a trade when the price hits a certain amount. A *stop order* tells your broker to sell when the price has gone down to a specific level, to prevent a big loss.

4. Most brokerages are covered by the **Securities Investor Protection Corporation** (SIPC), which insures your account up to $500,000.

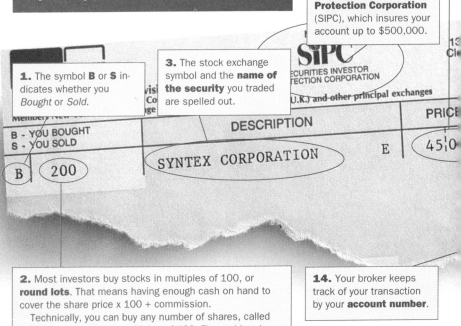

3. The stock exchange symbol and the **name of the security** you traded are spelled out.

1. The symbol **B** or **S** indicates whether you *Bought* or *Sold*.

B - YOU BOUGHT
S - YOU SOLD

DESCRIPTION

PRICE

SYNTEX CORPORATION   E   45 0

B 200

2. Most investors buy stocks in multiples of 100, or **round lots**. That means having enough cash on hand to cover the share price x 100 + commission.

Technically, you can buy any number of shares, called *odd lots*, if they aren't multiples of 100. The problem is that commission per share is likely to be higher.

14. Your broker keeps track of your transaction by your **account number**.

What Is a Reinvestment Plan?

Instead of sending you a dividend check each quarter, some companies will reinvest your dividend to purchase more stock in the company. The advantages are that the reinvestment is done automatically, and commissions are small or nonexistent. But there may be a service charge of about 5%. You owe tax on the reinvested amount just as if you had received payment.

A dividend reinvestment plan statement shows the amount to be reinvested, the cost per share at the time of the transaction, the number of shares—sometimes a fractional share—you purchase, and usually the total number of shares you have, both in the plan and separately. You also get a separate tax statement at the end of the year.

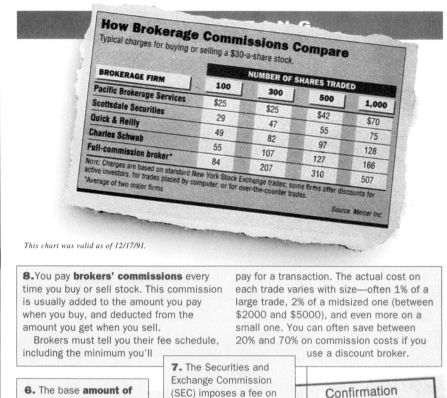

How Brokerage Commissions Compare

Typical charges for buying or selling a $30-a-share stock.

BROKERAGE FIRM	NUMBER OF SHARES TRADED			
	100	300	500	1,000
Pacific Brokerage Services	$25	$25	$42	$70
Scottsdale Securities	29	47	55	75
Quick & Reilly	49	82	97	128
Charles Schwab	55	107	127	166
Full-commission broker*	84	207	310	507

NOTE: Charges are based on standard New York Stock Exchange trades; some firms offer discounts for active investors, for trades placed by computer, or for over-the-counter trades.
*Average of two major firms

Source: Mercer Inc.

This chart was valid as of 12/17/91.

8. You pay **brokers' commissions** every time you buy or sell stock. This commission is usually added to the amount you pay when you buy, and deducted from the amount you get when you sell.

Brokers must tell you their fee schedule, including the minimum you'll pay for a transaction. The actual cost on each trade varies with size—often 1% of a large trade, 2% of a midsized one (between $2000 and $5000), and even more on a small one. You can often save between 20% and 70% on commission costs if you use a discount broker.

6. The base **amount of your purchase** is figured by multiplying the number of shares times the market price.

7. The Securities and Exchange Commission (SEC) imposes a fee on some transactions, and some brokerages impose a routine **handling charge** as well.

Confirmation

9. The **net amount** includes the cost of the security plus commissions and fees.

AMOUNT	INTEREST OR STATE TAX	S.E.C. FEE AND/OR HANDLING	COMMISSION OR CHARGE	NET AMOUNT
9000 00		2 25	190 24	9192 49

INV. OBJ.	ACCOUNT NUMBER	TYPE OF ACCT.	TYPE OF TRANS.	TRADE DATE	SETTLEMENT DATE
	AT1 234 567	1	25	10/30/91	11/06/91

11. The **trade date** is the day of the transaction—usually either the day you authorize a trade or the day the security reaches the price you specify.

13. Type of account, reported in code and explained on the back, confirms whether you made a cash trade, bought on margin, sold short, or any one of the other variations possible with the account you have set up. (See pages 128-129)

12. The **type of transaction**, given here in number code and explained on the back of the confirmation slip, tells you the exchange where the trade was made and details of the brokerage's role as agent in the transaction.

10. The **settlement date** is the deadline for paying your bill or getting your proceeds.

Other Broker Services—Brokerage houses will hold your stock certificates in *street name*, which means the certificate is made out in the brokerage's name instead of yours. This way the stocks can't be lost or stolen—as $2.6 billion-worth were in 1990—and selling is simpler because your broker can surrender your certificates immediately.

Buying What You Know—One investment strategy is to put money into businesses you know something about, provided you check their financial reports. If you like the product or service, the chances are others will too.

Tricks of the Trade

Though it's tough to beat the market consistently, knowing some of the tricks of the trade and how to recognize trends can help even the odds.

What Is Buying on Margin?

Buying on margin means borrowing money from your broker to finance part of a stock purchase. You use a *margin account* in which you deposit cash or securities to fund your share of the purchase. Under current rules, you can borrow up to half the cost of any transaction. You pay interest, but usually at less than market rates.

The advantages of *leverage*, or using a little of your own money to purchase something of greater value, is that your return on investment is magnified.

For example, suppose you buy $1,000 worth of stock with $500 of your own money and $500 from your broker, and it increases in value to $1,500. When you sell and repay the loan (plus interest) you've made almost $500 on a $500 investment—or 100% profit.

Without the margin loans, you'd have to lay out the whole cost yourself. If you didn't have the cash, you'd have to buy less initially and make less profit.

The disadvantage of margin buying is that if your investment loses money, you absorb the total loss and still pay back the loan.

What's a Margin Call?

Brokers protect themselves against losses by requiring you to deposit extra money in your margin account if the value of your investment falls below a specified percentage of its original value. If you won't—or can't—meet the *margin call*, you must sell and take the loss.

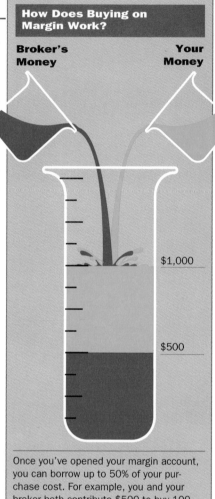

How Does Buying on Margin Work?

Broker's Money | Your Money

$1,000

$500

Once you've opened your margin account, you can borrow up to 50% of your purchase cost. For example, you and your broker both contribute $500 to buy 100 shares of a $10 stock (total cost: $1,000).

Professional Stock Analysts

Investment analysts make decisions about hot stocks in several ways. Fundamental analysts concentrate on the economic health—or balance sheet—of individual companies, their management, and their position in the industry. • Technical analysts use past performance to predict how individual companies, industries, or the market as a whole will do in the future. • A third perspective, called the efficient market hypothesis, argues that a portfolio of randomly selected stocks will do as well as one selected by experts. The Wall Street Journal tests this hypothesis regularly in the Investment Dartboard feature.

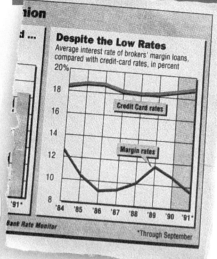

Despite the Low Rates
Average interest rate of brokers' margin loans, compared with credit-card rates, in percent

Credit Card rates

Margin rates

'84 '85 '86 '87 '88 '89 '90 '91*

Bank Rate Monitor

*Through September

What Is Selling Short?

Selling short is selling a stock before you buy it because you think the price is going down. To sell short, you use a *margin account*, and borrow the stocks you don't own from your broker. When the price drops, you *cover your short position* by buying the stocks for less than you sold them for. You give the stocks to your broker to replace the ones you borrowed and pocket your profit.

For example, if you sell short 100 shares at $10 a share and buy 100 shares two weeks later for $8, you make $2 profit per share (minus the interest you owe your broker plus commission costs). That's a 25% profit.

The risk is that the price of the stock might go up instead of down. Then you may have to cover your short position by paying more for the stock than you sold it for, so you can potentially lose more than the amount you invested.

What Are Warrants?

When you buy a *warrant*, you pay a small price now for the right to buy a certain number of shares at a fixed price during a specified period. For example, you might pay $1 a share for the right to buy the stock at $8 within 5 years. If you *exercise* (use) your warrant when the selling price is $12, you'll be $3 ahead ($12 – ($8 + $1) = $3).

If the price of the stock is below the *exercise price* when the warrant expires, the warrant is worthless. But before it expires, the warrant can rebound in value if the stock price rises. Because a warrant has a long life span, it is less risky than an option, which never lasts longer than nine months (see page 146).

Warrants are sold by companies that plan to issue stock, or by those that want to raise cash by selling stocks they hold in reserve. But once a warrant is offered, it has a life of its own, and can be bought and sold as well as exercised.

Could You Take a Fall? Historically, the stock market has declined most often in September and crashed in October.

September, October Vie for Worst Month
September is the month in which stock-market investors are most likely to sustain losses. But October is when a jolting decline is most likely to occur.

Month	Average Performance*	Worst Days	Performance
January	Up 1.1%	Oct. 19, 1987	Down 22.6%
February	Down 0.2	Oct. 28, 1929	Down 12.8
March	Up 0.7	Oct. 29, 1929	Down 11.7
April	Up 0.9	Nov. 6, 1929	Down 9.9
May	Down 0.3	Aug. 12, 1932	Down 8.4
June	Up 0.5	Oct. 26, 1987	Down 8.0
July	Up 1.4	July 21, 1933	Down 7.8
August	Up 1.4	Oct. 18, 1937	Down 7.8
September	Down 1.1	Oct. 5, 1932	Down 7.2
October	Down 0.2	Sept. 24, 1931	Down 7.1
November	Up 0.7	July 20, 1933	Down 7.1
December	Up 1.4	Oct. 13, 1989	Down 6.9

* Mean, for Dow Jones Industrial Average since Jan. 31, 1900

Source: Ned Davis Research Inc.

Taking Stock of Your Investments

To invest intelligently, and to track how well you're doing, you have to understand the language of stocks and the information that's available.

Stock tables, like the one reprinted here from The Wall Street Journal, provide a daily summary of what happened in the market. That information is the raw material for your buy-and-sell decisions.

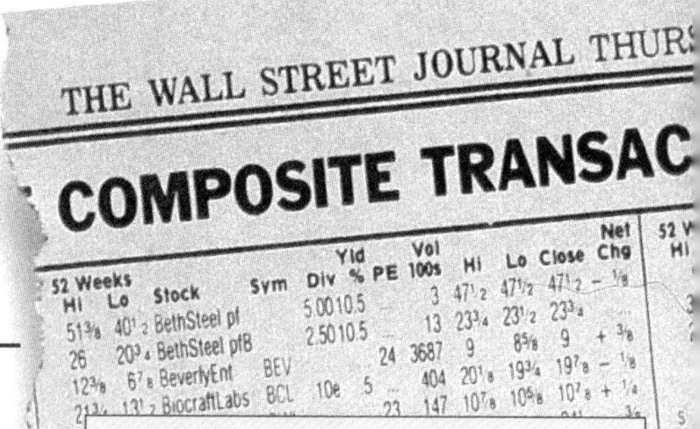

Company names are abbreviated, listed alphabetically, and followed by their trading symbol. Most symbols are closely related to the name of the company, like BIR for Birmingham Steel. Preferred stocks (see page 125) are indicated by a *pf* following the stock name.

Cash dividend per share is an estimate of the anticipated yearly dividend per share in dollars and cents. Notice that the prices of stocks that pay dividends tend to be less volatile than the prices of stocks with no dividend. Black Hills' yearly dividend is estimated at $1.86 per share. If you owned 100 shares, you'd receive $186 in dividend payments, probably in quarterly payments of $46.50.

52 Weeks				Yld			Vol				Net	52 Weeks		
Hi	Lo	Stock	Sym	Div	%	PE	100s	Hi	Lo	Close	Chg	Hi	Lo	Stock
51⅜	40½	BethSteel pf		5.00	10.5	...	3	47½	47½	47½	− ⅛	8⅝	1	CalFed
26	20¾	BethSteel pfB		2.50	10.5	...	13	23¾	23½	23¾	...	30¾	18	CalgnCart
12⅜	6⅞	BeverlyEnt	BEV			24	3687	9	8⅝	9	+ ⅜	28⅝	18¾	CalMat
21¾	13½	BiocraftLabs	BCL	.10e	.5	...	404	20⅛	19¾	19⅞	− ⅛	1¼	1¼	Calton Inc
n 13½	7½	BioWhit	BWI			23	147	10⅞	10⅝	10⅞	+ ¼	13/16	9/32	CampblR
27⅝	12⅝	BirmghamStl	BIR	.50	2.0	77	349	24⅞	24¼	24½	− ⅜	S 43⅞	34½	CampblS
26⅞	11¾	BlackDeck	BDK	.40	1.5	32	6542	26½	25¾	25⅞	− ½	20	14⅜	CdnPac g
44¼	32¼	BlackHills	BKH	1.86	4.4	18.	40	42¾	42⅜	42¾	− ⅛	15/16	7/32	Canal Ca
n 10¾	9⅞	Blackstn1998	BBT	.85	8.1	...	1494	10½	10⅜	10½		1⅛	3/8	Canal Ca
11⅜	10	BlackstnAdv	BAT	.98	8.8	...	243	11¼	10⅞	11⅛				

Highest and lowest prices of each stock are shown for the last 52 weeks. Stocks reaching a new high or low for the year are marked with an arrow in the lefthand margin. The range between the prices is a measure of the stock's *volatility*. (The more volatile a stock is, the more you can make or lose within a relatively short investment period.) The percentage of change is more significant than the dollar amount: a $5 change from $5 to $10 shows more volatility than a $5 change from $30 to $35.

Per cent yield is one way to evaluate the stock's current value: it tells you how much dividend you get as a percentage of the current price. For example, the yield on Black and Decker is 1.5%.

Per cent yield is one way to compare what you're earning on a stock with what you're earning on other investments. But it doesn't tell you your total return, which is the sum of your dividends plus increases (or decreases) in stock price.

When there's no dividend, yield cannot be calculated, and the column will be blank.

Price/Earnings ratio (P/E) shows the relationship between a stock's price and the company's earnings for the past four quarters. It's figured by dividing the current price per share by the earnings per share—a number the stock table does not provide as a separate piece of information.

P/E ratio is an important number because it indicates buyers' confidence in a stock, although there's no ideal ratio. The higher it is, the more unlikely it is that the high prices investors pay will be justified by their return.

A P/E ratio of 24, for example, shows that buyers are willing to pay 24 times the current earnings to buy a share of stock.

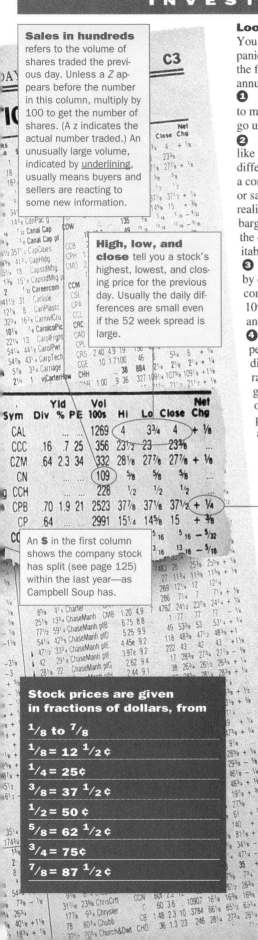

Sales in hundreds refers to the volume of shares traded the previous day. Unless a *Z* appears before the number in this column, multiply by 100 to get the number of shares. (A z indicates the actual number traded.) An unusually large volume, indicated by <u>underlining</u>, usually means buyers and sellers are reacting to some new information.

High, low, and close tell you a stock's highest, lowest, and closing price for the previous day. Usually the daily differences are small even if the 52 week spread is large.

An **S** in the first column shows the company stock has split (see page 125) within the last year—as Campbell Soup has.

Stock prices are given in fractions of dollars, from

$^1/_8$ to $^7/_8$

$^1/_8$ =	12 $^1/_2$ ¢
$^1/_4$ =	25¢
$^3/_8$ =	37 $^1/_2$ ¢
$^1/_2$ =	50 ¢
$^5/_8$ =	62 $^1/_2$ ¢
$^3/_4$ =	75¢
$^7/_8$ =	87 $^1/_2$ ¢

Look at the Companies, Too

You can get other information about companies that issue stock from your broker, the financial press, and prospectuses and annual reports.

❶ **Earnings per Share** is one way to measure the company's health: if they go up each year, the company is growing.

❷ **The Book Value** of a company is like your own net worth statement—the difference between assets and liabilities. If a company has more assets than it thinks or says it has, the book value may be unrealistically low and the stock may be a bargain. But if book value is low because the company has too much debt, its profitability may be hurt.

❸ **Return on Equity** is computed by dividing the earnings per share by the company's book value. Returns over 10% are generally considered healthy, and over 15% outstanding.

❹ **The Payout Ratio** shows the percentage of net earnings being paid as dividends, normally 25% to 50%. The ratio tells you if the company is struggling to meet its obligations. As a rule of thumb, a company should not be paying more than 70% of its earnings as dividends.

Net change compares the closing price given here with the closing price of the day before. A minus (–) indicates a lower price, and a plus (+) means it's higher. *Here, Campbell Soup closed at 37 1/2, up 1/4 point from the day before.*

Stocks that show a price change of 5% or more are in **boldface**.

Calculating Volatility — The Beta Factor

Some analysts measure the return on a given stock by comparing it to the average return on a group of stocks. This is called the stock's *beta*. If the average is 1, a stock with a beta of 1.8 is more volatile than the market as a whole, and a stock with a beta of .8 is less volatile. On that basis, analysts predict the first stock would rise 18% if the market went up 10%, for example, and fall 18% if the market fell 10%.

Some analysts say this method is faulty, while others dispute its validity entirely.

Investing in Bonds

Bonds attract more investors than any other security. One of the reasons is regular interest income. Another is the issuer's pledge to repay the amount of the bond.

Bonds are loans you make to corporations or governments. Unlike buying stocks (also called *equity* securities), which makes you a part owner in a company, buying bonds (or *debt* securities) makes you a creditor.

Bonds are called fixed-income securities because they pay a specified amount of interest on a regular basis. However, one of their limitations for individual investors is their cost: with the exception of U.S. Savings Bonds, few are sold for less than $1,000 and it's sometimes hard to buy just one. For many people, investing in a bond mutual fund may be a good alternative.

Types of Bonds

Type	Description	Features
Corporate Bonds	Bonds are the major source of corporate borrowing. *Debentures* are backed by the general credit of the corporation. *Asset-backed* bonds are backed by specific corporate assets like property or equipment.	• Sold through brokers • Fully taxable • Top rated bonds nearly free of risk of default • Higher yield than government bonds
Municipal Bonds	The greatest number (over 1 million bonds) are issued by state and local governments. *General obligation* bonds are backed by the full faith and credit of the issuer, and revenue bonds by the revenue of the particular project being financed.	• Sold through brokers • Lower interest rates than comparably rated corporate bonds and U.S. Government Securities • Tax-exempt interest
U.S. Treasury Notes and Bonds	Intermediate (2–10 years) and long-term (10–30 years) government bonds are a major source of government funding and a key investment for many.	• Bought through brokers or directly from any Federal Reserve Bank • Highest credit quality • Relatively low rate of return • Sold in amounts of $1,000 and up
U.S. Treasury Bills	These are the largest components of the money market—where short term (13 to 52 weeks) securities are bought and sold. Investors use T-bills for part of their cash reserve or as an interim holding place. Interest is the difference between the discounted buying price and the amount paid at maturity.	• Bought directly or through broker • Treasury Direct allows reinvestment for up to two years without a new application • Maximum safety but low return • Sold in $10,000 lots
Agency Bonds	The best known are federally guaranteed mortgage-backed bonds sold by GNMA, but other federal, state, and local agencies also sell bonds.	• Bought directly, through banks, or from brokers • Marginally higher risk and higher interest than Treasury bonds • Price varies widely from $1,000 to $25,000 and up

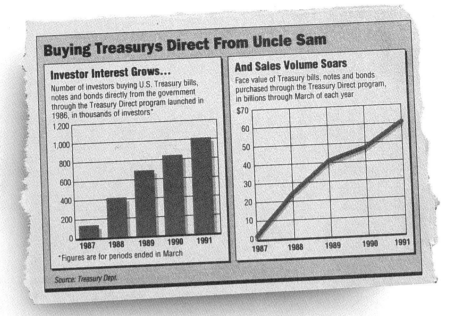

Buying Treasurys Direct From Uncle Sam

Investor Interest Grows...
Number of investors buying U.S. Treasury bills, notes and bonds directly from the government through the Treasury Direct program launched in 1986, in thousands of investors*

*Figures are for periods ended in March

And Sales Volume Soars
Face value of Treasury bills, notes and bonds purchased through the Treasury Direct program, in billions through March of each year

Source: Treasury Dept.

What Are Investment Grade Bonds?

High quality (or *investment grade*) bonds are considered safe investments because you're virtually certain of getting regular interest payments plus the amount of the bond when it matures.

Treasury bonds are considered as good as gold—they are backed by the "full faith and credit" of the government, which means it has the power to tax its citizens to pay its debts. Corporate and municipal bonds are evaluated by independent rating services—the best known are Standard & Poor's and Moody's—which measure the financial stability of the issuer and assign a rating—from triple A to D. Any bond rated Baa or higher by Moody's, or BBB or higher by Standard and Poor's, is considered investment quality. Usually, the higher a bond's rating, the lower the interest it must pay to attract buyers.

Avoiding Commissions on Treasury Bonds

The cheapest way to buy U.S. Treasury bonds is to buy them—without commission—from any Federal Reserve Bank or the Bureau of Public Debt. A system called *Treasury Direct* simplifies the process by storing records of the bonds you own and depositing your interest and principal electronically in your bank account. Using Treasury Direct, you can also reinvest Treasury bills automatically for up to two years.

Savings Bonds: Tried, True, and Better Too

You can buy U.S. Savings Bonds—up to $15,000 a year—from banks or through payroll deductions.

Ⓢ They're inexpensive—you can invest as little as $25—and get a guaranteed rate of interest if you hold them five years.

Ⓢ There's no commission and no state or local tax on the interest. Plus, you don't owe federal taxes until you redeem the bond. You may be able to avoid taxes entirely if you use the bonds to pay for your child's education.

The **long bond** is the 30-year Treasury bond. The going interest rate at Treasury auctions and the price of long-term bonds in the secondary market are used as benchmarks of investor attitudes toward the economy.

What Are Junk Bonds?

Investors willing to take risks for high yields buy corporate or municipal bonds with low ratings—or no ratings at all—commonly known as junk bonds.

Governments and corporations around the world also sell bonds which U.S. investors can buy, including some that are called "yankee bonds," which are sold in U.S. dollars.

The Value of Bonds

Some of the factors to consider in evaluating bonds as potential investments: the purchase price, the interest rate, and the yield.

If you buy a bond for face value (or *par*) when it is issued and hold it until it matures, you'll earn interest at the stated (or *coupon*) rate. For example, if you buy a 20-year $1,000 bond paying 8%, you'll earn $80 a year for 20 years. The *yield*, or your return on investment, will also be 8%. And you get your $1,000 back.

You can also buy and sell bonds through a broker after their date of issue. This is known as the secondary, or resale, market. There the price fluctuates, with a bond sometimes selling at more than par value, at a *premium* price, and sometimes below, at a *discount* price.

What Is the Relation of Bond Price to Interest Rate?

Changes in price are directly tied to the interest rate of the bond. If its rate is higher than the rate being paid on similar bonds, buyers are willing to pay more to get the higher interest. But if its rate is lower, the bond will sell for less to attract buyers.

Understanding Bond Prices

Corporate bond prices are quoted in incriments of *points* and eight *fractions* of a point, with par of $1,000 as the base. The value of each point is $10, and of each fraction, $1.25, as the chart shows:

$1/8 = \$1.25$	$5/8 = \$6.25$
$1/4 = \$2.50$	$3/4 = \$7.50$
$3/8 = \$3.75$	$7/8 = \$8.75$
$1/2 = \$5.00$	

So, a bond quoted at $86^1/2$ would be selling for $865, and one quoted at $100^3/8$ would be selling for $1,003.75.

Treasury bonds are measured in 32nds rather than in 100ths of a point. Each $1/32$ equals 31.25 cents, and the fractional part of the cent is dropped when stating a price. For example, if a bond is quoted at 100.2 or $100 + 2/32$, the price translates to $1,000.62.

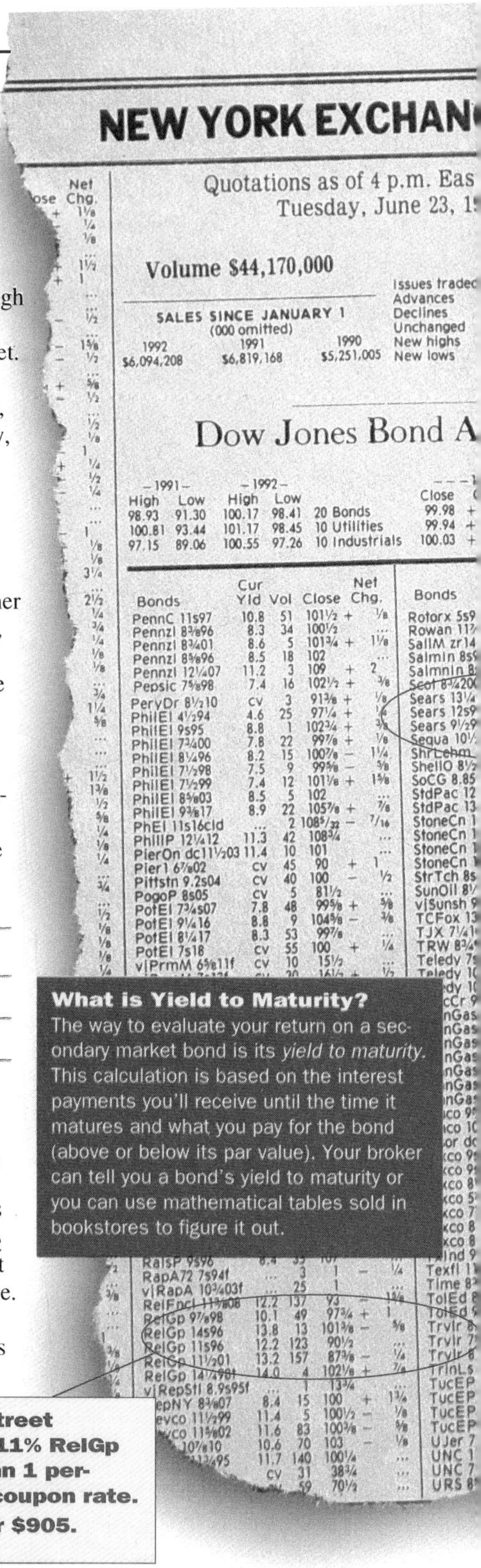

NEW YORK EXCHAN

Quotations as of 4 p.m. Eas
Tuesday, June 23, 1

Volume $44,170,000

Issues traded
Advances

SALES SINCE JANUARY 1		
(000 omitted)		
1992	1991	1990
$6,094,208	$6,819,168	$5,251,005

Declines
Unchanged
New highs
New lows

Dow Jones Bond A

−1991−		−1992−					Close
High	Low	High	Low				
98.93	91.30	100.17	98.41	20 Bonds			99.98 +
100.81	93.44	101.17	98.45	10 Utilities			99.94 +
97.15	89.06	100.55	97.26	10 Industrials			100.03 +

Bonds	Cur Yld	Vol	Close	Net Chg.		Bonds
PennC 11s97	10.8	51	101½ +	⅛		Rotorx 5s9
Pennzl 8⅜96	8.3	34	100½	...		Rowan 11⅞
Pennzl 8¾01	8.6	5	101¾ +	1⅝		SalIM zr14
Pennzl 8⅞96	8.5	18	102	...		Salmin 8s9
Pennzl 12½07	11.2	3	109	+ 2		Salmin 8
Pepsic 7⅛98	7.4	16	102½ +	⅜		Seot 8¾20
PervDr 8½10	cv	3	91⅜ +	⅛		Sears 13¼
PhilEI 4¼94	4.6	25	97¼ +	⅛		Sears 12s9
PhilEI 9s95	8.8	1	102¾ +	⅛		Sears 9½29
PhilEI 7¾00	7.8	22	99⅞ +	⅛		Sequa 10½
PhilEI 8¼96	8.2	15	100⅞ −	1¼		ShrLehm
PhilEI 7½98	7.5	9	99⅜ −	⅜		Shello 8½
PhilEI 7½99	7.4	12	101⅜ +	1⅝		SoCG 8.85
PhilEI 8⅝03	8.5	5	102	...		StdPac 12
PhilEI 9¼17	8.9	22	105⅞ +	⅞		StdPac 13
PhEI 11s16cld	...	2	108⅝/₃₂ −	⁷/₁₆		StoneCn 1
PhilIP 12¼12	11.3	42	108¾	...		StoneCn 1
PierOn dc11½03	11.4	10	101	...		StoneCn 1
Pier1 6⅞02	cv	45	90	+ 1		StoneCn ▮
Pittstn 9.2s04	cv	40	100	− ½		StrTch 8s
PogoP 8s05	cv	5	81½	...		viSunsh 9
PotEI 7¾s07	7.8	48	99⅜ +	⅝		viSunsh 8
PotEI 9¼16	8.8	9	104⅜ −	⅜		TCFox 13
PotEI 8¼17	8.3	53	99⅞	...		TJX 7¼1
PotEI 7s18	cv	55	100	+ ¼		TRW 8¾
viPrmM 6⅞11f	cv	10	15½	...		Teledy 7

What is Yield to Maturity?

The way to evaluate your return on a secondary market bond is its *yield to maturity*. This calculation is based on the interest payments you'll receive until the time it matures and what you pay for the bond (above or below its par value). Your broker can tell you a bond's yield to maturity or you can use mathematical tables sold in bookstores to figure it out.

RaisP 9s96						
RapA72 7s94f	...	3	1	−	¼	Texfl 1
viRapA 10½03f		25	1			Time 8
ReiFncl 11⅞s08	12.2	137	93	−	1¼	ToiEd 8
ReiGp 9⅞s98	10.1	49	97¾ +	...		ToiEd 9
ReiGp 14s96	13.8	13	101⅜ −	⅝		Trvlr 8
ReiGp 11s96	12.2	123	90½	...		Trvlr 7
ReiGp 11½01	13.2	157	87⅜ −	¼		Trvlr
ReiGp 14⅞s96f	14.0	4	102⅜ +	¾		TrinLs
viRepStl 8.9s95f			13¾			TuceP
epNY 8¾s07	8.4	15	100 +	1¾		TuceP
evCo 11½s99	11.4	5	100½ −	⅛		TuceP
vCo 11½s02	11.6	83	100¾ −	⅝		TuceP
...s10	10.6	70	103	−	¼	UJer
...s95	11.7	140	100¼	...		UNC 1
	cv	31	38¼	...		UNC 7
			70¾	...		URS 8

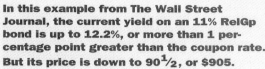

In this example from The Wall Street Journal, the current yield on an 11% RelGp bond is up to 12.2%, or more than 1 percentage point greater than the coupon rate. But its price is down to $90^1/2$, or $905.

Figuring Current Yield on Bonds

If you pay premium price for a bond, you still earn the same interest that was paid when the bond was at par. But since you paid more, the *current yield*—or the return on your investment—is less. *Using a par value 8¾ bond selling for 104 as an example:*

$$\frac{8.75\% \text{ Annual Interest}}{104 \text{ Current Market Price}} = 8.4\% \text{ Current Yield}$$

How Yield Changes

Yield from a $1,000 bond with an interest rate of 8%:	Interest Payment	Yield
If you buy it at a par price of $1,000:	$80.00	8%
If you buy it at discount price of $800:	$80.00	10%
If you buy it at premium price of $1,200:	$80.00	6⅔%

In contrast, bonds issued by Sears at 12% have a current yield of 10.9% — or more than 1 percentage point *lower* than the coupon rate. That's because the current closing price is 109⅝, or $1,096.25, which is more than par.

E BONDS

rn Time

| | Domestic | | All Issues | |
	Tue.	Mon.	Tue.	Mon.
	557	531	559	535
	192	188	193	191
	220	203	220	204
	145	140	146	140
	25	30	26	31
	5	8	5	8

erages

	%Yld	Close	Chg.
	7.96	94.07	− 0.16
	7.95	95.01	− 0.18
	7.98	93.14	− 0.14

	Cur Yld	Vol	Close	Net Chg.
	cv	10	70	
	11.4	99	103⅜	− ...
	...	100	13	− ⅛
	7.9	5	100¼	
	7.9	25	101	
	8.5	1	102½	− ¼
	13.1	4	101½	− ⁹⁄₁₆
	10.9	35	109⅝	− ⅛
	8.7	30	109½	− ⅜
	10.4	284	101¼	− ⅜
	496	9.7	19	110½ − ...
	8.3	22	102⅞	− ...
	8.7	2	102	...
	12.6	11	101½	...
	13.8	374	100½	...
	13.5	434	100⅜	− ⅜
	11.3	451	102	− ½
	11.3	128	105	− ½
	10.9	881	98½	+ ¼
	cv	47	112	+ 2
	8.4	5	101	+ ⅞
	...	5	29¾	− ⅛
	12.8	15	103½	− ½
	cv	5	98⅜	− ⅛
	8.5	6	103	+ 1¾
	7.4	41	94	− ½
	9.8	24	101⅜	− ⅛
	9.8	43	102	+ ⅛
	9.4	10	103⅜	+ ⅛
	8.9	10	103⅜	− ¼
	8.8	3	101⅛	+ 1½
	9.0	4	105	+ 3
	8.3	27	72¼	+ ⅛
	10.4	10	106½	+ ¼
	9.3	6	101	+ ¼
	13.6	60	100²²⁄₃₂	...
	8.8	5	110	...
	9.3	10	112	...
	14.9	132	85½	+ ¼
	8.3	3	108¼	+ ⅜
	8.4	5	104¼	− ⅞
	6.0	30	95¼	− ⅛
	7.8	50	100	+ ⅛
	8.6	31	103	...
	8.4	9	101	...
	cv	10	96⅝	...
	11.6	10	95	+ 5
	8.8	35	99	+ 1
	8.2	15	98	+ 1

Bonds

US West zr11
USAir 12⅞00
USG na16s08
USLICO 8s11
USX 4⅜s96
USX 5¾01
USX 7s17
USX zr05
UnAL 4¼92
UCarb 5.3s97
UCarb 7½12
UnEl 8⅞06
UPac 8.4s01
Unisys 13⅜92
Unisys 10¾95
Unisys 8.2s96
Unisy na15s97
Unisys 8¼00
Wean 12s99
Wean 10s01
Webb 10⅞00
Weingrt 8s09
Wendys 7¼10
Wendys 7s06
WstCNA 7¼41
WstDig 9s14
WstC 7.6s97
WstC 8⅜96
WstgE 9s09
Weyh 8.9s04
Weyh 5¼17
Whirl zr11
WilcxGb 7s1
WisB1 8s14
Witco 5½12
Xerox 8⅝99
Xerox 8⅛96
Zenith 6¼11

FC

Austia 12⅛0.
EurCS 8⅞96

AME

Vol

SALES
1992
$455,820,000

Issues traded
Advances
Declines
Unchanged
New highs
New lows

Bonds

Alza zr10
Arrow 13¾
Atari 5¼0
Atlant 14
BSN 7¾
BSN 9¼
BSN 9¼
CII Fn 7
CentBk 8
ChckFul
ChtMd 15.
ChtMd 15.
vjCntArHd
vjCntArH
DiagR 8½

To avoid losing any interest, you should redeem savings bonds right after the interest is credited. Banks where you cash in the bonds can tell you when.

Rating Savings Bonds

When held five years or longer, U.S. savings bonds pay the higher of a guaranteed minimum interest rate or a market-based rate that is reset twice a year. People who sell earlier get a lower rate based on how long they held. (Annualized rates, before semi-annual compounding, in percent.)

Current market-based rate (through April 30)	6.38%
Guaranteed minimum rate if held five years	6.00%

FIXED RATES FOR SHORTER PERIODS

Six months	4.16%
One year	4.27
Two years	4.64
Three years	5.01
Four years	5.50

This chart valid as of 1/16/92

Special Types of Bonds

There's something for everybody in the bond market. The trick is figuring out the best choices. If you don't have several thousand dollars to invest, a bond mutual fund may be a better idea than buying individual bonds.

What Are Zero-Coupon Bonds?

Zero-Coupons are sold at *deep discount*, or a fraction of their par value, by corporations and governments. Investors don't collect interest; instead the value of the bond increases to its full value when it matures. In this way, zero-coupons are like old Series E Savings Bonds that you bought for $37.50 and could cash in for $50 after seven years.

STRIPS are special types of zero-coupon Treasury securities. Brokerage firms offer a menagerie of zero coupons, including CATS, TIGRs, and LIONs.

ZERO-COUPONS HAVE SOME DRAWBACKS:

1. You must pay taxes on the interest which *accrues* (builds up) each year even though you don't receive it. This doesn't apply if your zero coupons are in a tax-deferred retirement account or you buy tax-free muncipal zero-coupons.

2. The prices are extremely volatile, so you can lose money if you have to sell during a downturn.

3. Rising interest rates can leave you stuck with a low-paying investment.

What are Munis?

Municipal bonds—known as *munis*—are sold by states, cities, and other local governments. Interest is exempt from federal tax. It's also exempt from state or city tax for people who buy munis of the state or city they live in. In a high tax area, like New York City, *triple tax-free* munis appeal to high income investors.

If a government's bond rating drops, it may have to raise the interest rate it offers to attract investors the next time it issues bonds. That can create a Catch-22: investors can earn higher interest—but taxes pay for it.

Mini-munis cost much less— often around $1,000—and are designed for investors who want the benefits of tax-exempt munis but not the big price tag of conventional ones.

Municipals vs. Treasurys

How yields on double-A-rated municipal bonds compare with U.S. Treasury notes and bonds, after adjusting Treasury yields for federal taxes based on a 31% tax bracket, in percent

■ Munis ■ Treasurys

3 YEARS   5 YEARS   7 YEARS   10 YEARS   30 YEARS

Sources: Delphis Hanover Corp.; Telerate Inc.

Munis

What Are Mortgage-backed Bonds?

Mortgage-backed bonds are backed by a pool of mortgage loans. They're sold by government agencies and private corporations to brokers who resell to investors.

With mortgage-backed bonds, each payment you get typically includes both principal and interest. When interest rates go down and people refinance their mortgages (see page 68), mortgage-backed bonds are paid off more quickly than you expect. *Collateralized mortgage obligations (CMOs)* are more complex versions of mortgage-backed bonds; evaluating their risks and rewards requires special knowledge.

What Are Convertible Bonds?

Convertible bonds offer the option of acquiring stock instead of getting your cash back. The terms of the exchange—generally a certain number of shares for each $1,000 bond—are spelled out in the initial offering. However, you don't have to exercise the option.

Convertibles appeal to investors who think the corporation is growing and that the price of its stock is going up. The question is whether the stock potential is worth the lower interest.

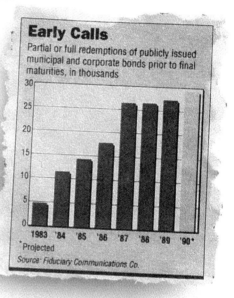

What Are Callable Bonds?

Some bonds are issued with a *call* provision, which means they can be paid off before their due date. Information about the first date on which a bond can be called should be included in the offering.

Issuers will sometimes call bonds when interest rates drop, so they can reduce their debt. Investors, however, can lose expected income if their bonds are called and they have to reinvest their money at a lower rate.

If your bonds are held by your broker (in *street name*), the broker should alert you when a bond is called. But if you hold coupon or *bearer bonds* issued before July 1, 1983, you have to keep track yourself because their ownership is not recorded. One place to start is The Wall Street Journal, which publishes a list of "Redemption Notices" every Tuesday.

Early Calls

Partial or full redemptions of publicly issued municipal and corporate bonds prior to final maturities, in thousands

*Projected

Source: Fiduciary Communications Co.

What's an Insured Bond?

Some municipal bonds have their principal and interest payments guaranteed by an insurance company. In exchange for that security, the bonds pay a lower interest and the insurance company collects a fee from the issuer. One catch: if the insurer has financial problems, it could jeopardize both the payments and the rating of the bond.

What about Bond Funds?

If you want to invest smaller amounts of money, want more diversity, and professional management, you can buy bond mutual funds. Most funds invest in specific types of bonds—like intermediate-term municipal bonds, long-term corporate bonds, or bonds of a particular state.

Unlike individual bonds, bond funds have no maturity date. The price you get when you redeem your shares may be more or less than you paid. So if you have to sell when prices are down, you might not get back what you put in.

It's a Fund-filled World

Mutual funds—more than 3,000 of them—provide a smorgasbord of investments. They offer growth, income, or both, and the chance to invest in everything from a country or industry to the movements of the markets themselves.

WHAT IS A FAMILY OF FUNDS?

Most mutual fund companies offer several different funds (known as a **FAMILY** *), and let you move money back and forth among them. Individual funds within a family have different investment goals and strategies, reflecting the different*

Type of Fund	Objective
Aggressive Growth Funds invest in new companies and industries, those in financial trouble or out-of-favor. They are sometimes called Capital Appreciation Funds.	• Above-average increase in price, with little current income • Very high risk
Growth Funds invest in well-established companies whose earnings are expected to increase. **Small Company Growth Funds** specialize in those companies.	• Strong price increases, with little current income • High risk
Growth and Income Funds invest in companies that consistently pay good dividends and also have strong growth potential.	• Combination of current income and long-term price increases • Moderate risk
Income Funds invest in income-producing securities such as dividend-paying stocks, bonds, or a combination.	• Current income • Moderate risk
Balanced Funds invest in a mixture of bonds, preferred stock, and common stock.	• Current income, growth, and safety • Some risk
Option Income Funds invest in dividend-paying common stock on which call options are traded.	• High current income • Moderate risk
International Stock Funds and Bond Funds invest overseas. **Global Funds** (in stocks or bonds or a combination) invest in both foreign and U.S. securities.	• Profit from strong markets abroad and offset changes in currency prices • Moderate to high risk
Bond Funds invest in government, corporate or tax-exempt bonds with different maturities.	• Current income • Some to moderate risk
High Yield Funds invest primarily in lower-rated corporate bonds (junk bonds). **Tax-Free High Yield Funds** invest in lower-rated municipal bonds.	• Very high current income • High risk

Mutual fund companies sell shares in a particular fund to raise money and then invest the money in securities. Some funds buy only one type of security—stocks of small companies, for example, or short-term tax free bonds—while others are more diversified. A typical fund portfolio includes between 30 and 300 different stocks, bonds, or other investments.

Should You Own Different Types of Funds?

Probably, if you have enough money to invest. Some funds do well when others are in the doldrums. By diversifing, you can do well during most market swings—through one fund or another.

interests of investors. The advantage is that you can respond to movements in the markets quickly. Check to see if there are sales charges: some funds impose them. One caution: profit or loss from exchanges among funds must be reported to the IRS just as if you redeemed or sold the shares outright.

Other Special Funds

• **Index Funds** buy stocks in the companies included in a specific market average, or *index*, like Standard & Poor's 500-stock average of large companies or the Wilshire 4,500 index of smaller companies. The fund mirrors the movements of the market—going up and down as it does.

• **Tax-Free Funds** invest in municipal bonds with tax-exempt interest. They pay less than corporate and agency bonds, but offer tax savings to investors who live in high tax states and buy funds investing in those states.

• **Sector Funds** focus on particular industries like biomedical, electronics, or energy. Each fund buys stocks in one field—so the risk level is greater than in more diversified funds.

• **Precious Metal Funds** trade mostly in mining stocks, with possibly a small portion of their assets in gold bullion. They're usually bought as a hedge against turmoil in the financial market.

• **Unit Investment Trusts (UIT)** put money into corporate bonds with fixed yields, agency bonds like Ginnie Maes, junk bonds, or even stocks. The investments are constant for the life of the trust, but there's no guaranteed return. And since their performance is not tracked by any index, it's difficult to assess how well they do.

As of June 1991, there were 3,300 mutual funds with $1.2 trillion invested, up from $135 billion in 1981. More than 68% was in load funds, despite their additional cost (see page 141).

You can get a current list of mutual funds for $5 from Investment Company Institute, P.O. Box 66140, Washington, D.C. 20035-6140.

Investing in Mutual Funds

Mutual funds come as close as anything to hassle-free investing. They offer diversification, professional management, and a strong safety record—though no guarantees of profit.

The Advantages of Mutual Funds
- **Convenience of buying and selling**
- **Diversity in investments**
- **Professional management**
- **Automatic reinvestments**
- **Distribution options**
- **Telephone redemptions and transfers**

Separate But Equal—At Least in Performance

Many people wonder if a broker's help will bring them a better-performing fund. But the table shows that whether load or no-load, fund performance is about the same—so long as you ignore the impact of the sales commission.

PERIODS ENDED JUNE 30, 1991	TAXABLE BOND FUNDS		STOCK FUNDS	
	LOAD FUNDS	NO-LOAD AND LOW-LOAD FUNDS	LOAD FUNDS	NO-LOAD AND LOW-LOAD FUNDS
1-YEAR	9.5%	9.5%	5.5%	6.0%
3-YEARS	8.6	8.9	11.8	12.0
5-YEARS	7.6	7.8	9.0	9.2
10-YEARS	12.5	12.0	13.5	13.4

Note: Figures are average annualized total returns before deducting any sales charge. Low-load funds are defined as those levying 3% or less. Table excludes single-sector and international stock funds, as well as those funds with less than $25 million in assets.

Source: Morningstar Inc.

How Do Mutual Funds Work?

Professional managers direct the funds, continually buying and selling. Investors are regularly credited with profits (or loss) in proportion to the number of shares they own. Profits are either paid out as dividends or reinvested in the fund.

For most funds you'll have to make an initial investment of $500 to $3,000. Once it's open, you can make additional purchases whenever you like, usually for as little as $50 to $100.

Dollar-Cost Averaging Can Help—or Hurt

Investing a fixed dollar amount at regular intervals can lower the average cost for shares. But while it can cushion a loss if the share price declines, it will retard a gain if prices rise.

IF SHARE PRICES FALL...

		MONTHLY INVESTMENT	SHARE PRICE	SHARES BOUGHT	VALUE
Avg. transaction price:	$25 a share	$200	$30	6.66	
		200	25	8.00	
Avg. total cost: ($600÷24.66)	$24.33 a share	200	20	10.00	
		TOTAL $600		24.66	$493

Value if lump sum of $600 were made at beginning: $400
($600 ÷ $30 share = 20 shares; 20 x current share price of $20)

IF SHARE PRICES RISE...

		MONTHLY INVESTMENT	SHARE PRICE	SHARES BOUGHT	VALUE
Avg. transaction price:	$30 a share	$200	$25	8.00	
		200	30	6.66	
Avg. total cost: ($600÷20.37)	$29.45 a share	200	35	5.71	
		TOTAL $600		20.37	$713

Value if lump sum of $600 were made at beginning: $840
($600 ÷ $25 share = 24 shares; 24 x current share price of $35)

	VALUE
	$1,576

If you dollar-cost averaged the entire 6-month period: $1,400
(Total shares bought [45.03] x current share price [$35])
If you invested $1,200 at beginning [40 shares]:

Source: Vanguard Group

What To Look For
- **Performance:** how much the fund returns, whether the returns are consistent, and how they stack up against the returns of comparable funds. Be careful of any fund whose high returns are based on 1 or 2 stellar years and 8 or 9 dull ones.
- **Risk:** how likely you are to earn money or lose it. Risk isn't bad if you're investing for the long term and you can tolerate some setbacks without selling in panic.
- **Costs:** if you pay high commissions or fees, less of the money you put into your account is actually producing investment income. For example, if you pay a 5% commission on each $1,000 you put in, only $950 of it is actually invested.

WHEN SHOULD YOU INVEST? ALMOST ANYTIME,
BUT NOT JUST BEFORE A STOCK FUND MAKES ITS
ANNUAL CAPITAL GAINS AND INCOME DISTRIBU-
TIONS, USUALLY IN DECEMBER. YOU'LL OWE TAX
ON THE DISTRIBUTION.

Payouts to Come

'Record dates' for year-end distributions at the 10 largest stock mutual funds. Actual payouts to investors who hold shares on those days may be later.

Fidelity Magellan	Dec. 13
Investment Co. of America	Dec. 18
Vanguard Windsor	Dec. 10
Washington Mutual	Dec. 20*
Fidelity Puritan	Dec. 20
Fideltiy Equity Income	Dec. 13
Twentieth Century Select	Dec. 28
American Mutual	Dec. 6**
Pioneer II	Dec. 13
Vanguard Index – 500 Port.	Dec. 26

*Previous distributions were declared Nov. 1 and Dec. 2.
**A total of 88 cents a share in income and capital gains will be paid today to holders of record Friday.

Open-end vs. Closed-end Funds

In an *open-ended fund*, the more you—and other investors—put in, the larger the fund grows. You can invest directly, by mail, or through your stockbroker or financial adviser.

Closed-end funds are traded on the major exchanges. There is a fixed number of shares available because the fund raises its money all at once. Shares often trade at a discount from their original selling price, but sometimes cost more if they're hot. Most funds that invest in a single country–like a Mexico fund–are closed-ended.

This chart valid as of 1/16/92

Dollar Cost Averaging

Dollar cost averaging means investing a fixed dollar amount every month, no matter what's happening in the financial market. That way, the price you pay evens out over time—you'll never pay only the highest or lowest price.

For example, if the price per share varies over a year from 10.65 to 8.45, you will have bought some high and some low. In the long run you may come out better than by trying to pinpoint the moment the price hits bottom or tops out. Dollar-cost averaging doesn't mean, though, that you can't lose money, or that you can't make more if you invest large amounts at the beginning of a market rise.

Load vs. No-load Funds

If you buy a mutual fund through a broker, it will probably be a *load* fund. With a *front-end load* you pay a commission on your purchase and sometimes on your dividend reinvestments as well. With a *back-end load* you pay when you redeem (or sell) your shares. Load fund rates range from 2% to 8.5%.

No-load funds, which you buy directly from the mutual fund company, have no commissions but may charge fees to cover sales and marketing costs.

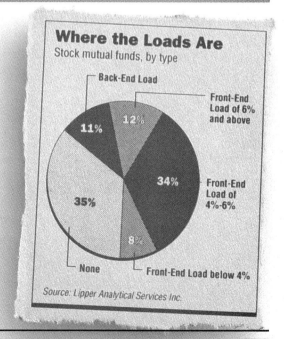

Where the Loads Are
Stock mutual funds, by type

- Back-End Load — 12%
- Front-End Load of 6% and above — 34%
- Front-End Load of 4%-6%
- Front-End Load below 4% — 8%
- None — 35%
- 11%

Source: Lipper Analytical Services Inc.

Anatomy of a Prospectus

By law, mutual funds have to provide detailed information before they accept your money. Dissecting the prospectus uncovers the workings of a fund.

Mutual fund companies provide a *prospectus* for each fund they offer. It includes a statement of objectives, a description of how the fund operates, often a summary of its investments, and information about its management. *Annual and/or quarterly reports* give details about past performance as well as the fund's investments. Companies will also supply a *Statement of Additional Information (SAI)* which has detailed financial information, if you ask for it.

What Does A Share Cost?

The dollar value of one share of a fund's stock is its *Net Asset Value (NAV)*. It's figured by adding up the value of all the fund's holdings and dividing by the number of shares. Unlike stocks, though, you can buy fractional shares. If you invest in round dollars—say $500—in a fund with a *NAV* of $60, you'll own 8.33 shares.

Load funds charge you more than the net asset value to buy because commissions are figured in, but they pay straight net asset value when you sell.

Fund Management

The person who manages the fund makes the decisions that determine how well a fund does. Find out if the manager responsible for the fund's success is still on the job and if the fund's management is achieving its objectives. If not, it may pay to look further—like finding out where the manager has gone.

You should also evaluate the manager's investment style: some styles do well at certain times—like buying undervalued small stocks—but do poorly at others. Check for a long-term success rate.

How the Fund is Invested

Make sure that you understand what the fund is buying and that you are comfortable with it.

Fees Can Affect Your Yield

Though mutual funds—especially no-loads—are the least expensive way to invest, you may still pay some or all of the following:

$ Annual management fees, which range from .25% to 1.5% of your investment and vary from company to company. They are stated in the prospectus, so you can check before you buy.

$ Fees (called 12b-1 fees) to cover marketing and advertising costs—and sometimes sales commissions. About half of all funds levy this charge, which can seriously erode your yield, especially if the charge is high.

$ Exit fees for leaving the fund, *redemption fees* for withdrawing funds before a certain time has elapsed, and deferred sales charges. You can choose funds that don't charge them, or you can wait out the minimum investment period, typically 5 years, after which the fee may disappear.

Automatic investment plans, also called *contractual plans*, let you contribute regularly, either through automatic transfers or direct deposit. The advantage is steady growth in your investment account.

Distributions are the way some gains are paid out. You can request regular checks, have the money deposited in another account, or have it reinvested in the same fund—or you can have a combination of payout and reinvestment. Taxable earnings are reported to the IRS even if they are reinvested.

Tracking Mutual Fund Performance

You can find out how well your mutual fund is performing by looking at your statements, calling your fund, or by checking out the Mutual Fund Quotations.

Checking Fund Rankings

Financial publications regularly review and rank mutual fund companies and their individual funds, rating their 1-year, 5-year, and 10-year performances. The Wall Street Journal publishes its mutual fund ratings four times a year and lists the best performers every day in the Mutual Fund Scorecard.

Once a week, they also publish the Lipper Indexes (named after Lipper Analytical Services which provides the information). The Indexes report the performance of several types of mutual funds over the previous week. You can compare the Indexes' performance with individual fund performances.

LIPPER INDEXES

Tuesday, June 23, 1992

Indexes	Prelim. Close	Prev.	Percentage chg. since Wk ago	Dec. 31
Capital Appreciation .	324.89	+ 0.45	− 1.74	− 8.34
Growth Fund	594.63	+ 0.47	− 1.53	− 4.73
Small Co. Growth	311.04	+ 0.47	− 2.63	− 9.63
Growth & Income Fd	918.29	+ 0.31	− 1.27	+ 0.84
Equity Income Fd	598.54	+ 0.30	− 1.14	+ 0.77
Science & Tech Fd ...	216.83	+ 0.45	− 2.55	− 10.20
International Fund ...	358.27	+ 0.11	− 2.02	+ 2.07
Gold Fund	137.20	− 0.53	− 2.99	− 2.49
Balanced Fund	714.78	+ 0.19	− 0.92	− 0.73

Source: Lipper Analytical Services, Inc.

Tuesday, June 23, 1992

The difference between the NAV and the Offer Price is the **load**, or commission, you pay to buy shares in certain funds. For example, you would pay $11.71 to buy a share in GT Global's Bond Fund, but get $11.27 if you sold. Most of the difference goes to the broker from whom you bought the fund.

NAV stands for net asset value, or the dollar value of one share of the fund's stock (see page 142). To compare performance, check the NAV of similar funds — growth stock funds offered by different companies, for example — rather than the NAVs of different types of funds sponsored by the same company.

The mutual fund company's **name** comes first, with its funds listed in alphabetical order. Evergreen Funds, for example, sponsors 7 individual funds. The details of each fund's performance are reported separately.

r after the fund name means the fund charges a fee to redeem shares for cash. This is also known as *back-end load*.

p after the fund name means the fund charges a fee for marketing and distribution costs.

t after the fund name means both r and p apply — or both types of fees are charged.

Tracking Fund Performance

You can measure the performance of a mutual fund by adding the dividend per share plus increases in share price, and then dividing by the price you paid per share. That lets you compare a growth fund—with small distributions but large price increases—to a fund with large distributions but a constant price.

$$\frac{(\text{Number of Shares} \times \text{Net Asset Value}) + \text{Distributions}}{\text{Cost of Initial Investment}} - 1 \times 100 = \text{Return}$$

If you're reinvesting your distributions, use this formula:

$$\frac{\text{Number of shares} \times \text{Net Asset Value}}{\text{Cost of Initial Investment}} - 1 \times 100 = \text{Return}$$

Calculating Gains or Losses on Mutual Fund Shares

To figure the taxable gain or loss on mutual fund shares you sold, you first have to determine your cost. There are essentially three basic approaches.

For many people, the best choice will be the "specific identification" method, in which you specify exactly which shares you sold. If you made a profit, you can minimize your tax bill if you are able to show that you sold the shares that cost you the most. The IRS can be tough: You should be able to show that you told your broker or your fund the particular shares to be sold at the time of the sale. The IRS also says you should be able to show you received written confirmation of which shares were sold, though many funds don't do this.

If you can't identify which shares you sold, the IRS says to assume that you sold those shares you acquired first. The big disadvantage of this "first-in, first-out" approach is that the shares you bought first usually have the lowest cost, so selling them results in the highest tax. On the other hand, if the value of your fund plunged, this may be the best approach because it would give you the biggest capital loss.

An alternative for some investors is the "average cost," or "average basis" method, which requires calculating the average per-share price for all your shares of the fund. Once you've used this method, you must continue to use it when you calculate gains and losses for that same fund in the future.

Three Basic Approaches

Suppose you bought 1,000 shares of a mutual fund at $10 each in January, 1990. Then, through automatic reinvestment of dividends, you received another 50 shares that July valued at $10 a share; 50 more shares in December, valued at $11 a share; 50 shares in July 1991 also valued at $11 a share; and 50 shares in December 1991 valued at $12 a share. Then you sold 100 shares late last December at $12 a share, or a total of $1,200.

SPECIFIC-ID	FIRST-IN, FIRST-OUT	AVERAGE-COST
Sale Proceeds $1,200	**Sale Proceeds $1,200**	**Sale Proceeds $1,200**
Highest-cost shares: − $1,150	**Cost of first 100 shares:** − $1,000	**Average-cost:** − $1,017
(Based on 50 shares at $11 in July 1991 and 50 shares at $12 in December 1991.)	*(Shares you bought in January 1990 at $10 a share.)*	*(Divide total purchase price of $12,200 by 1,200 shares. That equals $10.17 a share. Multiply by 100 shares.)*
Short-term* Gain: $50	**Long-term Gain: $200**	**Long-term Gain: $183**

*The shares sold were held for less than one year.

If the NAV and Offer Price are the same, there's no *front-load fee* when you buy, but there may be a *back-load fee* when you sell.

N.L. in the Offer Price column indicates a No Load Fund (see page 141).

NAV Change reports the change between the last trading day's NAV and the day before, measured in cents. First Investors Global Fund, for example, declined 5¢, from $5.25 to $5.20.

Should You Abandon A Fund?

Most people close out a fund because they need the money elsewhere, or want to change their investment strategy.

However, there may be sell signals that would make bailing out the right move:
• More than 3 consecutive years of poor performance, especially if other similar funds were doing well
• A move by a star manager to another fund
• A radical change in investment style
• A fund that gets too large or grows too fast

Gambling on the Future

Stocks, bonds, and funds aren't the whole story. With nerves of steel and money to spare, you can buy gold, soy bean futures, stock index options—often with relatively little cash. But the risks are enormous.

For some investors, the thrill of speculation is too great to resist. Dealing in *futures* and *options* lets them gamble on what something will cost down the road.

Futures and options are bought and sold in the *commodities markets*, where raw materials like agricultural products, metals, and petroleum are traded. Commodities prices can be volatile because the pressures of supply and demand can be disrupted by all kinds of natural and political forces.

You can also buy and sell futures in financial commodities—stocks, stock indexes, bonds, and currencies.

Who Trades Futures Contracts?

A *futures contract* is a deal you make now for commodities to be bought or sold in the future.

The futures market benefits *hedgers* who produce or use commodities (or who own and trade large investment portfolios) because they want to avoid risk by locking in a price.

Speculators aren't interested in the commodity, but buy or sell futures contracts because they're willing to take risks that prices will rise or fall. They can make the most money when they *leverage* their purchase, or invest a small amount to purchase a futures contract or option worth much more. The downside is that if the value falls, they are responsible for the entire loss.

WHAT'S THE RISK?

For hedgers, there is relatively little risk, because any loss they suffer on a futures contract is mostly made up in the cash price—and vice versa. Speculators, though, can make or lose a great deal of money as the difference between the cash price and the futures price fluctuates.

Where Do You Trade?

You can trade futures and options through commodities brokers at commodities exchanges in major cities. Stock brokers trade investment futures and options.

Why Buy Options?

An option gives you the right—for a fee—to decide whether or not you want to buy or sell futures contracts or stocks at an agreed-upon price—called the *strike price*—before a specific *expiration date*.

A Better Option...

If you speculate by buying options, you risk only the price of the option and know in advance what you can lose.

And a Worse One...

If you sell an option on something you don't own, it's called *naked writing*. You could be caught with a big loss if the buyer exercises the option. Since you must sell, you have to buy first, no matter what the price is.

What Kinds of Options Are There?

All options fall into two broad categories: puts and calls.

	Call	Put
BUY *(long)*	The right to buy the corresponding stock or futures contract at a fixed price until the expiration date	The right to sell the corresponding stock or futures contract at a fixed price until the expiration date
SELL *(short)*	Known as writing a call—selling the right to buy the stock or futures contract from you until the expiration date	Known as a writing a put—selling the right to sell the stock or futures contract to you until the expiration date

FUTURES OPTIONS PRICES

Tuesday, June 23, 1992.
AGRICULTURAL

CORN (CBT)
5,000 bu.; cents per bu.

Strike Price	Calls—Settle Sep	Dec	Mar	Puts—Settle Sep	Dec	Mar
240	20½	27½		5	11	11
250	14¾	21	27½	9¾	14	
260	11¼	17½	23	16	17¼	15½
270	8¾	13¾	18	23	23¼	21
280	6	10¾	14½	30½	30½	
290	4½					

Est. vol. 5,50...
Mon vol. 2,870...
Op. Int. Mon E...

CATTLE-LIVE (CME)
40,000 lbs.; cents per lb.

Strike Price	Calls—Settle Aug	Oct	Dec	Puts—Settle Aug	Oct	Dec
66		5.50		0.15	0.30	0.60
68	3.25	3.80		0.32	0.55	1.07
70	1.67	2.32	1.85	0.72	1.05	1.67
72	0.60	1.25	1.02	1.65	1.95	2.77
74	0.17	0.60	0.47	3.20		4.20
76	0.02	0.22	0.25			

Est. vol. 1,477;
Mon vol. 438 calls; 511 puts
Op. int. Mon 10,022 calls; 22,830 puts

HOGS—LIVE (CME)

5 YR TREAS NOTES (CBT)
$100,000; points and 64ths at 100%

Strike Price	Calls—Settle Aug	Sep	Dec	Puts—Settle Aug	Sep	Dec
10400			1-32		0-21	
10450			1-09		0-29	
10500			0-54		0-43	
10550			0-38		0-58	
10600	0-13	0-26		1-14		
10650		0-17				

Est. vol. 100;
Mon vol. 58 calls; 475 puts
Op. int. Mon 10,718 calls; 11,804 puts

EURODOLLAR (IMM)
$1 million; pts. of 100%

LONG TERM OPTIONS

CBOE

Option/Exp/Strike	Last	Option/Exp/Strike	Last	Option/Exp/Strike	Last	Option/Exp/Strike	Last
AT&T Jan 94 30	12¾	IBM Jan 95 85	20½	ASA Dec 93 35	7⅞	RJR Nb Jan 94 7½ p	¾
AT&T Jan 94 35	9⅛	IBM Jan 95 85 p	7¾	ASA Dec 93 60	1¼	RJR Nb Jan 94 10	1⅜
AT&T Jan 94 45	4	IBM Jan 95 105	11½	ASA Jan 95 35	9½	RJR Nb Jan 94 10 p	1⅛
AT&T Jan 95 40 p	4¼	IBM Jan 95 105 p	15⅝	AmExp Dec 93 15	9	RJR Nb Jan 94 12½	¾
BnkAm Jan 94 30	15¼	IBM Jan 95 135	5	AmExp Dec 93 20	5¾	Reebok Dec 93 17½	9
BnkAm Jan 94 40	9	IBM Jan 95 135 p	38¼	AmExp Dec 93 20 p	2	Reebok Dec 93 30	3
A.m Jan 94 40 p	4½	JohnJn Jan 95 55	2¾	AmExp Dec 93 30	1⅛	Tennco Jan 95 35 p	4⅞
		JohnJn Jan 95 40 p	4¼	AmExp Dec 93 30 p	7⅞	Texaco Dec 93 60	6½
		JohnJn Jan 95 45	9½	AmExp Jan 95 15	9½	TriTEn Jan 95 35	8⅛
				AmExp Jan 95 30 p	8¾	UCarb Dec 93 25	4⅞

Two Risk-Reducing Strategies

How an investor using long-term options to reduce stock-market risk would fare if stock prices rose or fell. Calculations (based on Wednesday's closing prices) ignore commissions and dividends; and all option values are at expiration.

OPTION-TREASURY COMBO

GOAL: Profit if Merck & Co. stock, recently trading at about $89.50 a share, goes up, while minimizing any loss if the stock price falls.

STRATEGY: Instead of buying 100 shares of Merck for $8,950, buy one July 1992 call with a $95 strike price for $863, and put $8,088 in Treasurys paying 7.10%.

STOCK PRICE AT EXPIRATION OF OPTION	PROFIT/LOSS ON OPTION	TREASURY INCOME	COMBINED PROFIT/LOSS	COMBINED RETURN
$ 60	−$ 863	$861	−$ 2	0.0%
80	− 863	861	− 2	0.0
100	− 363	861	499	5.6
120	1,638	861	2,499	27.9

A 'HEDGE-WRAPPER'

GOAL: Protect profits on 100 shares of Digital Equipment Corp. stock bought earlier for $38; stock currently at about $55.

STRATEGY: Sell one July 1992 call with a $70 strike price, receiving a premium of $513; buy one July 1992 put with a $45 strike price at a cost of $300.

STOCK PRICE AT EXPIRATION OF OPTION	PROFIT/LOSS ON STOCK	ON OPTIONS	COMBINED PROFIT/LOSS	COMBINED RETURN
$35	−$ 300	$1,213	$ 913	24.0%
45	700	213	913	24.0
55	1,700	213	1,913	50.3
70	3,200	213	3,413	89.8
80	4,200	−788	3,413	89.8

This chart valid as of 1/4/92

COMMODITY INDEXES

Tuesday, June 23, 1992.

	Close	Net Chg.	Yr. Ago
Dow Jones Futures	119.87	+ 0.09	
Dow Jones Spot	119.80	+ 0.19	125.90
Reuter United Kingdom	1552.6	− 23.0	129.39
C R B Futures*	209.11	− 0.05	1771.3
*Division of Knight-Ridder.			210.79

Commodities markets are zero-sum. For every dollar made, there is a dollar (or a little more) lost. But that doesn't mean half the investors win. It's more like one out of four.

Investing in Real Estate

You may buy property as a way to stake your claim, but on a practical level, real estate is a good way to diversify your portfolio. But remember, land is not *liquid*— you can't easily convert it back to cash.

Investing in real estate can range from owning your home to a partnership in a huge construction project, and from buying an empty wooded lot to a castle in Spain.

If you *leverage* (borrow money to pay for) your investment, selling at a profit means a healthy return. But leverage also magnifies your losses if prices go down. A primary drawback of real estate is that it's sometimes hard to sell, especially at the price you want.

Empty land, called unimproved or raw property, is usually the most speculative and the least liquid real estate investment. If you pay high taxes or have big carrying costs, it is hard to make money.

Real Estate Investment Trusts are funds that trade like stocks and work like mutual funds. Your investment is pooled with other people's, and the trust invests it.

For many people REITs are the most attractive real estate investments because the trust makes the investment decisions, it's easy to trade the shares, and the current yields can be high.

REIT share prices fluctuate in response to market conditions, the size of the dividend the trust pays, and changes in real estate values. Long-term profitability depends on the underlying value of the properties and the quality of the management.

Equity REITs buy properties that produce income or have growth potential. Some buy only certain types of property, while others diversify. In general, well-established equity REITs have been better investments than *mortgage* REITs, which invest in real estate loans, start-up offerings, or *blind* REITs that don't list the properties they own or intend to buy.

Vacation and retirement property appeals to investors who buy a second home either as an investment or primarily for their own use but welcome the extra income that renting can provide. Since 1986, complex rules have limited their usefulness as tax shelters, and overbuilding has cut resale value in some areas.

Single family rental houses, apartment buildings, and office space are traditional real estate investments. The key to making money is to earn at least enough to cover the mortgage, insurance, taxes, and repairs ▼

+ You can deduct all your repair and improvement expenses up to the amount of rent you collect. You may also be able to deduct losses on your investment against your regular income.

+/– Buying rental property to fix up and sell can produce a big profit if the market is right, but frustrations and big losses if it's not.

– If rents drop or space stays empty, you could end up subsidizing instead of profiting by your investment.

– Owning rental property makes you a landlord, which is an investment of time and energy.

The Plusses of Real Estate Investing ...

+ Provides a hedge against inflation
+ Permits some tax deductions
+ Produces big profits in some markets

And The Minuses.

– Can be difficult to get your investment back
– May be overpriced in hot markets
– Subject to zoning laws, environmental issues
– Frequently requires legal or other professional advice

Real Estate Limited Partnerships

invest in income-producing properties, often of a particular type (like shopping malls or low income housing) or in a specific geographic area.

The appeal is that several *limited partners* pooling their money can invest in larger properties with the potential for greater profits. The limited partners have no management responsibility and no liability beyond their investment.

Private limited partnerships are restricted to high-asset investors and established for a set period of time, often 7–12 years. *Public partnerships* require a relatively modest investment.

The drawbacks? Most RELPs have large fees, are difficult —maybe impossible—to get out of, and provide no assurance of return on investment. And they no longer serve as tax-shelters.

TAXES

Death and taxes, according to an old cliché, are the only

things you can be sure of. But you only die once.

You owe the U.S. Government part of what you earn

every year. The percentage, or rate, is set by

Congress. So are the rules for figuring your

tax liability, or the amount you have to pay.

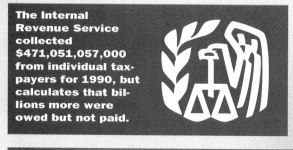

The Internal Revenue Service collected $471,051,057,000 from individual tax-payers for 1990, but calculates that billions more were owed but not paid.

A SHORT HISTORY OF INCOME TAX:

The U.S. government collected income taxes during 1863–1871

to pay for the Civil War, again in 1894–1895 (until the Supreme

Court declared them unconstitutional), and beginning in 1913

when the 16th Amendment was ratified. The average citizen

In 1990, the IRS processed almost 115 million returns. Over 50 million filers were eligible for refunds; but nearly 27 million had tax payments due.

The IRS

The Internal Revenue Service is the government agency that collects income taxes. It also provides tax forms, tax tables, and detailed instructions to help you figure your tax, not to mention an extensive list of tax publications.

Another function of the agency is to interpret the tax laws and administer the tax system. Not everyone agrees with the IRS's interpretation, or in some cases, with its methods of enforcement.

In 1643, The Massachusetts Bay Colony got the ball rolling by imposing the first recorded income taxes in the New World.

States without income taxes: Alaska, Florida, Nevada, South Dakota, Texas, Washington and Wyoming.

New Hampshire and Tennessee tax only unearned income.

didn't file a tax return—or pay taxes—before 1940, when the gross income required for filing was reduced from $5,000 to $800. Until the Tax Reform Act of 1986, tax law change generally meant new deductions and credits. Since then, the trend has been to cap deductions, or eliminate them altogether.

The Tax Structure

The U.S. has a *progressive* tax structure, which means the more you earn, the higher the rate at which you pay.

What's a Tax Bracket?

Under our progressive tax system, income is divided into specific ranges or *brackets*, each with a set tax rate. The part of your income that falls into each bracket is taxed at the rate for that bracket. In 1991 there were three tax rates:

15% *for the lowest bracket*

28% *for the next bracket*

31% *for the top bracket*

In fact, though, people with taxable incomes over $150,000 pay closer to 35% because they lose some tax advantages called *preferences* (like deductions for dependents and IRAs) that most taxpayers get.

Filing Status Counts, Too

The brackets themselves are pegged to your filing status — whether you are single or married, for example — so households with the same income pay different amounts of tax.

> Your *marginal* tax rate is the rate at which your last dollar of income is taxed—or the highest rate at which you pay.

$49,300

$20,350

$34,000

$75,000

$75,000

When everybody pays tax at the same rate, it's called a *regressive* tax. Sales taxes and Social Security taxes are typical regressive taxes.

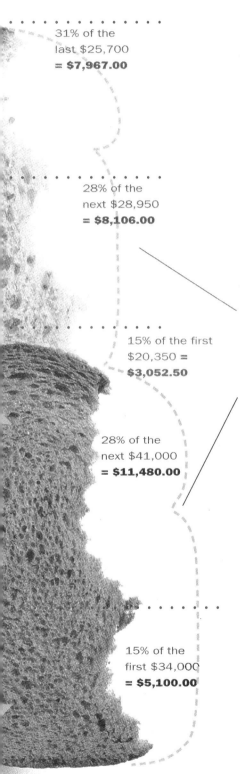

31% of the
last $25,700
= $7,967.00

28% of the
next $28,950
= $8,106.00

15% of the first
$20,350 =
$3,052.50

28% of the
next $41,000
= $11,480.00

15% of the
first $34,000
= $5,100.00

What's a Flat Tax?

With a *flat tax*, all taxpayers pay at the same rate. Advocates insist a flat tax system is simpler and fairer, in part because it eliminates most deductions that benefit high-income people. Opponents argue that a flat tax means the poor carry too much of the tax burden.

> **People paying at today's top rate of 31% might feel better knowing that it hit 94% during World War II.**

Filing Status—There are 5 *filing status* options—*single, married filing jointly, married filing separately, head of household, or qualifying widow(er) with dependent child(ren)*. The filing status you claim must reflect your actual situation as the IRS defines it. Some options can save you money—like filing as head of household instead of single, provided that you qualify. Others almost always cost more—like filing separately instead of jointly if you're married.

A single taxpayer with a taxable income of $75,000 pays **$19,125.50** in taxes, crossing three tax brackets. The taxpayer is in the 31% bracket since this is the highest rate on which part of his income is taxed.

But a married couple with $75,000 in taxable income who file a joint return would pay only **$16,580** in taxes. That's because the lower rates apply to a larger bracket of income, so they're only in the 28% bracket.

> **The average American in the 28% tax bracket worked 128 days — until May 8 — in 1992 to pay federal, state and local taxes.**

What's the Alternative Minimum Tax?

It's a separate, or parallel, system that taxes high-income people who have lots of tax-sheltered income. The tax rate is 24%, but few *preferences*, or tax breaks, are allowed, so the tax is assessed on a larger amount. The AMT doesn't catch many people—only about 109,000 in 1989—but the numbers are rising. It can catch you if you don't do tax planning. It's also complex, so you'll probably need a tax professional if you get stuck paying it.

The Reporting System

The IRS provides ❸ forms for figuring taxes: the 1040EZ, the 1040A and the 1040. The one you use depends on your filing status, the amount you earned and how you earned it, and deductions or credits you can claim.

In addition to the conventional 1040, 1040A and 1040EZ forms, the IRS is using some new filing methods.

File the 1040PC. Several commercially available software programs let you file a one-page, computer-generated answer sheet, called the 1040PC, along with your backup documents and payment.

File by Phone. TeleFile lets you call in basic information using a touch tone phone. The IRS figures out the tax due—or the refund—while you're still on the phone.

File by Computer. Some tax preparers offer the option—for a fee—of filing *electronically*, with the information transmitted directly from their computer to the IRS. Or you can pay an approved transmitter to file a return you prepared yourself. About 7% of all taxpayers used

the option in 1990, and the number is expected to grow. The bonus is you get a quicker refund. If you owe tax, you still have until April 15 to pay.

How Do You File?

You mail your return—and any payment that's due—to the IRS processing center that serves the region where you live. If you don't get a preprinted envelope with your return, you can find the address in the *Forms and Instructions* booklet. The return must be postmarked by midnight, April 15. (When the 15th falls on a Saturday or Sunday, you don't have to mail your return until the following Monday). *You can't pay in person.*

Choosing the Right Form

You can actually report your tax liability using any format you like—as long as you cover all of the required information. Publication 1167 spells it out.

❶ **1040EZ.** If your financial affairs are simple, the 1040EZ—only 9 questions long—can make short work of tax preparation. But you must be single to file it, and earn less than $50,000.

What's a Complex Return?

Complexity depends more on where your money comes from, and what expenses you have, than on how much you earn. If you have a good salary but no other income, your situation is usually much simpler than that of someone who makes less money but gets it from several different sources.

What If You Make a Mistake?

You can file an *amended tax return* on Form 1040X. It's used to report things you left out or figured wrong, or to get a refund. Some refund claims are limited to 3 years from the date the original return was filed or 2 years from the date the tax was paid.

What If You File Late?

You can get an automatic filing extension by sending in Form 4868, *Application for Automatic Extension of Time to File U.S. Individual Income Tax Return*, by April 15. That gives you until August 15. If you're still not ready, you may be able to get another extension, until October 15, by filing Form 2688.

The catch? You still have to pay the tax you owe by April 15 or face penalties and interest.

Where Can You Get the Forms?

If you filed a return last year, the IRS will send you a current version in January. Or, they'll send you a simpler one if that's all you need.

The forms you get in the mail come with a preprinted address label the IRS asks you to use when you file. The rumor that the label is coded, and makes you vulnerable to audit, has not been confirmed. The IRS emphatically denies it.

All the standard forms are available in local post offices, banks, public libraries, and regional IRS offices. You can get the other forms and schedules you need by writing to the IRS or calling 1-800-829-3676.

> The IRS estimates it should take you 3 hours and 23 minutes to fill out the 1040, plus 1 hour and 26 minutes for schedules A and B—after you've spent 5 hours and 38 minutes getting your records together and learning what you need to know about the tax law.

❷ **1040A.** You can use the recently expanded 1040A, an intermediate form, to report income from several different sources, subtract IRA deductions, and take child care credits. You can't use it, though, to itemize deductions or report taxable income of more than $50,000.

❸ **1040.** Nearly 70% of all taxpayers use the 65-question 1040 and file several of the more than 70 additional forms, schedules and attachments to explain their sources of income and the benefits they claim. The 1040 lets you report the full range of adjustments, deductions, and credits the law allows.

The Awesome 1040

The 1040 seems enormously complicated, and can take hours to complete. But it leads you ploddingly if not always logically through the process of figuring your income and deductions, and computing your tax.

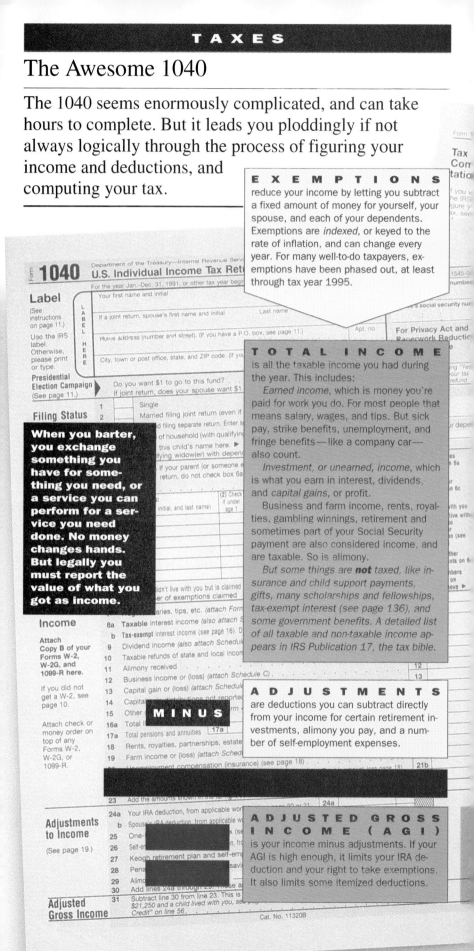

EXEMPTIONS reduce your income by letting you subtract a fixed amount of money for yourself, your spouse, and each of your dependents. Exemptions are *indexed*, or keyed to the rate of inflation, and can change every year. For many well-to-do taxpayers, exemptions have been phased out, at least through tax year 1995.

TOTAL INCOME is all the taxable income you had during the year. This includes:

Earned income, which is money you're paid for work you do. For most people that means salary, wages, and tips. But sick pay, strike benefits, unemployment, and fringe benefits—like a company car—also count.

Investment, or unearned, income, which is what you earn in interest, dividends, and capital gains, or profit.

Business and farm income, rents, royalties, gambling winnings, retirement and sometimes part of your Social Security payment are also considered income, and are taxable. So is alimony.

*But some things are **not** taxed, like insurance and child support payments, gifts, many scholarships and fellowships, tax-exempt interest (see page 136), and some government benefits. A detailed list of all taxable and non-taxable income appears in IRS Publication 17, the tax bible.*

When you barter, you exchange something you have for something you need, or a service you can perform for a service you need done. No money changes hands. But legally you must report the value of what you got as income.

MINUS

ADJUSTMENTS are deductions you can subtract directly from your income for certain retirement investments, alimony you pay, and a number of self-employment expenses.

ADJUSTED GROSS INCOME (AGI) is your income minus adjustments. If your AGI is high enough, it limits your IRA deduction and your right to take exemptions. It also limits some itemized deductions.

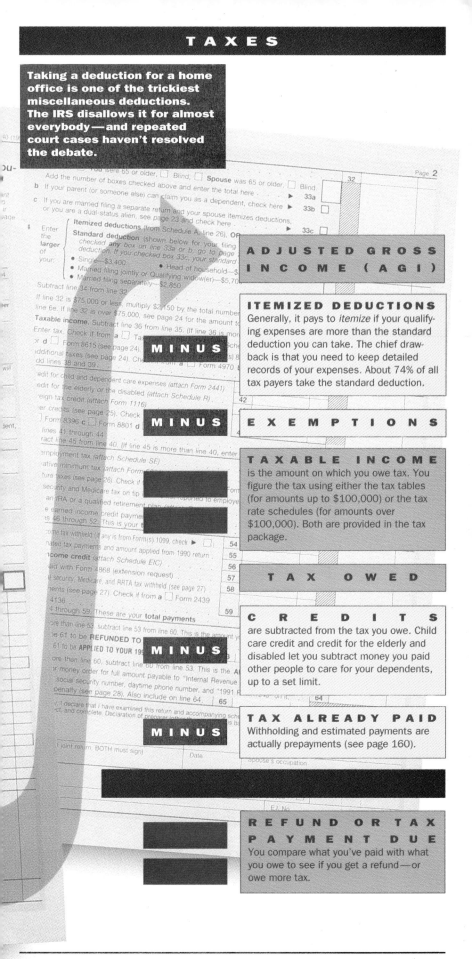

Taking a deduction for a home office is one of the trickiest miscellaneous deductions. The IRS disallows it for almost everybody—and repeated court cases haven't resolved the debate.

A D J U S T E D   G R O S S   I N C O M E   (A G I)

ITEMIZED DEDUCTIONS
Generally, it pays to *itemize* if your qualifying expenses are more than the standard deduction you can take. The chief drawback is that you need to keep detailed records of your expenses. About 74% of all tax payers take the standard deduction.

MINUS

E X E M P T I O N S

MINUS

TAXABLE INCOME
is the amount on which you owe tax. You figure the tax using either the tax tables (for amounts up to $100,000) or the tax rate schedules (for amounts over $100,000). Both are provided in the tax package.

T A X   O W E D

C R E D I T S
are subtracted from the tax you owe. Child care credit and credit for the elderly and disabled let you subtract money you paid other people to care for your dependents, up to a set limit.

MINUS

TAX ALREADY PAID
Withholding and estimated payments are actually prepayments (see page 160).

MINUS

R E F U N D   O R   T A X   P A Y M E N T   D U E
You compare what you've paid with what you owe to see if you get a refund—or owe more tax.

Forms and Schedules Aplenty

In addition to the 1040, there are dozens of forms and schedules you can file. They provide detailed information about deductions, investments and a host of special tax situations.

Some forms and schedules are used so often they're included in the tax packet the IRS sends you—like Schedule B for Interest and Dividend Income and Form 2441 for Child and Dependent Care Expenses.

Which Forms Do You File?

Each line on the 1040 that requires an additional form tells you which one to attach.

Schedule A lists the *itemized deductions* you can take. Many homeowners itemize because they can deduct mortgage interest and property taxes. If you pay big state income taxes, have a lot of job-related expenses, or give a lot to charity, it may also pay to itemize.

Schedule B reports *interest and dividend income.* You should have a Form 1099 for each item you include.

Schedule C is for filers who own their own businesses. You report your net profit or loss—and the numbers that back it up.

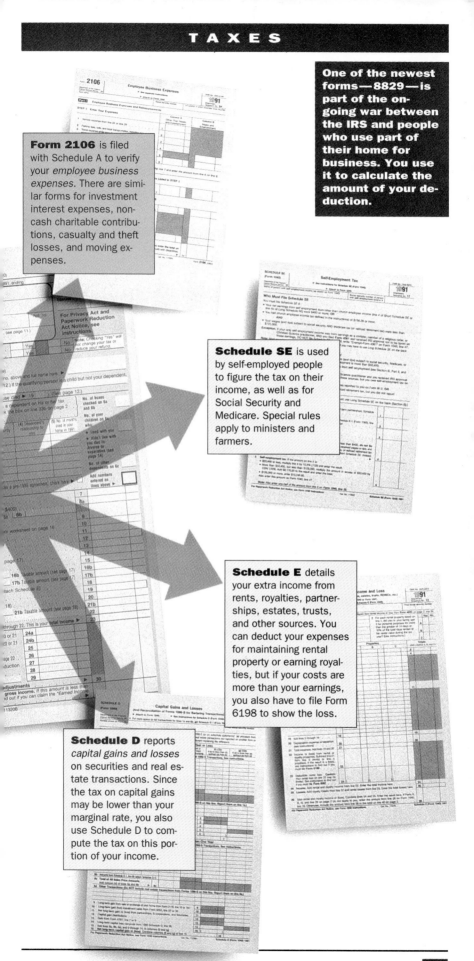

Form 2106 is filed with Schedule A to verify your *employee business expenses*. There are similar forms for investment interest expenses, non-cash charitable contributions, casualty and theft losses, and moving expenses.

One of the newest forms—8829—is part of the on-going war between the IRS and people who use part of their home for business. You use it to calculate the amount of your deduction.

Schedule SE is used by self-employed people to figure the tax on their income, as well as for Social Security and Medicare. Special rules apply to ministers and farmers.

Schedule E details your extra income from rents, royalties, partnerships, estates, trusts, and other sources. You can deduct your expenses for maintaining rental property or earning royalties, but if your costs are more than your earnings, you also have to file Form 6198 to show the loss.

Schedule D reports *capital gains and losses* on securities and real estate transactions. Since the tax on capital gains may be lower than your marginal rate, you also use Schedule D to compute the tax on this portion of your income.

Withholding—Prepaying as You Go

When you file your tax return on April 15, you're really settling your tax bill with the IRS. Most people prepay—and often overpay—the amount due through payroll *withholding* and *estimated payments*.

What Is Withholding?

If you earn a salary, taxes are ordinarily deducted or *withheld* from each paycheck. By year's end, you will have paid all or most of your federal, state, and local income tax for that year.

Besides your salary, you can expect to have money withheld from any tips you earn, as well as from sick pay, pensions, and annuities. Even gambling winnings—like lotteries, sweepstakes, and bets that pay over $1,000—are subject to withholding.

You may also have to pay *backup withholding* on your interest and dividends if you refuse to provide taxpayer identification, give it incorrectly, or have a history of underreporting your investment income.

Withholding was introduced in 1943, in the midst of World War II, to improve collection efficiency and to keep money flowing into the Treasury.

Estimated Taxes

If your withholding doesn't cover what you owe, or if you have no taxes withheld—because you're self-employed, unemployed, or live on unearned income—you have to pay estimated taxes.

IRS Form **1040-ES** can help you project your tax. It also provides a payment voucher. You can make a lump sum payment at the beginning of the tax year or pay estimated amounts quarterly. To escape penalties, you have to prepay 90% of your total tax bill.

If your income is constant, paying estimated taxes is relatively simple. But if your situation changes or your earnings are sporadic, meeting IRS requirements can be complex. You'll owe a stiff penalty if you underpay a quarterly amount, even if you get a refund back at the end of the year.

Making a Mistake on Estimated Taxes Can Be Costly

Penalties are relatively small for taxpayers whose estimated-tax payments are off by a few thousand dollars. But bigger mistakes get costly, as do mistakes repeated over several quarters.

Amount of Tax Deficiency	Maximum penalty if deficiency paid with next estimated-tax installment	Penalty for deficiency in second quarter if unpaid until April 15, 1993	Penalty for deficiency in second quarter that is repeated in third and fourth quarters and unpaid until April 15, 1993
$ 5,000	$150	$ 374	$ 745
10,000	300	748	1,490
15,000	450	1,122	2,235
20,000	600	1,496	2,980
25,000	750	1,870	3,725

Figures are based on a 9% penalty rate. There are no penalties for first-quarter deficiencies since taxpayers can rely on the previous year's tax bill for that payment. Source: KPMG Peat Marwick

1992 Form W-4

Department of the Treasury
Internal Revenue Service

Purpose. Complete Form W-4 so that your employer can withhold the correct amount of Federal income tax from your pay.

Exemption From Withholding. Read line 7 of the certificate below to see if you can claim exempt status. If exempt, complete line 7; *but do not complete lines 5 and 6.* No Federal income tax will be withheld from your pay. Your exemption is good for one year only. It expires February 15, 1993.

Basic Instructions. Employees who are not exempt should complete the Personal Allowances Worksheet. Additional worksheets are provided on page 2 for employees to adjust their withholding allowances based on itemized deductions, adjustments to income, or two-earner/two-job situations. Complete all worksheets that apply to your situation. The worksheets will help you figure

the number of withholding allowances you are entitled to claim. However, you may claim fewer allowances than this.

Head of Household. Generally, you may claim head of household filing status on your tax return only if you are unmarried and pay more than 50% of the costs of keeping up a home for yourself and your dependent(s) or other qualifying individuals.

Nonwage Income. If you have a large amount of nonwage income, such as interest or dividends, you should consider making estimated tax payments using Form 1040-ES. Otherwise, you may find that you owe additional tax at the end of the year.

Two-Earner/Two-Jobs. If you have a working spouse or more than one job, figure the total number of allowances you are entitled to claim on all jobs using worksheets from only one Form

W-4. This total should be divided among all jobs. Your withholding will usually be most accurate when all allowances are claimed on the W-4 filed for the highest paying job and zero allowances are claimed for the others.

Advance Earned Income Credit. If you are eligible for this credit, you can receive it added to your paycheck throughout the year. For details, get Form W-5 from your employer.

Check Your Withholding. After your W-4 takes effect, you can use Pub. 919, Is My Withholding Correct for 1992?, to see how the dollar amount you are having withheld compares to your estimated total annual tax. Call 1-800-829-3676 to order this publication. Check your local telephone directory for the IRS assistance number if you need further help.

Personal Allowances Worksheet

For 1992, the value of your personal exemption(s) is reduced if your income is over $105,250 ($157,900 if married filing jointly, $131,550 if head of household, or $78,950 if married filing separately). Get Pub. 919 for details.

A   Enter "1" for **yourself** if no one else can claim you as a dependent .... A ____

B   Enter "1" if: { • You are single and have only one job; or
• You are married, have only one job, and your spouse does not work; or
• Your wages from a second job or your spouse's wages (or the total of both) are $1,000 or less. } ... B ____

C   Enter "1" for your **spouse**. But, you may choose to enter -0- if you are married and have either a working spouse or more than one job (this may help you avoid ...

The gray overlay box reads:

In addition to your salary, the amount withheld will depend on three things:

❶ Whether you choose the higher *single rate* or the lower *married rate*.

❷ The number of *allowances* you claim. The greater the number, the less your employer will withhold. (However, if you take more than 10 allowances, your employer will send a copy of your W-4 to the IRS.)

❸ Any additional amounts you want to withhold.

For further information, get IRS Publication 919, *Is My Withholding Correct?*

Form **W-4**

OMB No. 1545-0010

1992

1   Type or ...

2   Your social security number

Home ad ...

☐ Married, but withhold at higher Single rate

City or t ...

5   Total nu ...   **5**

6   Additional ...   **6 $**

7   I claim ex ...
• Last ye ...
• This ye ...
• This yea ...

If you me ...

8   Are you a ...   **8** ☐ Yes ☐ No

Under penalties of ...

Employee's signature ▶

Date ▶

9   Employer's name and address (Employer: Complete 9 and 11 only if sending to the IRS)   **10** Office code (optional)

Cat. No. 10220Q

Changing Your Withholding

If you change jobs, take a second one, expect a lot of outside income, or get married or divorced, you should fill out a new W-4 to recalculate the right amount of withholding.

What's a W-4 For?

To determine how much your employer should withhold from each paycheck, you must complete an IRS Form W-4.

The form provides worksheets to help you figure the number of withholding allowances to claim. It may help to have your previous year's tax return handy, especially your itemized deductions (Schedule A) and your investment income (Schedule B), so you can estimate your current income and deductions.

What Affects Withholding?

There's no shortcut or simple equation for figuring the right amount of withholding.

Things that Increase Withholding:

• Having more than one job
• Both spouses working
• High income, which restricts or eliminates some deductions
• Large investment earnings that are not tax-free or tax-deferred

Things that Decrease Withholding:

• Home ownership—which generally increases itemized deductions for mortgage interest and real estate taxes
• A large number of dependents
• High state and local income taxes
• Large tax credits—for example, for child care expenses
• Filing jointly or as head of household

Some people use withholding as a forced savings plan, purposely withholding more than they'll owe in taxes. But there are better ways to save, since you earn no interest on the money you pre-pay and you have to wait for the government to refund it.

Tax Planning Is a Must

Short of breaking the law by not filing—and ending up like Al Capone—there isn't much you can do to avoid taxes altogether. But you can take advantage of several strategies to pay less tax.

Tax-deferred and tax-free investments, year-end tax planning, and taking full advantage of the tax laws can all save you money on April 15.

Tax-free means no tax is due, now or ever. Most tax-free income is interest paid on municipal bonds sold by state or local governments (see page 136). If you don't live in the state or city where the bond is issued, you won't owe federal taxes on the interest you earn, but you may owe taxes in your own state.

Tax-deferred means you don't owe tax on your earnings now, usually because you don't have the use of the money. Tax-deferred investments include money in 401(k), 403(b), and other qualified retirement plans, as well as IRAs and certain annuities. But you'll owe the tax later, when you withdraw the money. In theory your rate will be lower, so you'll owe less.

You can also defer taxes on investments that appreciate in value, as long as you hold onto them. For example, if you buy a stock for $5 a share and it goes up to $50 a share, you don't owe any tax on your "paper profit"—until you sell.

Shifting Income and Deductions

Sometimes you have the option of postponing income to next year, pushing it forward (*accelerating* it) into the current year, or bunching deductions so that your miscellaneous expenses exceed 2% of your adjusted gross income in alternate years. By planning those moves ahead, you can often save on your tax bill. But you should get tax advice when you use these strategies.

Selling Securities

You can avoid taxes on some or all of your capital gains by selling securities on which you are losing money—especially if you think they're not worth holding on to. That's because you can usually *offset* some investments earnings by subtracting losses from gains.

Home Equity Loans

Since interest on many home equity loans is deductible—while interest on consumer loans and credit cards is not—it may pay to use your home equity credit if you need to borrow money. The danger is owing more than you can repay comfortably (see page 72).

Borrowing for Investment

If you borrow money to make an investment, you can usually deduct the interest you pay on the loan. This and mortgage interest are the only deductible interest. IRS Publication 550 spells out the rules.

Paying Expenses with Pre-Tax Dollars

Many employers offer *flexible spending plans* that let you exclude a fixed dollar amount from your salary to pay certain medical and dependent care expenses.

Under these plans, you pay the expenses and are then reimbursed from your flexible spending account. Since this money is not included in your salary for tax purposes — hence the term pre-tax dollars — you pay less tax. As a rule, the higher your tax bracket and the more you contribute, the greater your savings will be.

For example, if you contribute $2,500 to a flexible spending plan, you owe no tax on that amount.

Compare two wage earners, each earning $75,000 a year, and claiming tax deductions of $15,000. Both have medical expenses of $2,100, and both file a joint return. The first wage earner covers the expenses under a flexible spending plan; the second one does not.		Wage earner using flexible spending	Wage earner paying expenses
	Salary	$75,000	$75,000
	Flexible spending	– 2,100	
	Reportable income	72,900	75,000
	Tax deductions	15,000	15,000
	Taxable income	57,900	60,000
	Tax	**11,792**	**12,380**

The wage earner using flexible spending plan **saves $588** *in taxes.*

Shifting Income to Children

If your children are over 14, their tax rate is determined by their individual incomes. If the rate is less than yours, you can shift money or investments to them and save tax on the earnings.

Children under 14 pay at your rate after their first $1,100 of unearned income, but at their own rate before reaching that amount. Since they'd need a substantial investment to earn more than $1,100 annually, it may pay to shelter some investments this way. There are some drawbacks to this strategy (see page 89).

Planning Now to Avoid Taxes Later

By planning ahead, you can also reduce the amount of tax the government will collect from your estate when you die. The surest ways are giving away your assets or setting up one or more trust funds for your heirs (see pages 112-113).

Giving to Charity

If you make a contribution of stocks or other securities that have *appreciated*, or increased in value, you get the same deduction as you would for giving cash, but you avoid the capital gains tax. As this chart from The Wall Street Journal shows, you come out ahead, as long as you've held the stock more than a year.

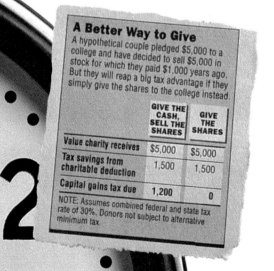

A Better Way to Give

A hypothetical couple pledged $5,000 to a college and have decided to sell $5,000 in stock for which they paid $1,000 years ago. But they will reap a big tax advantage if they simply give the shares to the college instead.

	GIVE THE CASH, SELL THE SHARES	GIVE THE SHARES
Value charity receives	$5,000	$5,000
Tax savings from charitable deduction	1,500	1,500
Capital gains tax due	1,200	0

NOTE: Assumes combined federal and state tax rate of 30%. Donors not subject to alternative minimum tax.

January Reading: The W-2

In addition to your wages or salary, Form W-2 shows the amount of tax your employer withheld, what you paid in Social Security taxes, and other contributions you made. But the sequence of information is not very logical—so check the numbers carefully when preparing your return.

You should receive a copy of Form W-2 from your employer by January 31. If the information is not correct—such as your name or Social Security number—make the corrections on your W-2 and notify your employer. If any dollar amounts are wrong, ask your employer for a Form W-2c, showing the corrected amounts.

Though W-2 forms vary in appearance, specific box numbers always contain the same kind of information, as mandated by the IRS. For example, federal withholding always appears in Box 9. Some customized W-2s may also omit boxes, such as those dealing with tips, where they don't apply.

Some countries impose a *Value Added Tax (VAT)*, a form of national sales tax. If you buy things in a country which imposes a VAT, you can often get a refund if you take or send them out of the country. Usually the retailer can tell you how to do it, but it's rarely a simple process. In some countries, visitors may be exempt from certain national sales taxes.

Box 1 is used by your employer for administrative purposes, and may not appear at all.

Box 5 shows your Social Security number (see page 101).

Boxes 24 and **27** show the amounts withheld for state and local income taxes. If you itemize deductions, report these amounts on Schedule A.

Other People's Taxes (1989 data)

Unbelievable as it may seem, US citizens pay less in taxes than their counterparts in most other developed countries.

Country	% of GNP paid as tax
France	44.4%
Germany	37.4
Britain	37.3
Italy	37.1
Canada	34.
Japan	31.3
U.S.	29.8

Boxes 25 and **28** show your salary and wages for state and local tax purposes. The amount is usually the same as your federal salary, except in states that don't allow certain exclusions, such as amounts contributed to flexible spending plans.

People who move when they retire can be—and increasingly are—hounded for income taxes by the states where they worked—even if they've changed their legal residence.

Copy B	File with your federal return
Copy 2	File with your state and local return
Copy C	Retain for your own records

Your employer submits Copy A to the Social Security Administration and Copy 1 to your state and local tax department.

Box 10 shows your salary or wages for the year. It does not include any pre-tax amounts you contributed to a 401(k) or flexible spending plan for medical or child care expenses (see page 162).

Box 6 shows if you belong to a pension plan and whether you contributed to a deferred compensation plan, such as a 401(k) or 403(b) plan (see page 96).

Box 9 shows the amount of federal income tax your employer withheld.

Box 18 shows the deductions for state disability insurance, if your state has such a plan. Otherwise, it will be left blank.

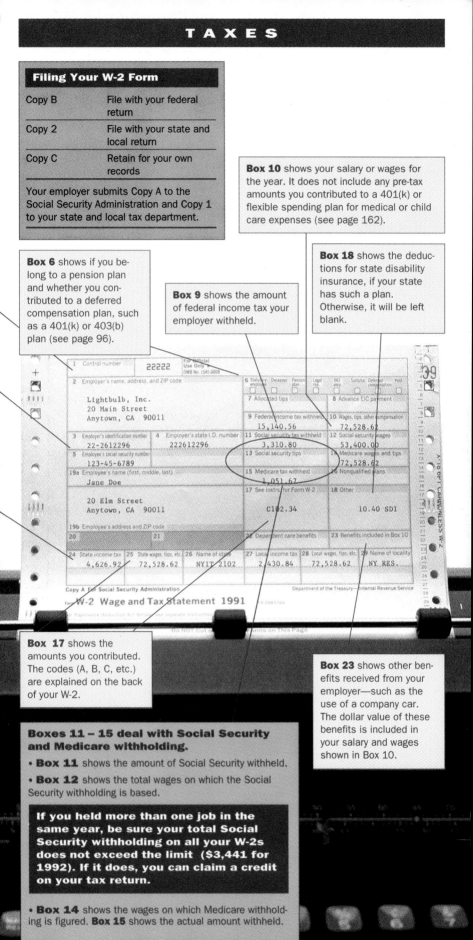

Box 17 shows the amounts you contributed. The codes (A, B, C, etc.) are explained on the back of your W-2.

Box 23 shows other benefits received from your employer—such as the use of a company car. The dollar value of these benefits is included in your salary and wages shown in Box 10.

Boxes 11 – 15 deal with Social Security and Medicare withholding.

• **Box 11** shows the amount of Social Security withheld.

• **Box 12** shows the total wages on which the Social Security withholding is based.

If you held more than one job in the same year, be sure your total Social Security withholding on all your W-2s does not exceed the limit ($3,441 for 1992). If it does, you can claim a credit on your tax return.

• **Box 14** shows the wages on which Medicare withholding is figured. **Box 15** shows the actual amount withheld.

Keeping Records

To figure your taxes, you need records that show what you earned and what you spent. For deductible expenses, be sure to write down the amount, the date, the place, and the reason, as well as the people or organization involved.

Your employer, the banks that pay you interest, and the companies that pay you dividends provide details of your earnings to you and to the IRS. You should have your copies by January 31.

Typical Tax Records	
Form	**What It Reports**
1099-R	Retirement income or distributions
1099-DIV	Dividend earnings
1099-INT	Taxable interest
1099B	Capital gains
1099M	Miscellaneous earnings
1065/Schedule K-1	Partnership gains or losses

If your broker holds your securities for you—which is known as holding securities in *street name*—you'll get a *Consolidated* or *Substitute* 1099.

Year-end statements that report your annual earnings are also important to keep. If you earn tax-free interest, you may not get a 1099 INT, even though you must report the interest to the IRS.

Keeping Your Own Records

You must keep your own records of earnings from other sources, like rental income, free-lance work, or royalties. These aren't reported directly to the IRS.

You must also keep records of your expenses if you plan to itemize deductions or plan to claim any exclusions or credits.

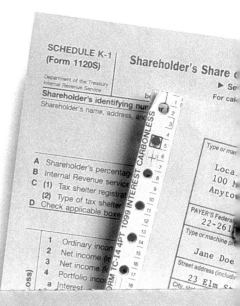

How Long Should You Keep Your Records?

The IRS usually has 3 years—called a *period of limitations*—to audit your return, so you should keep all the relevant records at least that long. But it's important to keep some records longer:

Type of record	How long to keep
Most records of income and expense	At least 3 years, 7 if possible
Property or investment	Until you sell
Real estate (initial cost, improvements, costs of selling)	Until 7 years after you sell
Tax Returns	At least 6 years, ideally forever

If you've underreported your income by 25% or more, the IRS has 6 years to audit. And if you don't file or file a false return, they have forever.

How Can You Verify Expenses?

Hold on to the evidence that you spent money for specific things. Your records should include who was paid, when, the type of expense, and the business purpose.

Receipts and cancelled checks are usually good records. If you have both, you're doubly protected.

Credit card charge slips sometimes provide a place on the back to record details of an expense. Or you can write on the back anyway, and keep the slip with your other records.

Regular entries in an appointment book or expense log, noting costs and other details of a meeting or purchase are also valid records.

There are special record keeping requirements for tips, business use of your car, travel and entertainment, and non-cash charitable contributions. For details see Publication 17, or Publication 526, *Record Keeping and How to Report*.

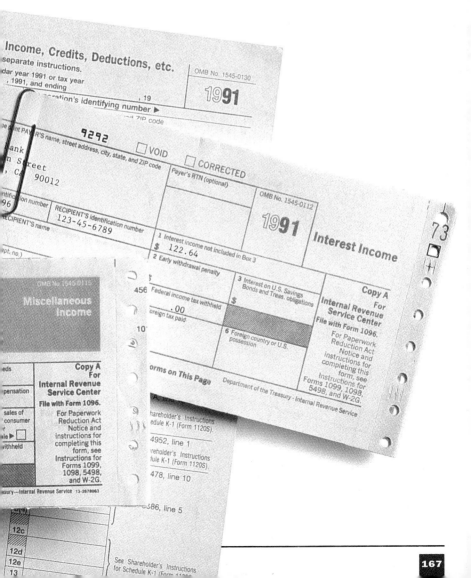

Tax Help

Whether people are buffaloed by the process, think they're missing out on ways to save money, or are terrified of an audit, they turn to tax preparers in droves.

ALMOST HALF OF ALL TAXPAY-
ERS USE A PROFESSIONAL PRE-
PARER OR ACCOUNTANT, AND
MOST OF THE OTHERS DEPEND

Professional Preparers

Preparers can find ways to save you money—legally—by taking advantage of all of the tax strategies that are part of the Tax Code. Legitimate preparers fall into 4 categories, plus volunteer groups:

Preparer	Comments
Tax Preparation Services (commercial preparers)	• 15% of all returns • Modest cost: $52 average • Prepare uncomplicated returns of middle-income people • Can go with you to audits, but can't represent you
Enrolled Agents	• Accredited by IRS, with continuing education requirements • Certified by Treasury Department • Can represent you before the IRS in an audit or appeal • Fees from $100-$300
Certified Public Accountants	• Clients are typically professionals, corporate executives or people with complex investments or financial situtations • Often maintain year-round relationships with clients for tax planning • Can represent you in IRS proceedings • Charge by the hour, with total fees in the $500 – $2,500 range • Not all CPAs are tax specialists
Tax Attorneys	• Provide advice rather than tax preparation • Familiar with details of tax law and tax rulings • Experts in interpretation and litigation • Can represent you before the IRS and in court • Hourly fees range from $150 – $500, with total charges running thousands of dollars
Taxing Questions What to find out before turning your return over to a paid preparer:	• Is doing tax returns a regular part of the preparer's business? • What kind of training does the preparer have? • Is the preparer available to answer questions throughout the year? • Is the preparer experienced with tax situations like yours? • Is the preparer conservative or aggressive in interpreting tax laws and regulations? • How much help would the preparer provide if you were audited? • How much will preparing your return cost?

IRS advice protects you against investigation and claims for more tax—if you've got it in writing. But they prefer to tell you what to do—and they're wrong 37% of the time.

ON ASSISTANCE FROM VARIOUS TAX GUIDES, COMPUTER PROGRAMS, OR HELPFUL FRIENDS AND RELATIVES IN FILING THEIR RETURNS.

Help from the IRS

The IRS provides several kinds of taxpayer assistance—though not necessarily with a view to saving you money.

There are more than 120 free IRS publications on specific tax subjects, including the comprehensive Publication 17, *Your Federal Income Tax*. You can order them by phone (1-800-829-3676) or by mail from three regional forms distribution centers.

Toll-free telephone assistance is also available—but it's often hard to get through, and the information is not always accurate by the IRS's own admission.

Tele-Tax, a pre-recorded information service, lets you call a toll–free number 24 hours a day, 7 days a week for information on about 140 topics—including a directory of the topics available. The IRS *Guide to Free Tax Services* provides a list of topics and the code numbers you need to access them. The basic telephone number is 1-800-829-4477, though large cities have individual numbers.

IRS Films and Tapes

Local libraries often have audio and video cassettes supplied by the IRS, with step-by-step instructions for filling out all three tax forms, plus Schedules A and B.

The IRS also produces films and video tapes in English and Spanish to explain the tax system, the audit process, and information about taxes for single parents and retired people. They're available for loan—free of charge—to groups and organizations.

Tax Guides

If you do your taxes yourself, you can find thousands of pages of instruction and advice in your local bookstore or library. J. K. Lasser, Ernst & Young, H & R Block and others publish voluminous guides to filling out tax forms. They're updated annually, with tax saving tips and tricks of the trade. The hard-core information is the same as the IRS's, but in the better books the format is friendlier and the information more helpful.

Computer Programs

Software programs for figuring taxes vary enormously in degree of sophistication and ease of use. However well they work, you still need to collect your tax records and enter the information.

The Dreaded Audit

When the IRS questions the details of your tax return, they can make you produce your records and explain how you figured your tax. The burden of proof is yours, and in most cases, you end up owing them money.

What's An Audit?

An audit is an IRS examination of your tax return and the records that back it up. They want to know if you've reported correctly— usually because they think you owe more tax. IRS computers flag most of the returns that are audited using a complex Discriminant Function (DIF) program based on taxpayer norms. For example, the program allows a certain —but secret—level of deductions related to your income. Not surprisingly, there are lots of educated guesses about "safe" deductions.

Types of Audits

A *Correspondence* audit is done by mail and is usually the easiest to deal with— though you may still end up owing money. The IRS asks you to send specific records to back up your return. One key bit of advice: send copies and hold onto the originals. An *Office* audit is held in an IRS office with a tax auditor. You are told which areas (up to 4) are being examined and the material you should bring with you. A *Field* audit is done by an IRS revenue agent, usually in your home or office — or anywhere that isn't an IRS office. It can also be at your tax professional's office if that person can practice before the IRS. Your whole return is open to examination, as well as the supporting documentation.

Automated Adjustments

are technically not audits, but notices, called CP2000s, that you owe additional tax. You do have the right to appeal—in writing within 60 days—if you disagree. The IRS can, and often does, make mistakes in matching the millions of pieces of information they get each year.

Taxpayers Compliance Measurement Program (TCMP)

is the IRS's way of establishing norms. Once every three years it subjects about 50,000 randomly chosen taxpayers to a line-by-line examination of their returns. The results of those inquiries are the basis of the statistical models—and the DIF formula— against which the next 3 years' returns are measured.

The Appeals Process

You have the right to ask for a review of any audit findings you don't agree with. You appeal first to the examiner's supervisor and then to the IRS Appeals Office. Publication 5, *Appeal Rights and Preparation of Protests for Unagreed Cases*, outlines the process you have to follow. You can represent yourself or have a tax professional represent you. Most appeals are settled at this level, often through a compromise.

What's the Taxpayer Bill of Rights?

IRS Publication 1, *Your Rights as a Taxpayer*, is often referred to as a bill of rights because it spells out the rules which the IRS must follow in questioning your return.

In 1988 Congress required the IRS to ensure that taxpayers knew their rights in any tax investigation, and also imposed some limits on the agency. For example, it's now illegal to use the amount of extra tax an auditor collects as part of the evaluation process for promotion.

As a taxpayer you can: get help from a Problem Resolution Officer or Ombudsman to prevent the IRS from seizing your property and wages or forcing you into bankruptcy
· have representation in IRS hearings
· end an interview in order to consult a tax professional
· record interviews
· propose installment payments
· appeal audit findings and tax liens

Tax Court

You can take your case to court, either before or after you pay the additional tax the IRS demands. But most litigation is expensive and slow. If the claim being contested is less than $10,000, you can argue your case yourself in Tax Court under "small claims simplified procedures." You can't appeal the decision, but you have about a 50% chance of winning. If your case involves more than $10,000, it's heard by the Tax Court, a federal district court, or the Claims Court—depending on whether you pay the disputed amount before bringing your case. You can represent yourself, but probably need professional help. The court of last resort— if your case goes on that long—is the U.S. Supreme Court. Supreme Court rulings are the only ones the IRS follows in setting its guidelines for future audits and appeals.

INDEX

NOTES